Language In The Blood

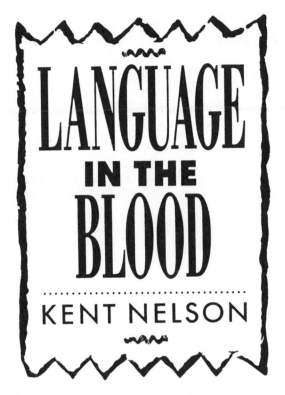

LANGUAGE
IN THE
BLOOD

KENT NELSON

For Shirley,
with thanks for stopping in to talk.
I hope you'll like This language.

All good wishes,

Santa Fe
9 Nov 1991

Kent

GIBBS·SMITH
P
PUBLISHER

PEREGRINE SMITH BOOKS
SALT LAKE CITY

First edition
93 92 91   5 4 3 2 1

This is a Peregrine Smith Book, published by
Gibbs Smith, Publisher
P.O. Box 667
Layton, Utah 84041

Design by Galie Jean-Louis
Cover illustration by Pete Spino

Manufactured in the United States of America.

Library of Congress Cataloging-in-Publication Data

Nelson, Kent, 1943-
Language in the blood / Kent Nelson.
p. cm.
ISBN 0-87905-394-1
I. Title.
PS3564.E467V63   1991
813'.54—dc20   91-8632
                                 CIP

In conformity with current practice and with the guidelines of the
American Birding Association, the complete names of bird species have
been capitalized in this book.

To my mother

Acknowledgments

With gratitude to the Ingram-Merrill Foundation, the Djerassi Foundation, and the New Hampshire Council on the Arts; and to all the friends who gave me time, help, and places to work.

PART ONE

Chapter one

One morning years ago, near Socorro, New Mexico, I photographed a Peregrine Falcon in midair. It was a hand-held shot with a 500-millimeter lens, lucky even at 1/1000th of a second. But the bird was in perfect focus: black cheek whiskers, black mottling in the tail, a bright yellow cere above the hooked beak. You can see in the photograph exactly the tilt of its pointed, slate blue wings, the compressions of the slender tail, and the fanatical concentration of its black eye.

But the background is blurred: behind the bird is a blaze of beige and orange and gray-black. You can't make out the cliff across the valley, or the shadows which would have indicated the time of day, or the thrust of the wings through the air. You don't hear the wind slipping through the Peregrine's feathers, or the gentle rush of the breeze among the crags where I had crouched for hours, or the calls of the nearby chicks in the nest. You're not driven to imagine the Cinnamon Teal the falcon may have spied taking flight from a slough a half mile distant, where, that morning, I had seen the mate of this bird strike a duck so hard it was dead in the air on impact.

A story is supposed to have a beginning and an ending, but I begin with the photograph, or really with the telephone call from Harriet Keating, because to tell what happened, there must be *something* first, before other things. Where I am now, seven years after that call, is part of what came before. Without order, events are merely like the moment captured in the photograph of the falcon, lovely in its still flight, but without particular meaning.

3

The phone call came on a Wednesday early in March. I lived then in Amesbury, Massachusetts, with my uncle, and I was about to go out to Smalley's Bar. My uncle was watching a Bruins play-off game against the Canadiens. He owned a small lighting-design company where, since graduate school, I had worked off and on as a bookkeeper, inspector of merchandise, and troubleshooter—almost anything he asked me to do. But mostly I thought of myself as a bird guide. I'd been through Harvard and the Cornell ornithology program, and when I'd come out of school, I'd wanted to do more than research. I wanted to be outdoors in the field, so I'd hired on with Top Flight and Big Birds, two of the companies which had capitalized on the birding boom. In those first years, while I was married to Demer, I'd led groups all over the country.

Then Demer had left me, and things had gone on a slow, downward spiral. I spent the winter around Amesbury, doing bookkeeping for my uncle and free-lance guide work, but the guide business was slow. It was easier and cheaper to hire me for $150 a day than to spend a week calling local Audubonists and consulting maps and muddling around Newburyport, Plymouth, or York, Maine, trying to find Glaucous Gull or Snowy Owl or Harlequin Duck, all of which I could turn up in a well-planned four or five hours. But I didn't get many birders. It was March, and the arctic birds had gone north, and the passerines had not arrived yet, so there weren't many birds around.

Harriet's call came like a bolt of whatever passed in those days for luck. She was a friend of mine in the biology department at the University of Arizona, a cetologist I had run into in far-off places like Alaska and Monterey, California, and she wanted to know whether I would come out to Tucson on such short notice to fill in for a professor who'd taken sick. "Fred Bentley's down with phlebitis. It would help us, Scott, if you'd come. You know the terrain out here and the places to go."

"I know the territory," I said, "but I haven't taught since graduate school."

"You don't forget how to teach," Harriet said. "You had a good record at Cornell. The committee, of which I am head, called Jack Watkins at Top Flight in Austin, who recommended you highly. So did the local birding elite here in Tucson, including Fred."

"Jack's a pal," I said, "and I'm grateful to Fred for the kind word, but I wouldn't take what they say too seriously."

4

"The committee is taking it seriously enough to ask you," Harriet said. "I know the guide business a little. You could come west and change your telephone number. That's the advantage in what you do."

"I'm working for a lighting company."

Harriet paused a meaningful time. "Are you interested or not?"

A list of negatives swam into view. I still had the idea Demer would come back, and she needed to know where I was. Jack wouldn't hire me for Top Flight anymore. (In fact he had fired me the previous fall, though he was still a friend.) And there was Tucson. But Harriet knew me marginally well, and if she and the committee were willing to give me a chance, I ought to be willing to take it. But I said, "No, I can't do it."

"Why not?"

"I can't, that's all."

"We'll pay you forty-six thousand dollars a year, prorated. That's close to three thousand dollars a month. Jack Watkins said you could use the money."

"I don't think Tucson's the place for me," I said. "Not at this time."

"Are you afraid?"

"Yes."

"Someone here or someone there?"

"There."

"Me?"

"Not you, no."

"Another woman?"

I paused on the line. "Not another woman, either."

"Scott, Tucson is a big city. You don't have to see anyone you don't want to see. Even me."

I considered that. Maybe I could dodge Tilghman for as long as the term lasted. That wouldn't be so hard. Maybe it was time to move. "When do you need me there?" I asked.

"Monday is your first class."

After I hung up, I took a bottle of Ancient Age from my closet and went downstairs to talk to my uncle. He was my mother's brother. When I was eight, my parents had been killed in a highway accident, driving back from Buffalo, and he'd assumed the burden of raising me. Not that I'd been much trouble, at least not until recently. He thought my problem was too much intelligence and not enough spine. I ruminated too much. At thirty-two I should have been able to carry things through. I ought to have settled down. When was I going to pay my bills? Demer would have said, "When are you going to *do* something?"

So I didn't go to Smalley's Bar. I sat down on the sofa and opened the bottle of whisky and poured two glasses.

"It's three-one," my uncle said. "Second period."

"Who's ahead?"

"Guess." He took the glass.

My uncle was serious about sports. The Celtics, the Bruins, the Red Sox who always folded. Except the Patriots. He hated the Patriots. I waited until we'd made a serious fender dent in the Ancient Age, and the Bruins were down five-two in the third.

"I'm going out to Arizona," I said. "The university has offered me a job in the biology department."

"Bullshit," my uncle said. "Is that what the phone call was?"

"I'm leaving tomorrow."

He threw a punch through the air when a Canadien defenseman hauled down a Bruin breaking in on goal. The whistle blew, and while the man was being sent to the penalty box, a commercial came on. My uncle looked at me. "You mean leaving town?"

"I have a little money coming from the company. I'll need that to get started."

He measured me closely. "And then what?"

"Then, when I get a place and get paid, I'll send you some of what I owe for rent."

"I don't mean that."

My uncle was what in the old days was called a flake. He had started the lighting company with the idea of producing natural light, *arctic light*, he said. The trouble with the world was that people relied on light that wasn't true. No one could make the proper judgments under false light. So he wanted to create the real light that existed in the far north. He'd been stationed in Greenland in the army, and it had been the best time of his life.

His company had been moderately successful, which meant it was still in operation. It had outlets in the big cities of the Northeast—Boston; Burlington, Vermont; Portland, Maine; Manchester, New Hampshire. I knew he had hopes that someday I'd take over. "I thought you were going to stay here," he said.

"This other job is temporary."

"Teaching about birds?"

"They're paying me four times what I make with you."

"But with me you have a future."

I didn't answer. The TV camera panned back to the Forum in Montreal. There was a face-off in the Canadiens' zone.

"Well, shit," my uncle said.

That was that. He turned back to the game, and I went upstairs to pack. I left the rest of the bottle on the table.

That night I didn't sleep well. Maybe it was the whisky. Or maybe it was doing something without talking it over with Demer. Or maybe it was what I thought Demer's reaction would have been if she'd known I was going to Arizona at the invitation of Harriet Keating. Demer knew about Harriet. I'd met Harriet on a pelagic trip to Grays Canyon off the coast of Westport, Washington, on a gray day several years before, and I had seen her again the next summer on the ferry to Kodiak, Alaska. It was the kind of coincidence that was expectable—meeting someone in an unlikely, but likely, place. (That's how I'd become friends with Jack Watkins, too. We'd kept seeing each other at places rare birds showed up—the Dry Tortugas; San Ygnacio, Texas; Cave Creek Canyon, Arizona.)

But Demer didn't believe in coincidence. "So who is this woman?" she'd asked.

"Nobody."

"Come on, Scott. Don't lie to me."

"I'm not lying. She's a whale fanatic."

"And you're a whale?"

We'd argued about it. That wasn't the only time Demer had accused me of something that hadn't happened. She'd said I'd slept with one of my tour women in Maine. Someone had sent me a photograph of the group, and Demer had picked out the prettiest woman. And she'd been sure I'd stayed with a woman the night I'd had a flight mix-up in San Antonio and had got home a day late. That was the way guilty people operated: they projected their own malfeasances on others.

I learned it was better not to say much. When I ran into Harriet a third time in Monterey, I didn't tell Demer. When I got home, I went on as if nothing out of the ordinary had happened.

Of course that was past. The marriage was over. I tried to make it over by thinking it was, but I couldn't help the way Demer's presence intruded, even after nearly a year, even when she was, then, off in Costa Rica, where her last letter had been from. After all the time together—four years—and the hours of talk about what she had to do, I still thought she'd come home again.

So there I was in Amesbury, trying to sleep, thinking of Arizona and whether Demer would find me. Then I did sleep finally, and I dreamed. I was crossing an expanse of saguaro and greasewood outside of Tucson, walking on desert dust. A Cactus Wren's slurred song and the pale whine of an airplane overhead were the sounds I walked with. Far away in the rocky hills was a canyon illuminated by the clear, late-afternoon sun. I didn't know the place or the name of the mountains, but as I got nearer, I could hear water flowing. The water was so far away that even in my dream I knew I couldn't reach the stream before dark. I walked and walked all night amidst the night sounds of animals, and before dawn I woke up in my own room.

Chapter two

I was going to make the trip in one strike. Fifty hours was what I figured, including coffee breaks and gas stops. I'd promised Harriet I'd be there Sunday night, and given my recent track record, I was going to make it or else. Amesbury to Tucson was three thousand miles.

I was used to marathon travel. During college I'd been a bird lister— the sort who tried to see as many different species in a certain geographic area as possible. A lister had to be wild, a crazy person willing to toss aside everything when the phone rang. One could never tell how long a rare bird would stay in one place. Failing money for airfare, one had to have the ambition or foolhardiness to get in the car and go. Once I cut class and drove from Cambridge to Key West to see a Bananaquit, and after two hours' sleep, raced out to Austin where I hooked up with Jack Watkins to drive another seven hours to the Rio Grande Valley, where a Crimson-collared Grosbeak had wandered over the river from Mexico. Another time, in graduate school, I drove from Ithaca to St. Louis for a Slaty-backed Gull, then to Arizona on a rumor that a Streak-backed Oriole was frequenting someone's feeder in Bisbee. Such was my insanity in the early days.

Listing had made my reputation in the birding world—I'd discovered one North American record in Florida (a hummingbird from Trinidad and Tobago), and I'd had a stretch of good fortune with the camera in Arizona and south Texas. My Roadside Hawk appeared on the cover of *Birding* magazine, and the Peregrine series I'd shot in New Mexico was featured in *The Realm of Birds*. As a result Jack had hired me for Top Flight right away.

9

All of that was before I'd met Demer. She was in college then at Georgetown, starting, she thought, a career in the foreign service. Her father had been an embassy doctor in Peru and Guatemala and Mexico, and she'd grown up speaking Spanish. The diplomatic corps seemed a natural choice for her, but in her junior year she became suspect of American foreign policy. The history of U.S. involvement in hemispheric politics troubled her, so she dropped out of school for a while, worked for Amnesty International, went to rallies, made posters. The summer I met her, she was at a crossroads and had taken time off in Maine to help some friends build a house.

This was in Sorrento. It was June, and I'd been leading a three-day bird tour around Maine, looking for gulls and Purple Sandpipers and guillemots and the wealth of warblers that inhabited the spruce knolls along the coast. We'd spent that particular morning on Machias Seal Island taking close-up photographs of Arctic Terns, puffins, and Razorbills, and we were headed back to Bar Harbor. I promised the group a Black-backed Woodpecker and delivered that bird in the burned-over dead trees off the main highway near Jonesport. After that we hugged the coast, in no particular hurry. We stopped in Sorrento to scope the rocks.

I can still see the round hole of vision through the spotting scope: sea, rocks covered with kelp at midtide, trees, and islands blurred beyond focus. I passed over cormorants, gulls, sea ducks. Then I paused on one bird. Someone less intent, perhaps less knowledgeable, would have missed it. The bird was in a group of other, larger gulls, mostly Greater Black-backed and Herring gulls on a rock ledge. I focused more closely, fixed the scope dead still on the tripod. This gull was softer looking and much smaller than the others and ghostly white. Its shape was different, and it had a yellow-tipped bill and a black eye.

My blood raced. I stepped away from the scope and spoke to the group in a hushed tone, as if the bird, well away from us beyond the surf, might hear. "On the ledge," I whispered, pointing. "Ivory Gull."

A few of the group had heard of the bird. Some knew it was rare. No one but me knew how rare. The Ivory Gull was a bird of the high Arctic, wandering occasionally as far south as Massachusetts in a hard winter. This was June. The bird was out of range and out of season. I left my scope for the others to look through and went to call Jack Watkins.

The closest house was across the road and up a wide lawn. That was where Demer was staying. She was sitting on the veranda on a swing, reading.

"I need to use your phone," I said. "May I?"

"Help yourself."

"There's an Ivory Gull . . ."

She got up and showed me where the phone was inside. I dialed Jack's number from memory. "Can I leave this number?" I asked. "He'll call me back with his flight."

"Who? Oh, sure. The number's there. Bangor's the closest airport."

"I forgot to make it collect," I said.

Demer was amused. "You can give me your name," she said, "and I'll bill you." She was amused, too, about the Ivory Gull. "Is that what you were doing down there? Looking at birds?"

Jack answered. "Listen, it's me, Scott. I'm in Maine, and I've got an Ivory Gull. I kid you not. How soon can you make it?"

We were off the phone in less than a minute.

"You mean this friend of yours is going to fly here from Texas to see a seagull?"

"*Seagull* is a misnomer," I said. "There are inland gulls, too."

I took Demer out to the lawn and gave her my binoculars. "Most people think gulls are white," I said. "But they aren't white. They have black on the trailing edge of the primaries, and some have black on their heads or tails or backs. Some go through phases of brown. But this one gull is white."

Demer scanned the rocks, licking her lips as she held the glasses to her eyes. She had on a loose sweatshirt with sawdust stuck to it and worn jeans. She was medium height, dark haired, solid. I liked that, in her demeanor, looking through the glasses, she was going to prove me wrong.

She didn't care about the Ivory Gull. She checked through the flock. "You're right," she said, "they aren't white." She lowered the glasses. "Who are you, Scott? What are you doing here?"

That was the first fragile thread from which the rest of it was woven.

The next fall Demer went to nursing school in Boston, and we saw each other whenever I was off the tour, or in a slow time when I worked for my uncle. She thought my life was what she wanted— always on the lookout, moving around, seeing how the world fit

---

together. I was traveling then to Texas, Colorado, Florida, and all along the New England coast.

"What about Belize and Costa Rica?" she asked. "Why don't you do tours there?"

"Other birders are more expert."

"Mexico, Guatemala, Panama? I've heard there are wonderful birds there. I remember the hummingbirds and toucans and trogons."

"In Central America there are stories of birders being robbed," I said. "Not to mention wars."

"You wouldn't do that, would you?"

"What?"

"Let rumors affect you. Don't you want to branch out? Go to new places?"

"There's a lot about birds here that I don't know."

"Jesus Christ, shit," Demer said.

Demer finished nursing school and took a job caring for people in their homes. Mostly her patients were older people or children recovering from surgery or people dying. She had a friend in Boston, Paige Jones-Ruiz, who gave Demer medical-technical translations from Spanish. That paid well. That was about the time, too, that we decided to live together. We got a duplex on Queen Elizabeth Street in Newbury.

The first year went well enough. We had to sift out whose stereo we'd keep and what to do with too many blankets and books. Demer supplied furniture. I donated lamps from my uncle's company. We each had a car. Hers was a Honda Prelude she drove to work. Mine was a Toyota Corolla wagon with 150,000 miles on it.

My recollection is that when I wasn't on the road, we were in bed. Long nights and long mornings. Demer had desire. Sometimes we'd have a slow breakfast, read the paper, and then spend the rest of the morning in bed. Demer had beautiful long hair then, and a darkish skin that was smooth as oil, and small breasts which, when I touched them, or she did, elicited from her a sigh. We often started with that sigh and went from there.

We were married the next year. It was what Demer wanted to do, though I was content with what we'd had. She wanted children, and I wanted to please her. Top Flight flourished, and so did the other birding tour companies. I was called to do more traveling. Annette Burns of Big Birds offered me Alaska, the Rio Grande Valley, and Big Bend. Jack Watkins at Top Flight countered with

Arizona. I was a kind of superstar of birding. In this one small world-among-worlds, the name Scott Talmadge was common knowledge. I was courted, admired, desired. Within limits I could name my price.

I liked being in the field. What could be better than being where you liked to be and getting paid for it? But I didn't like being away from Demer. When I was away, the rest of it started— Demer's craziness, the jealousy, her search for herself. I don't know how much of it I was to blame for. I only know that when I came back one day, there was a darkness around her. And once the darkness had begun, it was impossible to erase. I couldn't shine a light into it. I couldn't see inside.

I left for Tucson very early on that Thursday. My own confused, internal longing had always been to head west, perhaps for a place I wished was home, and I had allegiance to spaces. The trick days of March and April in New England were to me the definition of unfulfilled hope, and even before Harriet had called, I'd been restless. Getting into the Toyota— all those miles and counting— made me take heart. I slid out along the Mass Pike to Interstate 84, on through the leafless trees in the Connecticut hills into Pennsylvania and the Alleghenies. I gained momentum. The land flowed out before me in brilliant disarray. I rolled into the middle of the country—millions of acres of farmland which secured the nation by its sheer weight. Ohio, Indiana, Illinois, Missouri. By Friday morning I had dropped down on I-44 into Oklahoma.

Demer's postcards and her one letter were in the glove compartment, and sometimes as I drove, I thought of her descriptions of the Costa Rican countryside—the milpas, the lush hills, the cloud forests. "Birds are everywhere around us," she wrote once. "Their calls are so loud I'm reminded of an open-air market where men and women sell the vegetables and fruits. Why wouldn't you have wanted to come here, where waterfalls of thin mist fall from the leaves?"

I-44 through Oklahoma. I prayed the Toyota would hold together. My eyes burned from the hours awake. I listened to the radio. Once in a while I wondered whether Harriet had made an error entrusting to me these classes at the university. Then I would think how good it would be to live in the dry desert. Then I would think of Tilghman.

Thinking of Tilghman was the mistake. Of course Harriet was right: I didn't have to see anyone I didn't want to see. I could do my teaching, waltz around Tucson's barrio bars, do my stint in the mountains just south of town. Tilghman was nothing to me.

But somewhere west of Tulsa, I bought a six-pack of Budweiser. Late that afternoon, sliding on alcohol, I read aloud one of Demer's postcards:

Dear Scott, I'm staying in a dormitory with other volunteers. Huge spiders and lizards roam freely. We all share one room, undress, even urinate and defecate without privacy. There's a man from N.J., two nurses from Houston, a priest from Toronto, and several others. I swear if someone were interested in romance, it could happen with everyone else present and no one would care. In spite of the conditions, it's a relief to be here. Remember the joke? For so long I've thought of doing this. I wish you felt that, too, Scott.

Love, Demer.

"Felt what," I asked myself.

Romance was the postcard word. What other word applied? Fucking? Making love? Copulating? Sometimes Demer called it therapy. Therapy was cheaper than seeing a shrink, she said, and more pleasurable.

The Bud soothed me, brought me to my senses. I'd have preferred it if Demer hadn't mentioned the convivial times, which, barreling along the interstate, made me laugh. I did remember the joke. I'd imbibed some wine at dinner once with Eric and Annie Minter, and we were watching the World Series afterward. In a commercial Tommy LaSorda, the Dodger manager, gave his pitch for Rolaids. "How do you spell relief?" The first thing I said was "B-L-O-W-J-O-B." Annie laughed, but Eric, the little prick, feigned shock. Demer had to tease him out of it. During the seventh-inning stretch, I went to the bathroom, and Demer sneaked in and made me come in her mouth.

I was glad to have the postcards. She sounded well, and I was happy for that. But the letter, which had arrived back in the winter, worried me. She'd written vaguely of new projects she was working on, and it was framed with bolder rhetoric. It mentioned Tilghman, too. "I think you should know, Scott, that I've been in touch with Tilghman. I know this will make you nervous, but . . ."

Driving sixty, feeling the car shimmy, absorbing beer and hours indiscriminately was how I longed to live. I pieced together a slender trail across the Texas Panhandle, that barren, flat, gray country of the Old West. I was by this time well into a new six-pack of Lone Star.

Tilghman: my classmate in college, my friend afterward, my rival now? The irony that of all the cities in the country in which I might have been offered work, I had got Tucson was not lost on me. I kept reminding myself, drunk, what Harriet had said.

A few miles past Amarillo, I stopped in broad daylight in Wildorado, aching with fatigue. I dialed Tilghman's number from a pay phone. I got an answering machine with a voice like Jack Nicholson's. "Howdy. I might not be here right now. If you turkeys will leave a name and some numbers, and I feel like it, I might call you back." The machine farted for a beep.

I left no message. I drank a Lone Star and drove on over the last of the flat Texas Panhandle into New Mexico.

Suddenly—it seemed sudden to me—somewhere near Socorro, a clear light washed the land. It was a pure light, not muted by smoke or humidity or the aura of flat ground, but a serene, clear light which emanated from the mountains in the distance. The light gave to the amber and beige and tan hills a brilliance I understood. The horizon was rimmed with mesas and hills and mountains, powder blue and lavender and nameless, and I felt at last as though I was driving to a place I wanted to go. I was driving toward a country which gave weight to the few things I knew I still believed in—birds, mainly, and the idea of dreams.

I had to stop in Socorro for a while. I ate dinner and then drove south a few miles to the bird refuge at Bosque del Apache. I slept in my car outside the gates of the refuge, and when I woke, there was frost on the windshield. Thousands of Snow Geese and Sandhill Cranes were in the air on their way to feed in the fields along the riverbank. The birds rose from the water and the flats, honking and squawking and composing as they flew their layered patterns against the burnt yellow hills. The ducks mostly stayed put—Green-wings, Blue-wings, Northern Shovelers, Mallards, a few Gadwalls. A Northern Harrier dipped and glided over the reeds at the edge of the pond. It was Sunday morning and crystal clear, and I sat too long on the hood of my car when I should have been driving, shivering, scanning with my binoculars the geese and the cranes as they drew their sinuous lines in the air.

Chapter three

I got to Tucson late Sunday night and called Harriet right away, hoping she'd suggest I stay with her for a couple of days. I knew about her incontinent mother, and when the invitation wasn't forthcoming, I arranged to have breakfast with her early the next morning. Then I faced the choice of a motel or camping. I decided to save money, and I slept in my car again, on a side street near the university.

The next morning I met my first class. I was hardly more awake than they were, though my nervousness, plus some coffee, made me hum. Harriet at breakfast had given me Fred Bentley's syllabus, but it resembled *Robert's Rules of Order* more than a plan to interest students in birds. Not to knock Fred: he was a consummate ornithologist who'd done population research which suggested that several heretofore distinct species—juncos, flickers, orioles—were not so distinct where their ranges overlapped. His work on desert bird voices was the finest in the field. Besides, I no longer considered myself one of the young lions. I didn't believe in Big Days (how many species you could log in twenty-four hours: who cared?) or Big Years, which, with the blitz travel back and forth from Alaska to Florida and one coast to the other, cost big bucks. I considered myself in the mainstream—a man a bit out of shape, a reader of a few ornithological journals, daily newspapers, *Harper's* and *Rolling Stone*. I viewed my task as not so much teaching about birds as getting the students to look around at the possibilities for revelation in the natural world.

I opened class with a question. "What would you do," I asked these faces, "if suddenly it got dark outside and the temperature dropped to twenty below?"

"Go to Safeway," said a man with a beard.

"And the Safeway and the A & P were closed," I said. "Out of business."

"Go to L.A." The students clapped, and a woman in the second row with buzzed hair on one side stood up and took a bow.

"Anyone else?" I surveyed the room.

"Acapulco?" asked the lone man in back.

A titter of laughter ran through the class.

"You're all correct," I said. "You'd migrate."

We took it from there. We discussed how the animals of the Serengeti wandered according to rainfall and the availability of grasses at different seasons, how elk moved from higher pasture in summer to lower ranges in mountain parks in winter. The buzz-haired woman knew that nomadic people summered on the plains and wintered in sheltered canyons where animals also sought refuge.

"It happens that we in America have largely solved the problems which force others to migrate. The dust-bowl Okies were the last of a breed. Now we can heat and air-condition our houses and cars. We can drive wherever we want. We travel, but we're not forced to travel. I just came out from Massachusetts. I can find a place to live, buy food in the Safeway, turn on the water tap."

"And you can leave, too," said the man in back, "if it gets dull."

At the end of the hour, I told the class that rather than lecture in the traditional manner, I wanted to move the course outdoors. Instead of three meetings a week with a lab, we'd meet once a week in the classroom and twice a week at 6:00 A.M. in the parking lot next to the science building. From there we'd take a van into the Santa Ritas or to a brushy draw in the Rincons or maybe up into the pine forests on Mount Lemmon. We'd track the spring migration through the region, and in the van, going to and from, we'd talk about how birds navigated, the various theories of birds' interpretation of atmospheric and climatological data, the paths they took and why. I wanted to operate a mist-net project which would give us evidence of when the birds appeared and in what weather conditions and how they were eating.

No one was thrilled, but no one groaned, either.

Harriet Keating was a smallish woman just past forty by a year or two. She studied whales, wrote about them, and took every chance she got to be with them. She was fit and agile, and she had about her a worn look I liked, as if she'd never made much effort to play to an audience. "Who's watching?" she seemed to ask. She usually wore her hair loosely bunched in a horn or turquoise barrette, and her clothes were sturdy and workmanlike—khaki shirts and light sweaters over blue jeans, comfortable leather gum-soled shoes or jogging sneakers. She had a good complexion from being outdoors in rough weather, a cheerful smile tinged occasionally with melancholy, and lovely warm brown eyes which were, I thought, devoid of bitterness or envy.

I'd liked her from that day I had met her in Washington on the high seas. It had been rough, and despite being veterans of such excursions, Harriet and I were both enervated by the pitching and yawing of the boat. Scopolamine saved our stomachs, but our legs and arms ached from the constant ups and downs and sideways. Harriet, more than I, wanted to stay on deck, but I kept her company. We talked. She said most of the words. She loved whales and the sea, and she knew a fair bit about seabirds. As the day wore on, we cheered our good fortune. We had South Polar Skuas, several species of jaegers, dozens of shearwaters and gulls, including four Sabine's, and as many Black-footed Albatrosses as I'd ever seen at once. And we saw whales, grays mostly, but one mammoth blue which surfaced close off starboard and showed its tiny dorsal fin and then the immense flukes.

A year later I ran into her again on the *Tustumena* going from Homer to Kodiak. She was involved in a joint effort of scientists filming humpbacks in the waters around the Barren Islands, and as usual, I had come for the birds—puffins, kittiwakes, auklets, shearwaters—which nested on the cliffs and plied everywhere around us the nutrient sea. I was alone then, killing time between Big Birds tours to Denali National Park.

It was a rare day of sun for Kachemak Bay. Harriet and I stood on deck in short sleeves and passed through one swarm of seabirds after another. Now and then, off to port in the Gulf of Alaska, a monolithic humpback would breach, sometimes bursting so high above the surface that for the moment aloft the whale seemed unearthly, as if it were taking wing when we knew it couldn't. Then it would drop back into the sea with a resonant thunder so loud the compacted air shook the whole boat.

In the afternoon we steamed past Afognak toward the mountains of Kodiak, and that night I lay in my sleeping bag in my tent at Fort Abercrombie, where we were all camped. I listened to Harriet and her friends talking late, thinking that twice meeting made us friends. The sea tide scoured the rocks near us, and I drank from a pint of Jack Daniels I'd brought, wishing Harriet would desert her friends and speak to me. But she didn't.

The third time had been the fall before Demer had left for Costa Rica. I met Harriet at Sam's Fishing Shop on the Monterey Pier embarking with her cetology class from the University of Arizona on a boat called *The Big Tiny*. I was leading one of my first groups asea, a dozen crazies from Maryland who wanted to check off Pacific pelagic birds—Laysan Albatross, mainly, and Xantus' Murrelet, which were possible that time of year in Monterey Bay. I was in turmoil about Demer. She'd been talking about leaving. I was drinking a lot then, and seeing Harriet was a freshet on a scorching day. I talked to her too much on the boat and paid too little attention to my group or to the birds, either one. We saw lots of whales—blues, humpbacks, a minke—and hundreds of white-sided dolphins. One humpback rolled up onto its back beside the boat and cast its glinting eye at us for half an hour. It sounded, swam under the boat, waved its flippers. I understood how Harriet could be entranced. We had a few seabirds, too—storm-petrels, shearwaters, alcids, gulls, terns—but we missed the albatross and the murrelet. The guide was blamed. Several of them wrote Annette Burns, the head of Big Birds.

In the evening, instead of tending to the van and doing my preparation for the drive the next day to the Salton Sea, I went out with Harriet. We had dinner at a restaurant near the wharf. I talked her into a bottle of chardonnay. We were in California after all. She told me more about her life. Her mother had an unending series of invented maladies and psychological ploys that kept Harriet a virtual prisoner. How could she escape? She supposed she could send her mother to her brother's in Chicago, but it was so cold there. And Harriet was forty and wanted to get married and have children. It was getting late. "I'm a biologist, remember," she said.

"We're in California now," I said. "Far from your mother."

"Oh, my mother doesn't mind my seeing whales. She thinks a whale isn't a threat."

We drank the wine and ate bay scallops. I came to understand how avidly Harriet admired whales. She spoke so lovingly of them, of their singing, of their family life, of their agonies at being hunted. She recounted the story of a whale, trapped in a tidal pool, which was killed by speedboaters who ran over its back while its mate languished in the sea just beyond the mouth of the inlet. She told of whalers using a whale calf as bait to lure the parents within range of the harpoons. I'd never heard a person so deeply religious over a subject, and I, a lover of flight, was taken with her zeal.

She had been aboard the Greenpeace vessel, the *Rainbow Warrior*, when it had been flagged by the Russian Coast Guard in the Bering Sea in July, 1983. The Russians had taken captive a few of the protesters trespassing at a Russian whaling station and had tried to keep the *Rainbow Warrior* from returning to Nome. Harriet described the incident with such fervor that she had several nearby tables in attendance on her story.

Afterward I walked her back to her hotel. "I don't usually drink," she said. "Did I embarrass you?"

"Everyone was enthralled," I said. "You should write a book."

She took my arm, which pleased me. "It's just that I don't want my friends destroyed," she said. "Do you know what the world would be like without whales?"

I didn't answer, but turned my glance into the breeze off the water and toward the stars in the high, misty sky. Harriet steadied herself on my arm. As we neared the hotel, I felt her tighten like a spring. The awkwardness of the imminent moment when she would ask me in or not, when I would say yes or no, disturbed her. And I confessed to ambivalence, too. Demer was still home, I thought, waiting for me.

I stopped a little way from the hotel. I thought of kissing Harriet then to ease the decision. I often intuited what others wanted without knowing myself what I wanted. But as soon as I stopped, she looked me straight on and said, "I can go alone from here."

Chapter four

Before Demer left me, she had a patient she cared for in Boston, an Argentinian woman who'd been flown up to Massachusetts General Hospital for treatment of leukemia. The treatment had been ineffectual, and the woman was in pain day after day. The doctors didn't understand why the radiation hadn't worked. The woman seemed better for a while, but then she would lapse into a near-hypnotic state in which she couldn't speak or open her eyes. Demer watched over her. She sat by the woman's side and spoke to her in Spanish for long minutes at a time. Now and then the woman stirred or moaned or shuddered.

This went on for weeks. "It's as if the rhythm of the language is reaching her through muscle and bone," Demer told me. "She hears me."

"And what do the doctors say?"

"They don't know whether it helps."

"How could it not help?"

"It may make her homesick."

Over the days Demer grew anxious. She'd stare out the window at the snowy field behind our house or sit in front of the TV without watching it. More than once she burned something in a pan on the stove because she'd forgotten to turn off the burner.

"So what is it?" I asked her one afternoon. We were sitting in the bay window, looking out at a solitary deer crossing the meadow. "You've had other patients. You know the rules."

"What rules?"

I didn't need to explain them.

"There's something about this woman," Demer said. "She's from a little village in the mountains. Can you imagine how she got from that place to here?"

"Money."

"The church collected alms from the villagers," Demer said, "and the diocese contributed some. And now she's going to die."

"You don't know that."

"I know it."

The deer moved away from the trees and into the open meadow. Demer's face shone in the calm, diffuse snowlight.

Then she looked at me. "Don't you think anything bad ever happens?"

"Of course bad things happen."

"You think because we live here in this apartment with the TV on, nothing bad will happen." Her voice was soft.

"I see the news," I said. "I know . . ."

"I don't mean the news. What, there was a train crash? Or maybe an explosion somewhere that killed people? An earth-quake? Do you think those are bad things?"

"Aren't they?"

Demer got up from the table. The deer moving across the snowfield saw her and froze stock-still, and Demer stopped, too. "I'm not talking about *events*, Scott," she said. "I mean something worse than events."

The Argentinian woman died two days later. I thought Demer had prepared herself for it, and at first she seemed to take it well. Her supervisor, acting on policy, assigned her another patient right away. But Demer wanted to take some time off. "Let's go skiing," she said. "Let's go out to Colorado and see Clarice and Tilghman."

I agreed it was a good idea. We had money saved, and a vacation from New England was never a bad thing. And it would get Demer's thoughts off the woman's death. Clarice said we were welcome. They had plenty of room. The snow was excellent, she said. We'd all sit in the hot tub and drink manhattans.

We bought our tickets. Then at the last minute, Jack Watkins called. He had an unscheduled tour lined up for New England—some doctors who wanted to sort through wintering gulls and maybe pick up a few arctic strays. "It's bigger than usual," Jack said. "Doctors. Good for business."

"Demer and I are going skiing," I said.

I could imagine Jack nodding. I knew how these things worked. If I didn't do the tour, Jack would give it to someone else. The field was getting tougher. More birding fanatics were pressing for jobs. Competition was tightening. Whoever got this trip might get first call the next time. And I was a little worried that news about my performance in Monterey for Big Birds would have seeped over to Jack at Top Flight. "All right," I said, "if it's good for business."

I tried to postpone the trip to Colorado, but Demer wanted to go then, so she went alone.

She was different when she came back, though I didn't notice it much right away. We made love the first night she was home, and I don't remember its being unusual. (Only the bad times really stick in the mind.) She sighed. We coiled in our ordinary embraces. I told her I loved her.

She was tanned from wind and sun on snow, and was more relaxed than I'd seen her in months. But she drifted through the weeks doing nothing. We had my earnings from the special tour, so Demer turned down two more patients. She wasn't ready to begin work again. The tour money thinned out, and no new trips were scheduled till the spring migration. I went to work for my uncle putting aluminum shields on two hundred experimental arctic lights he'd sold to a theater company.

Then one night, while I was doing the dishes after dinner— we'd had broiled chicken, a salad, Uncle Ben's rice—Demer sat at the table and had a cigarette.

"I didn't know you smoked," I said. She was using her dessert dish as an ashtray.

She looked at me. "What would you say if I told you I'd slept with Tilghman?"

I turned off the water in the sink, pulled a towel from the door rack, and dried my hands. "Did you?"

Demer watched the smoke rise from her cigarette. "I said 'what if.'"

I sat down. "What would you say if I'd fucked Paige?"

"I didn't say 'fucked.'"

"Well, Christ, Demer."

"Why do you always answer a question with a question?"

"What kind of question is that?"

"I was wondering whether you'd care."

"Of course I'd care."

"Would you, really?"

Her voice conjured up cold fear. What was she thinking? I loved her more than I could tell her. She knew that. Why was she asking whether I'd care when she knew I would?

23

Chapter five

The second night in Tucson, I drove past Tilghman's house. It was a low-slung cottage made of adobe with a wire-mesh fence around the small front yard. Some kind of animal had torn up what had once been a lawn and had chewed to death the plastic webbing of several yard chairs. I made a pass by the gate.

I couldn't see much along the side of the house. A low adobe wall blocked my vision, but a gray Land Rover was parked at the gate in back. On the bumper were two stickers side by side: JESUS KNOWS ALL and QUESTION AUTHORITY. In the back window was another, which said CHEW MORE SKOAL AND FUCK GOATS. I drove around front again.

That I hadn't heard from Tilghman since Demer's trip to Steamboat wasn't exactly true. I'd had one note from him just after he'd moved to Tucson. Demer and I were living apart then. She hadn't left the country yet, but she was getting ready to. I knew she was corresponding with Tilghman because she'd told me he'd split with Clarice. He was moving from snow to sun, mountain to desert. She said he was going to make his own money for a while. Tilghman's note had given me an address and telephone number. "You can visit anytime, as always."

I pulled the Toyota to the curb and shut off the headlights and the engine. All the way across the country, especially after Socorro when I'd sobered up, I'd tried to convince myself I should stay clear of Tilghman. He would get me into more trouble than I could invent alone. He'd done it before. And what kind of friend was he? I didn't know exactly what had happened between Demer and him, but she'd left me and he'd left Clarice. At the same time

I made counterarguments. He was a sympathizer from the early days. In college we'd run track together, hung out. He'd written me twice or three times as many letters over the years as I had him. I could deal with Tilghman. What kind of friend was *I?*

I sat in the Toyota for a while in front of his house. A line of palm trees and street lamps slid together toward the buildings of the city in the distance. A sign far away flashed the time—9:45 P.M. Monday, March 10—and the temperature—59.

The front door was open behind the screen, and a light was on inside. I got out, went through the fence gate, climbed four steps. In the living room was a small desk without a chair, a ratty sofa, a small Indian rug. The chipped walls had no posters on them, no paintings. It didn't look as if Tilghman had got any of Clarice's money, or had made any himself.

I knocked, and a dog barked from one of the back rooms.

"Go around back," a voice shouted. "Read the sign."

The porch was unlit, but I made out a small placard under the broken bell. Beware of Dog. No Solicitors. Deliveries in Back.

"Tilghman?"

"The door doesn't open," Tilghman shouted. "Go around back."

I went out the gate and around the low adobe wall. Two huge oleanders encroached over the cement, and I detoured into the street to get around. The back gate was broken and hung askew on one hinge. I looked into the yard. The back-porch light illuminated a construction zone—a heap of broken concrete piled next to a neat cube of red bricks, a stack of new lumber near the garage, a mountain of cinder blocks. Hoes, tubs, bags of ready-mix were all jumbled together beside a wheelbarrow by the back door.

"Watch out now," Tilghman said from behind the dark screen door. "I'm going to unleash the dog."

The door sprang open and before I had a chance to move, a smallish mongrel shot out at me, squealing, barking, yipping. He jumped up and wriggled his rear end and peed on my running shoes. Tilghman came out and shielded his eyes from the glare of the light. He had on baggy shorts and a T-shirt and loafers without socks. He was thinner than I remembered him. He looked wiry and in good shape, dark skinned from the sun. His curly hair was cut short. "Who are you?" he asked. "Zapata knows you."

"Me," I said. "Scott."

"Well, Talmadge." Tilghman jumped off the stoop and

shook my hand and gave me a long hug. "God dammit, Scott. Are you chasing some woman, or a bird?"

"I have a job," I said.

"A tour?"

"No, at the university. Got here last night. Started today."

"You want to hole up here?"

"Maybe for a day or two. It would help me out till I find a place."

"Sure. As long as you want." Tilghman leaned down and roughed the dog's throat. "This is Zapata. You can keep him for me when I go to Mexico."

"And you're doing okay?"

Tilghman smiled. "I got my house. I got Zapata. We're doing some building." He waved his free hand toward the yard. "I'm doing fine." He stood up and flung an arm over my shoulder. "What about you? Come on in and tell me what's happened to you, Talmadge. All this fucking time."

This encounter seemed innocent enough at the time. I needed a place to stay, and Tilghman had plenty of room. I brought my bags in—I hadn't brought much with me except my cameras and scope and binoculars and a few clothes. It was easy to settle in.

We had roomed together our senior year at Harvard in Eliot House, had made our leaps of faith from the same bridges over the Charles, had bathed our wounds with the same bottles. One summer we'd worked Forest Service trails in Colorado, and another I'd stayed at his parents' house in St. Cloud, Minnesota, and sold clothes in a department store while Tilghman was a lifeguard at a summer camp. We had been friends in the best ways.

Tilghman had majored in art history, and after college had won a Fulbright to study in Yugoslavia. He'd gone to Belgrade, Split, Dubrovnik, and afterward, when my first year at Cornell was over, I'd met him in France. We'd hitched and ridden trains all summer—Spain, Portugal, France. We'd wanted that last time before the world really got hold of us.

But the world had never got hold of Tilghman. His father wanted him to go to business school, and he'd been admitted, but he never went. He spent a year in Vista helping black businesses get started in Selma, Alabama. He worked on a salmon boat in Alaska one long summer. Then he went back to St. Cloud for a while and tried the family insurance business with his brother.

That ended in hard feelings, so he took off to Steamboat Springs to ski. He rented a trailer outside of town, waited tables at a restaurant, made pizzas, moonlighted for an office cleaning company. He wrote me hilarious accounts of finding executives—both women and men—hidden in closets with unclad paramours. Then he hooked onto doing feature articles for the local tourist magazine. Mostly he wrote about fishing in the Elk River or high-country backpacking or skiing in blizzard conditions. He interviewed celebrities who came through Steamboat—Gerald Ford, Nancy Lopez, Jean-Claude Killy. He sent the magazines to me and said half, maybe three-quarters, was invented.

Then he met Clarice. She'd donated twenty thousand dollars to the Steamboat Springs Art Alliance, and he had to talk to her for the magazine. He did a background piece about her family in Virginia—horse farms—and how she'd landed in Steamboat (Rhodes Scholar from Johns Hopkins, magna cum laude, women's field hockey), and why she'd given all that money to the arts (she believed in them). Tilghman said at the end of the interview he'd asked whether there was anything else she wanted to tell him about herself, and she'd answered, "Yes, I want to sleep with you."

Even after the wedding, though, which I attended in Lynchburg, I never thought of Tilghman as married. It was not so much Tilghman as my image of him. He didn't have the roving eye, but the generous spirit. He liked drama and changes, and he often had his mind set on what was to unfold next. When I thought of him from a distance, I pictured him still running the hurdles. That had been his event in track. He was tall and lithe and he floated above the cinder oval, his stride untroubled by competition, his leap feathery over each striped board. His gaze was always on the next hurdle. At two hundred yards he pulled away from the other runners, and the margin between him and them lengthened until, by the end of the race, he was alone.

My misgivings about seeing him were oddly discordant with the daily business of house and garden. Of course it troubled me, looking back, that I had given in so quickly to the need for company. I didn't want to demean myself in my eyes or his, but I had, though Tilghman would never have seen it that way. I suppose, finally, it was my desire to explain what had happened with Demer that made me stay there. Tilghman, I thought, had some insight. He knew details I didn't know. But it wasn't a subject lightly broached. I didn't want to ask him point-blank. He was my friend, and I didn't want to accuse him. And it was my character *not* to ask, so that an issue could evolve without the distortion questions engendered. I wanted Tilghman to tell me what had happened of his own volition and in his own time. I wanted him to confess.

In the first few days I was there, Tilghman said half-a-dozen times how much he'd missed writing letters. He'd intended to write, but he'd been preoccupied getting started in Tucson. But that was not an excuse. Friendship shouldn't require a reply. It was just that he'd been focused on making his half million in a hurry.

"Only a half million?" I asked.

"That's all I needed."

"And where is it?"

He smiled. "In a bank."

"So you own this house?"

"Oh, yes, it's my house. That's why I'm building the wall in back."

"There's already a wall."

"And then I'm going to plant trees and restore the garage into an apartment."

"And not bother with the house?"

"The house comes last. That's where I live."

"You really made a half million?"

"In real estate," he said. "A little more, maybe. It was easy."

He had let the house go. All the rooms needed patching and paint. The windows needed glazing. Those were long-term necessities. The dirt in the corners, cobwebs on the ceilings, dishes in the sink, cockroaches were shorter term. The scarcity of furniture and the blank walls hadn't been Tilghman's intent. I came to understand gradually someone else had lived there with him and had moved out. That was why there was room for me.

I had always been lazier about friendship. My contribution was over the telephone—the quick fix. I'd call my uncle, for instance, or Demer when we were apart, or Tilghman occasionally. The phone bill was the price I paid for not taking the time to write.

Tilghman's letters were the kind I took with me when I traveled. He described the paintings he was studying in Yugoslavia, discussed the struggle for art in a poor land where the spirit had been submerged in politics. He wrote about loneliness on the salmon boat, though he was with five other crew, including a woman who liked him. He was frequently lonely, he said, though he had understood it only later when he was happy. He used to tell me how lucky I was to have a passion for birds. He'd never had more than his father's expectations.

He wrote me about drinking sprees and fights in bars, about encounters with women who cared too much for him too soon, about daring, sometimes-pointless acts he could not explain, even to himself—river rafting in spring flood on the North Platte, sky-diving one summer in St. Cloud, solo climbing in the Zirkel Wilderness outside Steamboat. Before Demer had gone to visit, I used to get a letter like that every month or two.

There was resonance in the letters, too, the kind of resonance you feel in a friend like that. It wasn't so much that he was a mirror of me—we weren't so much alike really—but rather an echo, another voice of myself. He gave me a way of hearing myself speak, a test of whether what I said meshed with what I saw around me and heard myself say. For a long time I had depended on Tilghman for that pure tone.

Chapter six

Harriet came to my class lecture on a Thursday when we were talking about geography. I drew on the board a shape I thought resembled North America—Alaska, Canada, the continental United States. "What's missing?" I asked.

"The islands," said Cynthia Turner in the front row.

"Islands." I drew in some token islands off California and Maine. I dotted in the Florida Keys and the Aleutians and added Afognak and Kodiak for Harriet's benefit. "What else?"

"State lines," said the bearded man, Laszlo Kornyei.

I didn't draw the state lines. "Why are state lines important?"

"The Mann Act," Laszlo said.

Rosalie Hull took exception. "First of all, men are pigs. Second, state lines are of no significance to avian habitat, which happens to be the topic under discussion. There are no boundaries for birds except climate and terrain. What's missing from the map are Mexico, Central America, and South America."

"Way to go, Rosalie," someone said.

"Correct." I drew in approximations of Mexico and Central America and erased the border between the United States and Mexico. "Now, who can give me some details of topography?"

"What's topography?" asked the woman with the buzzed hair.

"Let's start with the local area," I said. "What does Arizona look like?"

"Square," she said.

Most of them knew Arizona. The Colorado River ran through the Grand Canyon. The San Francisco Mountains were north of Flagstaff. There were mountains around Tucson—the

Rincons, the Santa Catalinas, the Sierritas—which we could see out the window. There was desert. It was hot in Phoenix.

"What about Mexico?" I asked.

"More desert?" said Holly.

"Are you asking me or telling me?"

"Yes."

"What about Popocatepetl? What about jungle? Have you ever heard of the Yucatan? Who knows the terrain around Acapulco?"

Rosalie Hull raised her hand, but I didn't call on her.

"How can you know birds if you don't know the landscape?" I asked. "We need maps. We need reports. You and you," I said, pointing to students at random, "bring in charts of Mexico—rainfall, mountains, and all that. I want a topo map of Arizona, too. Does anyone know how much rainfall we get in Arizona?"

"Not enough," Lazslo said. "My father's got to irrigate all the time."

Rosalie Hull spoke up without raising her hand. "You can't ask a question like that," she said. "It's not a question of judgment. We get the rainfall that comes to us. Plant life evolves its own response to moisture. Ocotillo rolls its leaves during drought and unrolls them when it rains. Saguaros store the water they need. Birds and mammals adapt to heat and the allotted water just like plants. If there were more rain, we'd have a radically different ecology."

"Way to go, Rosalie," I said. "Why don't you bring to class a climatological map of the Southwest?" I turned to the class. "Now, will anyone volunteer to help me set up mist nets on Sunday afternoon?"

No one raised a hand. The bell rang.

Harriet and I walked down the hall to my office, or really, Fred's office. We stopped in front of the door where Fred had pasted a huge picture of two whooping cranes dancing. They looked like vaudeville performers, their long legs high stepping, their white wings raised.

"Alberta," I said. "Wood Buffalo National Park, Alberta. That's where the cranes dance." I unlocked the door. "Would you like to come in?"

"Another time," Harriet said.

"Is that a promise?"

Harriet nodded. "What time Sunday?" she asked. "I don't

know much about the desert birds, but I'll help you with the nets."

I searched her expression for signs of intent, but there weren't any. "Later rather than earlier," I said. "Maybe around four. The sun won't be so hot then."

"All right."

"The mist nets are in the science building. You want to meet me here?"

"Fine. I hope you weren't offended that I came today."

"Should I be?"

"I was checking up."

"Oh?" I had been standing by the door, and suddenly, though I didn't mean to be rude, I turned and went in and let the door swing to.

Harriet caught the door, pushed it open, and stepped into the office. Fred had nests everywhere around the room—tiny nests of hummingbirds mounted on plasterboard, exotic nests of bowerbirds, orioles, becards, weaver finches. They were draped from the ceiling and hung from the walls. He even had a hawk's nest of sticks and feathers and bones on a wide shelf above the bookcase.

"The museum," Harriet said. "I forget sometimes how odd Fred is."

"Each in his own way."

"I was concerned about you, Scott. I had to be for the committee's sake. None of us questioned your skills as a birder, but we took a risk hiring you to teach. I've seen you lead a group once well and once not so well, but I know you can be good with people. Jack Watkins praised you to the skies. But the woman at Big Birds said you'd missed a group one morning and that you argued with clients."

"I get the picture," I said.

"Don't be that way, Scott." Harriet smiled, but it wasn't a smile. "You're here, aren't you? I couldn't have had too many doubts."

"I don't let my work interfere with my personal life," I said.

Harriet was hurt. She stared at me, and then turned and went out the door without another word. I was angry, too, but mostly at myself. I closed the door gently and heard it click.

Chapter seven

That first week or two I looked for apartments. There was a place on Seventh Street, a motel-room condo, for $660 a month, and a duplex out on Tanque Verde for $800. How could I pay that? It wasn't so much that I was in Tilghman's way as that I wanted to make an honest effort to prove I couldn't afford other housing. Tilghman proposed a work-for-rent scheme. I'd help in the backyard when I had the spare time, and I could sleep free. Food was extra. A deal.

The house was quirky. There was no shower, for instance, so Tilghman had adapted by swimming every day at the university pool. Crickets lived behind the refrigerator, and when it went on, they chirped. The screen door had holes in it, but Tilghman kept chameleons leashed on fishing lines to eat the insects that might enter. He put sugar in the salt shakers. None of these were oddities I couldn't live with.

There was something else, though, that I couldn't put my finger on. Tilghman was preoccupied. He was busy in a way I didn't understand—all the while he was building his wall, rearranging his backyard, making lists of things to do, something else was on his mind. I knew Tilghman well enough to know he wasn't telling me something.

The afternoon Harriet visited my class, I worked with Tilghman in the backyard. He'd begun a trench for the foundation of the new wall, and while he wielded the pick, I shoveled the loose clay from the ditch. The trench ran the boundary of the setback requirement, about two feet from the existing sidewalk, and a foot or so from the already-existing adobe wall. It was a warm day, perfect if we hadn't been digging in the hard earth.

"So why don't you build the other wall higher?" I asked.

"I want more space."

"For what?"

"Privacy."

I stopped digging and wiped my forehead on my bare arm. "If you have this half million, why not buy a better place?"

"I don't want a better place."

"You could buy privacy."

"If I spent my money for a bigger house, I wouldn't have any time," Tilghman said. "This way I can live on the interest and do what I want. Besides, people in big houses have to work at privacy. I was married to Clarice, remember? People were always bugging her. I want anonymity."

"Like building this huge wall?"

"No one will notice the wall," Tilghman said. "Are you going to talk or dig?"

We worked another hour without saying much. Once I rested and went inside for a beer, but Tilghman kept on. "You want one?" I called from the kitchen.

"Can't," he said.

I brought out a cold Rolling Rock and drank a little. "You used to like a beer once in a while."

"Still do," Tilghman said, "but I'm in training."

I looked at him. Tilghman swung the pick down into the crust of the earth. His legs and arms were taut sinew. "Training for what?"

"The right moment." He stopped and leaned on the pick. He was sweating hard. "You drink, Scott, and your life goes down the drain. And if you don't drink, nobody likes you."

"I'll drink to that." I raised the green bottle to his wisdom and took another swallow. "Who doesn't like you?"

"Francie."

"She's the one who owned the furniture that isn't there and the paintings that aren't on the walls?"

"The paintings were mine," Tilghman said. "I sold them."

"She made you stop drinking?"

"No, Francie thought I was nicer when I drank. I was gentler, she said. She didn't ask me to stop. I stopped on my own. Anyway she's a dancer, not a psychiatrist. She models to pay her bills. Can you believe this world? She has slim ankles, so some idiot pays her seventy-five dollars an hour to model stockings and shoes."

"You stopped drinking and she moved out?"

"Something like that. She was free to choose."

Tilghman lifted the pick and wheeled it above his head. His back glistened with sweat, but he barely breathed hard from the work. I wondered what the right moment was he was training for. I swigged the last of the Rolling Rock and tossed the bottle toward the door. Zapata got up from the shade of the grapefruit tree and licked the top. I picked up the shovel and went on digging.

Chapter eight

Demer had spent her childhood in rich gardens of embassies. Banana trees, mimosas, birds, scents of flowers had been her environment. Her mother read books and went to lavish parties. Demer thought of her father dressed in tuxedos or hunting clothes more often than she thought of him in a doctor's white coat. They had servants, too. In her household there was always someone to take a message to the minister of justice or to the Committee on Economic Development, or an invitation to the wife of a general; always someone to fetch a drink, wash the floor, do the laundry. There were secretaries, bodyguards, caterers, gardeners.

Once when they lived in Mexico, a man attempted to assassinate the U.S. ambassador. The man climbed the embassy wall in broad daylight and hurled a grenade through one of the grilled windows on the second floor. The grenade exploded in a bathroom and killed a cleaning woman who was polishing the ornate mirror that formed one entire wall. The toilet was blown up, and water leaked down the brocaded wall of the West Room.

The man had been summarily shot by embassy guards before anyone could ask his motives or identify his cause. Demer had been downstairs with her father when he was summoned, and she'd followed him up to the bedroom. The woman's blood was all over the bathroom and the shards of the blown-apart mirror. From a window she saw the man lying on the cobblestone drive, bleeding.

The Mexican government apologized to the embassy personnel and assured them it was nothing personal. But Demer never forgot what had happened. She talked of the incident as both real and imagined, and each time I heard her tell the story, it was a little different, slightly embellished, and I was conscious of its powerful influence on her. A dream can be as persuasive as death, and Demer kept talking about the man lying on the stones.

She wanted to go back to Guatemala. She said it was a land so beautiful it made her ache. But she was torn. Her nursing mattered to her; her friends meant something. We had a marriage. Once she went back with a team of nutrition experts who were to advise villagers of ways to improve the health of their children. Demer had lived in Guatemala City growing up, she said, and the only times she had been to the country were to someone's fancy *finca*. But on that visit she spent three weeks in the villages.

Not long after she came back, we had a dinner party for friends—Annie and Eric Minter, Paige Jones-Ruiz, and a couple of others. Demer showed slides. She described the people and the villages she'd visited, what the volunteers had done in each place. Every day they had traveled out from the provincial capital to a village and spoken to the women there. The men were at work in the milpas or away at jobs in the capital, so the women were isolated with the children and old people. One woman demonstrated the use of powdered milk by pouring it on her children's heads. That was all she knew.

Demer laughed, telling about it, and in the midst of laughing, she cried. She was sitting between Paige and me on the sofa, and she leaned over and said, "God, Scott, I'm so sorry."

I put my arm around her. "Sorry for what?"

She looked at me and then at everyone else in the room, and I knew what she was sorry for. The slide on the screen showed the woman and a handsome young Guatemalan man in a white coat.

Demer composed herself and showed more pictures. She told about the army troops which had invaded one of the villages they had gone to. It had been the night before a wedding. The army was supposedly looking for guerrillas. Most of the men in the village were in the city because no one had money, and the crops had been burned in the fields by the army which suspected the villagers of providing food to the enemy. Somehow one of the old men had learned of the attack, and a few of the women delayed the advance by setting off fireworks along the road into town. That allowed the others to flee into the hills.

One woman had a sick child to carry and a little boy who held her hand. It was dark, and the hills were steep. The mother had to let go of the little boy's hand to keep her balance, and the boy ran under a bush to hide. The woman thought he was following her, and when she discovered he wasn't, she had to go back. She called for him. The government troops heard her calling, and they killed her and the baby and the little boy—all three. Then the soldiers burned the village to the ground. There was no wedding. The bride had been caught and raped and killed, too.

Demer had told me this story before the dinner party, but in company the story was different, like her childhood memory of the man lying on the stones. It was different for me, too, because now I had seen the man in the white coat.

Later, after the guests had left, I asked, "Who was he?"

"No one you know."

"One of the nutritionists?"

"A man named Rafael, who was the liaison for us to the villages."

"And everyone knew about you?"

"Everyone knew? Is that what you're worried about?"

That was what I'd thought of first.

"Everyone knew," Demer said.

That was the first infidelity I found out about. I don't know how many others there were. Nursing gave her a ready excuse for anything because there was no routine to her work. Sometimes she worked nights if her patients needed her then. Sometimes before or after her duty, she put in a few hours at the American Field Service office in Boston or stuffed envelopes for Amnesty International or made telephone calls to raise money. She told me where she was, and I believed her. I never asked her where she'd been.

For this I suffered. Not every day, but often enough. Sometimes when I was on the assembly line at my uncle's factory, I'd wonder where Demer was, whether she was taking pledges for Amnesty International or fucking someone else. Or when I was in the field leading a tour along a trail in south Texas, I'd wonder whether she was sleeping with someone else when I wasn't there.

Even when we were together making love, when I felt her body around me, arms and legs, and I heard her sigh, I wondered who the sighs were for. I would say silently, "I forgive you, I forgive you."

But I didn't forgive her. I wanted to. I loved Demer that much. But already the darkness had started.

Chapter nine

Sunday afternoon I drove over to the science building to get the mist nets. I had the idea Harriet wouldn't show up. She hadn't spoken to me since our disagreement in my office, and I assumed her grudge would linger at least through the weekend. I didn't blame her. As usual when something went wrong, I blamed myself.

But when I pulled into the semicircular, palm-lined driveway, there she was, talking to a tall man in a red AU jacket. He was slightly stooped, middle-aged, gray. I wondered who the competition was. Harriet was laughing at something the man was saying. I stopped and gave a tentative wave and got out.

"This is Jaime Arguello," Harriet said. "He's the maintenance man for the building and knows where everything is."

"You going to use those nets finally?" Jaime asked. "No one ever used them before. I got them checked out for you. No holes."

"Thanks."

"Jaime said you'd asked for them," Harriet said. "It's Sunday, and he came down to make sure you had what you needed."

Jaime nodded. "I hear you give a good class, professor."

Jaime helped me put the mist nets into the Toyota, canting the poles out through the open window on the passenger's side. They were a little shorter than volleyball poles, and the nets were thinner mesh. The university had ten of them.

Harriet threw her day pack on top of the netting in back. "I brought sandwiches," she said, "in case we break down on the highway."

Harriet was dressed for the desert—long pants, a light canvas shirt, boots, a light green scarf around her neck. She had coiled her hair on top of her head, which was new for her, I thought. At least I hadn't seen it that way before. We both thanked Jaime and were off.

Speedway to the interstate: we headed south. I knew the way. Once we got going, with the windows rolled down and the air whirling through the car, Harriet tied the green scarf over her hair. We slid from the city into mesquite and creosote flats. The highway was warm, slippery. Harriet chatted about Jaime, about whales, about Fred's phlebitis. She had apparently forgotten my rudeness of a few days before.

"There's a conference coming up in California on the state of the oceans," she said. "The greenhouse effect is warming the water and endangering the life of the sea. The university will pay for its faculty to attend. Maybe you'd like to go. There are never any ornithologists at these meetings."

"I don't want to press my luck as a visiting professor," I said.

"You can think about it."

The light soothed as we drove. Clouds swarmed over the Sierritas, and the sun broke into visible rays. We eased past the greasewood salt flats which supported no birds at all. In that country even the jackrabbits had to carry their lunches. To our left was the Santa Cruz River, and when we intersected that, the terrain changed. Willows and cottonwoods graced the wide river bottom. Foothills rose in arcs from the river and ascended gradually toward Mount Wrightson in the distance.

"Jack Watkins also told me about your wife," Harriet said. "I'm sorry."

Exit sixty-three, Madera Canyon. We drove east a mile from the interstate to a crossroads called Continental, where I pulled into the dusty parking lot of a store. The last time I'd been there it had been a one-family store, a place to buy gasoline, groceries, hardware, clothes. Campers stopped there for fuel, frozen hamburger meat, sunscreen. Now it was a package store with iron bars on the windows.

I asked the Asian woman at the cash register what had happened to the groceries. What about the Maestases who'd run the place? The woman shook her head. "Food down at Safeway," she said. "Other side of freeway. This is Green Valley now.

People live all around here."

I bought a six-pack of Budweiser and peeled one from the plastic ring before I got back into the car.

We turned southeast on a narrow paved road that transected the state experimental grasslands on both sides. The gently sloping bajadas were covered with cholla, ocotillo, and saguaro, and lush broom grass that hadn't been grazed in years. It was perfect habitat for desert birds and wintering sparrows from the north. Madera Canyon was farther on, six miles more, where oaks and sycamores billowed out from the barren rocks of the mountains.

I wedged open the beer, drank, and set the can between my legs as I drove.

"Do I get one?" Harriet asked.

"Help yourself."

"Is that where we're going? The trees?"

"I think we'll set the nets first in the wash. It's not that hot anymore, but hot enough so the snakes will still be in cover."

We crossed a bridge over a sandy dry creek, and I pulled the car over. I'd been there before, too—Florida Wash. It was a good spot because the grassland ran right up to the steep, rocky bank. Water was the life of the desert, and even a dry bed provided nutrients and cover. Along the wash was a tangle of paloverde, cactus, hackberry, and ironwood. We got out and unloaded five nets.

A slight breeze skittered off the foothills and down the bajada, but it wasn't enough to break the heat on the sand. We walked downstream. A gnatcatcher scolded us, and far away, an early Bell's Vireo sang its staccato song from a thicket. I carried my open beer in one hand, one in my back pocket, and three mist nets over my shoulder.

The idea was to set the nets where birds would encounter them in their normal feeding patterns along the banks. They couldn't see the netting, and a fair sampling would get caught in the mesh. The nets didn't hurt them, so long as the nets were checked regularly. We'd log the species by date, weight, length, and fat content, and we'd chart food supply, weather, and the number of individuals and species. In that way, as spring proceeded, we could determine the bird movements, together with the variations of migrant and indigenous populations. Naturally I hoped to trap some rare vagrant—a Mexican warbler or an exotic oriole which might wander a little north of its normal range in the Sierra Madre Occidental.

It took nearly an hour to find a good place to stake the nets and to set them right. Afterward we sat in the sand and shared the warm beer I'd carried in my back pocket. The light in the wash eased, and the shadows of the Sierritas edged toward us. The air cooled. We listened to birds call—a Curve-billed Thrasher, a Northern Cardinal, a Phainopepla.

A bird guide had to pay attention to all the signs in the natural world. He had to see everything clearly, without imagining. It was a learned ability, one I prided myself on. I'd discovered birds in the fourth grade, not long after my parents were killed. A lady named Miss Watham, who lived next door to my parents, had kept feeders in her backyard, and I'd sit at her window in winter and watch the nuthatches and woodpeckers and chickadees, the juncos and wintering sparrows, and now and then a few crossbills. I remember once, on a snowy day, a flock of birds descended out of nowhere into the crab-apple tree by her clothesline. I was stunned by the birds' sleekness, their black masks, their warm brown backs and the beautiful yellow fringe on the ends of their tails. They were like ornaments on the leafless tree. Then, as a horde, they took off again, and it was as if I had dreamed them. Bohemian Waxwings.

That spring Miss Watham gave me a bird book and sat with me in her yard. We figured out the warblers and thrushes and vireos and tanagers that passed through her small orchard. She knew them all, but pretended she didn't. I was enthralled. What I learned I wanted to know and didn't forget. Ever. It had nothing to do with school.

That was how I had started to learn, and the lessons, years later, were translated into guide work. The brain sifts out codes, the names which fit the empirical evidence. Even a distant bird, one not seen well through binoculars, may still be identifiable by family. A woodpecker, for example, flies in rhythmic flaps and glides in the motion of a wave, and a pipit, flushed from a grassy field, will spiral and call high into the sky. A Turkey Vulture soars on upraised wings, while a Black Vulture flaps wildly and turns in tight circles. A Northern Harrier twists and skims low to the ground. A kestrel hovers, as do Ospreys, kingfishers, terns (but not gulls), and hummingbirds. A silhouette can sometimes be sufficient: a Mourning Dove perches on a wire at a certain oblique angle; a kingbird is more erect; a kestrel is larger.

Habitat and range. Where in the realm of air do you see the bird? On the coast: which coast? In the forest: where is the forest? What kind of trees does it contain? Is the bird in the forest on the ground (grouse, thrushes, *oporornis* warblers), in the middle story (kinglets, certain *vermivora* warblers, flycatchers), or in the highest branches of the trees (Blackburnian Warbler, for one)? If by fresh water, is it marshland or mud flat or running water? If in the mountains, where are the mountains and how high in the mountains is the bird? In Arizona, for instance, Red-faced and Olive warblers are only found above six thousand feet. Grace's Warbler and Painted Redstarts are lower. In the Rockies above timberline, you'll find Rosy Finches, but not House Finches; White-tailed Ptarmigan, but not Willow or Rock Ptarmigan; eagles, but not harriers.

A bird close in, or one seen clearly in binoculars, is easy: a shiny, blue-black bird, slightly smaller than a robin, with a crest and a red eye, and white on the outer primaries—I'd know that bird immediately as a Phainopepla, family Ptilogonatidae. It flutters when it flies, makes a syrupy *wurp*, as if asking a question. Even if I saw the bird in Ohio or Vermont, though its range is Texas, Arizona, and California, I'd know it. I was always attuned to birds' normal ranges, the seasons they moved, the habitat, though I never dismissed the fundamental fact that birds can fly. I didn't expect to see Ivory Gull in Maine in summer, but there I had found one. There is a photograph, too, of a Laysan Albatross on a sidewalk in Yuma, Arizona.

The bird guide had to see the smallest details in the shortest time: the flash of wing bars on a flycatcher, say, or the shape and banding on an accipiter's tail. He looked at the length and shape of the beak—a vireo's bill is thicker than a warbler's, smaller than a tanager's. He recognized patterns on the head and throat—how extensive is the black on the face or cap? How far down the breast does yellow extend? Are there stripes, speckles, streaks, or spots on the breast? He knew songs. The Cassin's Sparrow sings a more lilting melody than a Rufous-winged Sparrow which occupies the same grassland. I knew all these things absolutely, without any doubt, which was not the way I knew other things.

Sitting with Harriet in the sand wash, listening to the birds' distant singing, I felt at ease. The mountains had lost their rocky sharpness in the evening light and had receded to pink and gray. But even as I heard the birds' calls, I put names to them.

Harriet touched my arm. Something had rustled in the grass near the edge of the bank. "Do you think it's a snake?" she asked.

"We should go on up into the canyon anyway," I said, "before it gets dark."

Madera Canyon had a running stream, and because of the flowing water, a different flora and fauna from the nearby grassland and desert. The stream emptied from the Wrightson Basin and, fed by springs, rushed down the rocky corridor between slashes of tall oaks and sycamores toward the Santa Cruz River.

By the time we reached the lower canyon, the sun had fallen below the Sierritas, and we could see how much higher Mount Wrightson was than the surrounding mountains. The top quarter of the rocky summit was still in the sun.

I stopped at Proctor Road. A few people were picnicking in the area just above us, and children's voices ran along the streambed. Farther up, I knew, were a campground, summer homes, and then, at the end of the road, another picnic area and the trailhead for the mountains.

I turned left onto the gravel and parked near the stream, where the canyon opened out into the plain. "This is the best we can do," I said. "If we went higher, I'm afraid someone would disturb the nets."

The birds here were of the riparian woodland. A Black Phoebe we wouldn't have seen in Florida Wash darted from its perch, snared an insect above the water, and returned to its snag, flicking its tail as it sat. A towhee scratched in damp leaves under a sycamore tree. We set the nets in the understory on the far bank where people were less likely to come across them. One double net extended the width of the split in the stream, and we set two others in scrub oak and chokecherry on the hillside.

When we were through, we were in no hurry to leave. Harriet got her backpack and sat on a boulder above the water. I carried the rest of the beer.

The Sierritas were blue-black then, and along the sloping bajada beneath us, saguaro and ocotillo blended with the grass and the distant cottonwoods along the river. The headlights of cars going up and down the canyon scattered light into the canopy of leaves. Now and then, above the murmur of the stream, the lights of fires and the voices of children slipped in and out of the air.

Then the air darkened, and the arc of what we could see tightened around us. The stream lost its light, though we could hear it still. The sun was gone, but remained in the rock on which we sat. I felt its heat with my bare hand. I could feel, too, Harriet's silent pressure, so different from before in Monterey. This was her territory, where she lived. I was at hand longer than for a night.

To explain why we were there, I would have said we were listening for owls. Elf Owls called from the deep sycamores and screech owls gave their eerie whistles. But I didn't explain it or need to. Night is only a shadow the sun makes, a cone of darkness which extends behind the earth like the tail of a comet. The sun is a star, and lying back on that smooth warm rock, I wondered how many other nights I was seeing in addition to our own moonless one. For outside this cone of night was light, and we were only temporarily in the shadow.

Chapter ten

That night when I got back from Madera Canyon, I found
Tilghman standing in the backyard. The streetlights shone
through the oleanders and bloomed in the dirt like silver flow-
ers. Tilghman was in the dark by the side of the house.

At first I thought he'd been drinking. He didn't acknowl-
edge me, didn't say hello, though he must have heard my car
drive up and me stumble through the broken gate. I was a little
tight from the six-pack of Budweiser. "You all right?" I asked.

He didn't answer for a minute. I looked around the yard.
He hadn't made any more progress that I could see. The broken
adobe from the old wall, the cinder blocks, the ready-mix—all
were where they had been. We had finished the trench days
before.

"I'm going to Mexico," he said. "Will you watch Zapata?"

"Okay. When?"

"Now. I'm ready to go."

"In the middle of the night?"

He nodded vaguely. "There's a man coming tomorrow to
work on the wall. Will you be around?"

"As far as I know."

"I have to count on you, Scott."

"I'll be here," I said. "Where are you going in Mexico?"

"A fishing village called Puerto Peñasco on the Gulf of
California."

"Never heard of it," I said.

Tilghman's tone lightened. "Now you have. I have a friend
there, Ellis Carmichael. We smoke a little dope, lie in the sun,
eat squid and flounder and shrimp."

"For that you leave now?"

"Yes." He didn't explain further, and I didn't ask. We stood for a minute more and listened to a mockingbird sing in the dark.

"Do you remember that night in Cambridge we picked up that girl," Tilghman asked, "that one in front of the Brattle Theater?"

"The one with the beret. Lots of sweaters and coats."

"We gave her a ride home. I had that Datsun with the seat that wasn't bolted to the frame."

"She said she lived on Mass. Ave. Yes, I remember."

Tilghman took a breath. "I think of her sometimes. I wonder about her. When I get very tired, I settle on her."

"And you're very tired?"

"You don't know how tired I am."

I sat down on the cube of red bricks in the lighted part of the yard and positioned myself so a branch of the oleander shielded me from the beam of the streetlight. I was half drunk and had reading to do for my class, but Tilghman was in a mood, and I didn't want to miss it if he'd talk.

I remembered that night we'd picked up the girl. It must have been ten, eleven years ago, maybe twelve. It had been January, late at night. We were on our way back to Eliot House, and the girl was sitting on the curb. Her hair was tucked under her beret, and she had on so many sweaters and coats she looked fat and shapeless. It was freezing out. Tilghman pulled over, rolled his window down, and took the beret off her head. "We're the Jesse James Cab Company," he said. "We'll take you anywhere you want to go."

"You got any grass?" the girl asked.

"No grass. Where do you live?"

The girl had a dazed look. "Duluth."

"I'm from St. Cloud," Tilghman said. "Are you waiting for someone?"

"Jacksonville," the girl said. "I want to go to Jacksonville."

"I'm from Jacksonville, too," Tilghman said. "Come on, we'll drive you home."

The girl snatched her beret, which Tilghman was dangling over her head. She got to her feet. "I live on Mass. Ave.," she said.

I got out and helped her into the front seat between us. Tilghman jolted forward and the seat snapped back. We picked up speed toward the old trolley barn. The girl hadn't said which direction on Mass. Ave., but Tilghman headed toward Central Square.

Traffic was thin. The sidewalks were deserted. The cold made the light seem brittle. Streetlights and an occasional headlight shimmered through the icy air. We crossed Western Avenue. "Whereabouts?" Tilghman asked.

"Farther," the girl said.

We passed through Central Square, whizzed by the dwindling buildings until M.I.T. loomed up in front of us.

"Over the bridge," the girl said.

"Why don't we get her a real cab?" I asked. "Go over to Copley Square to the hotels."

The girl closed her eyes. Tilghman ignored me. We crossed the river, skimmed over Storrow Drive, whose lights curved away along the river ice. We dropped down into Back Bay. It was one in the morning, and then suddenly we were in Roxbury. Three white faces stared through the frosted windshield. There were no numbers on the buildings. Blackened brick, stone walk-ups, blocks of rundown stores. Tilghman nudged the girl, and she leaned forward and opened one eye. "Maybe you passed it," she said.

She watched for a couple of blocks. Finally she recognized a dilapidated walk-up. Lights were on in the windows. Business transpiring. Tilghman double-parked. He wanted to go in.

"I'll wait in the car," I said.

Three black men came out of one of the apartments and crossed in front of the car. I decided to go in, too.

The girl's roommate was named Pearl. Pearl was a he. He offered us a drink and a smoke. Tilghman said yes. We sat around for an hour listening to music, listening to the sharp voices in the next apartment come through the thin walls. A man and a woman were fighting, breaking things, and then afterward, sighs. Pearl offered the girl in payment for the ride home, saying it had saved him from going all that way across the river.

Tilghman declined politely. We had another beer and then left. We never saw the girl again.

I shifted my place on the bricks when a breeze moved the oleander. Light rushed through. "Why do you think of her?" I asked.

He shrugged. "I wonder what happens to people is all. Where is she now? What's she doing?"

"She's probably married to a doctor and lives in Newton."

"She's probably dead," Tilghman said.

I didn't say anything. The light burned my eyes.

"Disappeared," Tilghman said. "No trace."

Tilghman went inside and threw some clothes from a cardboard box into a satchel. In a few minutes he was ready. "Zapata needs food and water," he said. "The vet's number is by the phone. Take him to the park to run once in a while. The guy who's building the wall is named Ramon. He's supposed to work all week and the weekend. If you want, give him a hand."

"You won't be back for a while?"

"If Ramon has questions, you can call me. I'll give you Ellis's number."

"I take it Ramon has instructions?"

"One of these days he's supposed to bring some orange trees. Maybe you can help him plant them. I've marked the places on the ground."

Tilghman carried his satchel to the kitchen and pulled open the door of the refrigerator. He took out bread, sandwich slices, a Coke. He got peanut butter from the cupboard.

"Don't forget the number," I said.

"Right, the number." He wrote the number on a piece of paper.

"Who's Ellis?"

Tilghman went to the bookshelf in the living room and brought back a book with a red, white and blue dust jacket. "This is Ellis," he said, turning the back of the book to me.

The jacket photograph was a profile of a dark-haired man gazing downward. His hair was long and hung over his ears and covered his cheek. His eyes were in shadow, and the effect was of a man hiding in his own portrait. "Ellis in 1965," Tilghman said.

I turned the book over. "*Carte Blanche*," I said. "I've heard of that."

"It was a best-seller in the sixties," Tilghman said. "When it was written, we were ten."

I read the jacket flap:

Carte Blanche *is the first novel of a major new talent. It strikes like lightning and sizzles in the hand. This is the tragic story of two people immersed in a world of false values and relentless egotism, who fight the system and each other in search of truth. Tim Argus and Clare Wood reflect the new vulnerability of those who struggle to assert the glory of the human spirit. Ellis Carmichael is a voice everyone who fears for his country should heed.*

Tilghman zipped his satchel and carried it and the paper bag full of food into the living room. Zapata jumped down from the sofa, and Tilghman scratched the dog's neck. Tilghman was nervous about going, I could tell.

"You can come with me sometime, Scott," he said. "It would do you good to get some sun. Take good care of Zapata, right?"

"Right."

"Oh, one other thing. If Francie shows up, don't let her in here. Under no circumstances."

I nodded. "Is that likely?"

"Maybe." Tilghman nuzzled Zapata. Then he picked up his satchel and went out the back way. I was still holding Ellis Carmichael's book.

Chapter eleven

On Monday I drove my class to Florida Wash and Madera Canyon to check the mist nets. I showed them how to extract the birds from the mesh—to figure out first which side of the net the bird had flown into, to ruffle the net gently so the wings wouldn't be damaged, to pick the netting gingerly from the legs and feet. We had a good sampling the first day—two Bell's Vireos, a half dozen Blue-gray Gnatcatchers, a Curve-billed Thrasher, four cardinals, a Pyrrhuloxia, a Virginia's Warbler, a dozen Yellow-rumped Warblers, a Gray-breasted Jay, a Western Meadowlark, a Ladder-backed Woodpecker, an early Lazuli Bunting strayed maybe from the river, and a Sharp-shinned Hawk. We speculated about the drama enacted before the hawk had hit the net, since next to it, only three or four inches away, was a gnatcatcher whose life had been spared when both birds had struck the mesh.

We measured the birds, weighed them, sampled tactilely their fat content and the condition of their feathers. We ran through the various field marks of each species. Most were straightforward: who could miss the Lazuli Bunting's brilliant blue? Or the thrasher's bill (though there were other thrashers with curved bills)? But some were tougher. The Western Meadowlark was not so easily distinguished from the Eastern, and though we had no direct comparison in hand, it was possible to see the wider yellow on the breast and to listen to the Western's song in the nearby grassland. We noted the differences between a female cardinal, which was brownish, versus the grayer, but similar, Pyrrhuloxia.

We had only one casualty. The Gray-breasted Jay, a common species, of the desert mountains, had broken a wing when it had tried to untangle itself from the net.

A day later I went to Harriet's for dinner. She lived north of town just off El Camino Way in one of the older neighborhoods which, in recent years, had been inundated by developments like Desert Rose, Sunset Village, and Flaming Rocks. Harriet's place, though, was an original frame bungalow surrounded by a few eucalyptus trees and a small, fenced-in yard. Yellow paint was chipping from one side of the house, but the yard was neat— a little grass, some saguaros and prickly pear, and bare ground. Gambel's Quail scurried along the brushy margins, and a pair of Cactus Wrens had nested in a clump of cholla at the corner of the lot. Off to the east Mount Lemmon rose like a block of beige quartz in the full light of the sun.

Harriet greeted me at the door in a blue dress. I handed her a magnum of Mondavi white in case she hadn't had time to buy liquor. "Thank you," she said. "I don't know that I own a corkscrew. I don't entertain much."

"I have a Swiss army knife," I said. "For emergencies."

"I was just making my mother a gin and tonic," she said. "Would you like one?"

"Perfect," I said. "And you look wonderful in that dress."

She turned around and laughed. She'd done up her hair again, too, wound it at the nape so her bare neck showed. It made her face fuller, I thought, and set off her eyes.

Harriet pointed toward the screened porch. "Mother," she said, and she rolled her eyes. "Why don't you take this gin and tonic in to her? I'll bring yours in a minute."

I carried the drink out onto the porch. Mrs. Keating was sitting with her back to me. A metal cane was hooked around the armrest of her chair. When she turned, I saw she was as striking as Harriet, but a little taller and finer boned. "Are you the ornithologist?" she said.

"The bird guide," I said. I set the glass on a coaster on the table beside her.

Harriet brought in two more drinks. "Scott is the man we hired to take Fred's place," she said. "This is Scott Talmadge."

"Do you know Fred?" Harriet's mother asked.

"A little."

"He's a bore, isn't he? If everyone were as dull as Fred, there wouldn't be any children in the world."

Harriet sat down on the wrought-iron chair and straightened some magazines on the table. "Be nice, Mother."

Mrs. Keating eyed me. "Have you ever seen a California Condor, Mr. Talmadge?"

"I've seen three."

"I mean in the wild."

"These were in Los Padres National Forest north of Los Angeles," I said. "One flew over me at two hundred feet."

"I've always wanted to see a condor. I could see one in a zoo, I suppose, but that wouldn't be the same."

"In a few more years, a zoo will be the only place to see anything," Harriet said.

Her mother turned in her chair. "Be nice, Harriet. Don't start a fight."

"I'm not starting a fight."

"Harriet's always complaining about the human race," Mrs. Keating said.

Harriet rose to the bait. "Acid rain, ozone depletion, global warming, pollution of the seas. Look around us, Mother. That doesn't happen without people."

"She's a pessimist, isn't she?" Mrs. Keating asked me.

"Look at Desert Rose," Harriet said. "Where's the water going to come from for all those people? And if they *get* water, what will happen to wherever *doesn't* get water?"

"Icebergs. Someone will make a fortune in icebergs."

The dinner didn't go smoothly. Mother and daughter sparred with one another, and sometime around the fifth round, I opened the bottle of wine, hoping to have everyone drink himself or herself to amiable distraction. We talked a little about birds and the early spring weather which had melted most of the snow from Mount Lemmon. Then Harriet's mother asked me about my apartment hunting. "Have you found something?" she wanted to know. "I'm thinking of moving from here."

"My mother thinks moving is the answer to everything," Harriet said. "She has a Tolstoy complex."

"Do you know Tolstoy, Mr. Talmadge?" Mrs. Keating asked.

"Not personally."

"Have you read *War and Peace* and *Anna Karenina?* Tolstoy

was a miserable soul. At age eighty-eight, he tried to leave his wife."

"And died in a railway station," Harriet said. "My mother thinks that's romantic."

"I think it's right to change your circumstances if you're unhappy."

"I haven't found any apartments I can afford," I said. "Tucson's not cheap."

"So you're staying with this friend of yours," Mrs. Keating said. "Are you gay?"

"Oh God, Mother."

"If he is, I'm not offended."

"I'm not gay," I said calmly. "I was married once."

"That means nothing these days," said Mrs. Keating.

"I'm staying with a friend from college," I said. "He happens to live in Tucson."

"What business is he in?"

"Real estate."

"This is the person you weren't going to see, isn't it?" Harriet said. "The one you mentioned on the telephone."

"I didn't intend to see him," I said. "I had to."

"Does he owe you money?" Mrs. Keating asked.

"No."

"Money explains a good deal," Mrs. Keating said. "Tolstoy had money, so he was free to indulge his misery. I wish my husband had been rich. Then I could flee, too."

"What did he do?" I asked.

"He was a welder."

"He was a sculptor," Harriet said.

"Still he wasn't rich."

"If you moved out, who would watch over you?" Harriet asked.

"Maybe Mr. Talmadge and I could pool resources. That would solve both our problems."

I laughed. "I might not stay in Tucson beyond the spring," I said.

When we finished eating, I cleared the table while Harriet got her mother settled in the living room to watch "Mystery" on PBS. I put the coffee on.

As unlikely as it might have seemed at the time, Harriet and I had not made love that evening in Madera Canyon. The time and place and mood had all conspired to that end, and I had thought she wanted to. I had thought *I* wanted to, and if she had made the first move, it might have happened. If she had leaned her head against my shoulder, had touched my arm, it would have been simple to interpret such a sign as a symptom of desire. But she hadn't. Perhaps it was a matter of vocabulary. She didn't know what words to say to me, and I didn't know what words to say to her. I wanted to say not the ordinary words of love, but something more, words which wouldn't have lost their meaning in a few hours. A promise maybe. I didn't know whether, in a different moment, I would be able to say such words or not.

But Harriet had let the moment pass. I hadn't spurned her. I hadn't done anything. She might have assumed (we never talked of it then, but later we did briefly) I hadn't perceived her unspoken intention, her motives for going with me in the first place to set the mist nets. That I hadn't been affected by the ebbing light or the fading songs of birds settling into their roosts for the night might have put Harriet off. I didn't know whether such a moment would come again, or whether, if it did, I would feel the same. If the opportunity to be on that boulder came some other twilight, I would be a different person altogether. Maybe the next time I wouldn't think of Demer.

The British do this so well," Harriet's mother said. "There's never any violence. Come and sit by me, Mr. Talmadge."

I sat on the sofa. After a few minutes Harriet came in with coffee and gave me a cup. She leaned close and whispered, "She'll go to bed after this."

"Are you talking about me?" Mrs. Keating asked.

"Yes," Harriet said. "I was telling Scott he didn't have to accede to your every wish." She sat on a chair to the side of the sofa.

I felt obliged to watch the TV, though I had no interest in the people speaking with British accents. I couldn't tell what they were doing or why, and they all moved at half speed.

But Mrs. Keating's attention was like the vortex of a whirlpool pulling everything down to its center. There were no commercials or breaks, no pauses to ask questions. I sipped my coffee. When I glanced at Harriet, her gaze was as riveted as her mother's to the TV screen.

Harriet wasn't like other women I'd known, not that I'd known that many. She wasn't like Demer. Demer had experimented with men before I knew her. She understood that men could hurt her or not love her enough. She risked harm. I think that's why she liked me at first: I would never harm her. Perhaps later that's what troubled her, too. She wanted danger from me, and I couldn't give it to her. She wanted to be at the edge, to be afraid I would leave her, to be fearful I would love someone else. But she wasn't at the edge. She was herself: petulant, selfish, zealous, expansive, needy. She didn't get tension from me, so she created the tension on her own.

But Harriet was calm. She was dedicated to her work. Where Demer was cantankerous, Harriet was a shimmering, slow-moving river. She was cautious about love. The night in Monterey when she had left me on the sidewalk outside her hotel—had she wanted to invite me in? I didn't know. *She'll go to bed after this.* What did that mean?

When the show was over, Harriet turned off the television with the remote control. "Well? What did you think, Scott?"

"I gather it continues."

"For six weeks," Mrs. Keating said. "You'll have to come back."

"And then someone is arrested?"

"We'll see."

There was a pause during which Mrs. Keating's silence was pervasive. Harriet looked at me. "I guess I should go," I said. "It was a fine meal."

"No more coffee?" Harriet asked.

I stood up, helped Mrs. Keating to her feet, and handed her the cane.

"Do you really have to go, Mr. Talmadge?"

"I have some work to do," I said.

Harriet walked me to the door. Her mother didn't follow, but waited in the living room where she could see us. Harriet and I exchanged a few pleasantries about school. She invited me to her class. I asked whether, since I was only filling in for Fred, I had to go to faculty meetings. She kissed me lightly on the cheek, afterward pressing her cheek to mine and pulling me down a little with one hand.

Then her mother coughed. She coughed and turned away, still coughing, and Harriet said good night and went to her.

Chapter twelve

It's hard to think well of someone who's left you. You're angry. You're depressed. You throw around in your mind all the things you could have done differently. There are wild swings between good riddance and I-wish-you-were-here. And it's harder still when you don't know where the other person is. Demer had sent those postcards and the letter, and then nothing. Where was she at that very moment, when, after dinner at Harriet's, I was sitting with Zapata back at Tilghman's?

I took out Demer's letter and read it again. It was dated January. That was all.

> *Dear Scott,*
>
> *We are being sent to Guatemala now on assignment to count the dead and to listen to the stories of survivors, the stories the villagers tell, and to try to estimate as best we can what is happening there. The* campesinos *are not political people. They're uneducated, silent, and distrust what's new. They were born here, and they don't understand why they are being killed.*
>
> *Of course there are some who know why. These are the ones who know what a nation is—the rebels and the clergy, for instance. To think of all this makes me numb. There is so little progress, almost no change. One regime is like another, only richer. In Guatemala a few days ago, we toured Quiché Province where the fighting has been bad—villages destroyed, the farms firebombed, many people killed. During our visit to Chichicastenango, we found a man's body at the side of the road. He'd been eviscerated, his hands and feet cut off, and his face hacked with machetes. Nailed to the man's skull was a sign*

which said Habran muchas mas. *There will be more.*

I could tell you other stories, too. I'm keeping a journal of them, along with my reflections from before. Do you remember I told you of my friend, Inez Montera? She went to grade school with me, and sometimes she stayed weekends with me at the embassy. I've visited her several times since I've been here. Her father was a coffee grower in the north, but they lived in Guatemala City most of the year. Now she teaches agronomy at the university. She's a beautiful person, and it's been wonderful to see her again. Sometimes she goes with us to see for herself what is happening in the provinces.

In a few days I'll know more about what AFS wants us to do. I'll write more later. I hope you're doing well, Scott. Think of me.

Love, Demer

I folded the letter back into the envelope and sat down in the kitchen with a beer. Zapata was outside in the yard, tethered to the grapefruit tree, sleeping. If I'd been back in Amesbury, I'd have gone out to Smalley's Bar.

Demer always said I worried too much. What worried me most was that she never worried enough. She had the idea she could go anyplace and she'd be all right.

Once she accepted the offer of a drink from the son of a man she was caring for—a Cuban. "I was interested in learning about Cuba," she said. "The old man is sweet."

"Just because the old man is a saint doesn't mean the son is one. What made you think the son knew anything about Cuba?"

"He's from Cuba."

"Do you think the man in the street knows anything about America?"

"You're right, Scott. I should be more careful."

"So what happened?"

"Never mind."

That was in Demer's phase of experimentation. She was building her independence. Coming from Mexico to college, she hadn't passed through the stage of culling from her education the things that were true. Or maybe she'd never been taught the things that weren't—democracy works, the president is honest, our representatives do what their constituents want them to. She talked to her mother on the telephone for hours during that time, asking what it had been like living in those countries. Demer wanted to know because she had been too young to remember the truth she now needed to know.

"I thought you wanted to be a nurse," I said once after she'd had a long talk with her mother. I'd overheard part of the conversation.

"I can't be a nurse in some other place?"

"Of course you can. But we live here."

"We live here, but you're gone half the time," Demer said.

"That's my work."

"Are you saying being interested in what goes on in Central America is a hobby?"

"I didn't mean it like that."

"I can make choices, can't I? What's so impossible about being a nurse and caring about politics and history? I want to *do* something."

"You make it sound as if finding birds is not doing anything. What's wrong with it?"

"Nothing."

We glared at one another.

"You think there's something wrong with being a bird guide?"

"I don't think there's anything wrong with it, Scott. That's what you want to do. This is what I want to do."

"Okay," I said.

"Okay."

We'd gone to bed cold and woken up cold.

In the morning I was up early before the sun broke through the palm trees behind the garage. Zapata had barked and wakened me. Ramon was in the backyard. I guessed him to be nineteen or twenty, thin, with a face so smooth it looked as if he didn't shave. Tilghman had led me to expect he'd be older. Ramon, he'd told me, had a regular job in the orange groves, but the work wasn't steady. When he was laid off, Tilghman gave him work.

I put some water on, and while it heated up, I walked down to the Circle K. The neighborhood was moderately safe, except for the park where transients slept on the grass and it was rumored drugs were bought and sold. I got some instant coffee and a newspaper. The headline was CHEMICAL SPILL KILLS FOUR. An event, according to Demer, not something bad.

Ramon was grateful for the coffee, though he didn't stop

working. He took a sip every once in a while and grimaced, then smiled at me. "Gracias," he said.

I read the paper on the strip of cement outside the sliding screen door. House Sparrows chattered in the palm trees. Far-away, over on Speedway, cars revved and squealed and hummed. It was strange to think of Tilghman's hiring someone to work for him. In college he'd had less money than I, and he'd worked a bursary job buttering toast and pouring milk. In summers he'd done construction work and lifeguarding, except that one summer we'd worked on the trail crew. Now he was paying Ramon to build a wall.

I checked the newspaper ads for apartments. A couple of new listings had come up—one in the neighborhood for $550 a month. That was manageable, and I told myself I'd go look at it. I knew if I didn't go right away, it would be gone. I had another cup of coffee and read the sports page.

I was about to get up and help Ramon when a yellow-green VW pulled up at the gate. Zapata didn't bark. Ramon, who was mixing cement, paused and leaned on his shovel. It was the only time all morning he'd rested. The woman extricated herself from the driver's seat and stepped to the curb. She was tall. That was what struck me first—maybe five feet eight or nine. Her brown hair was shortish, barely visible under a wide-brimmed straw hat. She had on a beige blouse and a white skirt. Bare feet. I had the impression, watching her pass through the broken gate, that she couldn't sweat.

Ramon pretended to examine the cement he was mixing. He looked at me. I looked at him. The woman came right up to me and shook hands. "You must be Scott," she said. "Tilghman said you were staying with Zapata."

"Just visiting," I said. "You must be . . ." I paused, not want-ing to make any mistakes.

"Francie Slocum," she said. She turned and shook hands with Ramon, too. She seemed to know him from before. "Hola," she said. "¿Hace mucho calor, no?"

Ramon wiped his brow. "No es tan mal."

Francie stepped into the wedge of shade which the eave of the house cut across the patio. She took off her hat, and for the first time I was aware of her face—red lips, blue eye shadow, pale skin. She was aware of my stare. "I don't usually look like this," she said. "I'm on my way to a session. I dropped by to pick up the photographs Tilghman left for me."

"He's not here," I said. "He went to Mexico."

"I know. That's why I came now. He said you'd be here."

"He didn't mention any photographs."

"Didn't he?" She peered through the screen behind me. I glanced at Ramon, who was still looking at Francie.

"Tilghman said I wasn't supposed to let you in."

Francie looked puzzled. "He told me you'd know where the photographs were."

"He was pretty clear about the instructions," I said. "No entry."

"Are you the doorman?" Francie said. "Fuck that." She was through the screen door before I could stop her.

"Hey!" I threw the paper down and got up to follow.

"You're not letting me in," she said. "I'm going in on my own."

"Tilghman said . . ."

"I don't give a damn what Tilghman said."

She headed straight for Tilghman's bedroom closet, where she pulled out the cardboard boxes he kept his clothes in. She checked the shelves and under the bed, where Tilghman kept more boxes of clothes. "He ought to buy a bureau," Francie said, "instead of letting his clothes rot in these boxes."

"You're sure he has these photographs?"

"He has them all right. But they're mine."

"What kind of photographs?"

"The kind he has no right to keep."

She went from Tilghman's room across the hall to the room I was staying in. My gear was strewn all over—cameras, binoculars, books. My duffel bag spewed clothes out onto the floor. "Not very neat, are we?"

"The photographs aren't in here," I said.

Francie lifted the mattress and made a cursory tour. Then she went out to the desk in the living room. She hovered there, long winged, sleek. Then she turned to me. "They aren't in the house, are they?"

I shrugged.

"He set this up."

"What?"

"He told me to come over, and he told you not to let me in. He told me you'd know where the pictures were, but he neglected to tell you. You didn't even know there *were* pictures."

"So he forgot to tell me."

"He didn't forget," Francie said. She glided to the kitchen and looked out through the screen at Ramon, who had gone back to mixing the cement. "How long have you known Tilghman?" she asked.

"A long time."

"But not lately. You haven't been around him lately."

"No, not that lately. Maybe a couple of years now. He was in Steamboat when I saw him last."

"Do you know his father has had two strokes?"

"No."

"Both times Tilghman went back to St. Cloud. It was hard on him."

"Is his father all right? Tilghman was never all that fond of his father. You probably know that."

"His father is convalescent," Francie said. "That's when Tilghman quit drinking."

"And you moved out."

"I didn't move out for a while. It's only been a month or so ago. And it wasn't that I wanted to, either. I had to. Tilghman got pretty intense, pretty strange. I didn't want him to take me down, too."

I didn't know what Francie was talking about exactly. Tilghman had been evasive. He'd been quieter, but not withdrawn. Suddenly she turned around at the screen door and went back into the living room. "Come with me a minute."

I followed her.

She stood on the Indian rug on the floor. "Do you know what I'm standing on?"

"A rug."

"What kind of rug? Who made it?"

I hunkered down, lifted a corner of it, felt the rough texture of the wool. "Navajo? Maybe Pima."

"Ixil," Francie said. "Demer sent Tilghman this rug from Guatemala."

I let the corner of the rug drop with a soft slap to the floor.

"I know a little, but not enough," Francie said. "Demer's got something to do with it, and so does Ellis."

"Not drugs?"

"No, not drugs. It's people," Francie said. "That's how Ramon got here. He's from Honduras."

Chapter thirteen

The rest of that week, when I wasn't in class or out in the field, I worked on the wall with Ramon. Between the two of us who couldn't speak to each other, we got three times as much done as either could have alone. Day by day we made progress. We laid the foundation in the trench, set in rebar, tamped down cinder blocks into cement. I carried the blocks. Ramon did the masonry. The wall grew to three feet, four. Ramon kept the tiers even with a taut string, and he checked them using a beer bottle half full of water as a level.

One day, the day Ramon had brought the orange trees to plant, Francie showed up to see whether Tilghman was back yet from Mexico. I barely recognized her when she came through the gate, except she was tall. She looked so casual without makeup. She had on jeans and a red-and-yellow striped shirt and a San Diego Padres baseball cap to fend off the sun.

Ramon and I were driving steel rods into the ground to shore up the wall around the archway.

"What are those for?" Francie wanted to know.

"The gate. Tilghman wants to hang a three-hundred-pound wood-and-iron gate."

"For what?"

"Exercise. Every time he comes through, he'll be pumping iron."

"I told you Tilghman was a mental case," Francie said.

I smiled at her. "He's protecting himself. If someone's really after him, he's not paranoid."

"So he's not back yet?"

"No. Was he supposed to be?"

Francie took off her cap, scratched her head, and tugged the cap back down again. She looked at her watch. "He doesn't tell me anything," she said.

"What did he tell you?"

"Nothing." I backed away from Ramon, who was chipping the edges from the cinder blocks he was going to use for the archway. "I don't know anything more about the photographs. You want me to call him?"

"It's okay. Never mind."

She stood for a moment in the shade of the grapefruit tree, and for that moment, the way the sun and shadow mixed on her face, she looked gritty. Already I admired what I saw as her struggle with Tilghman, but maybe it was one with her memory of him. She was determined not to let Tilghman get the better of her. "You need some help?" she asked. "I have some time."

Sometime during the morning, while we were letting the cement harden in the new rows (we could only put up two tiers at a time), Francie went inside to make iced tea. Ramon was going to start planting the orange trees, and I walked down to the Circle K to get Ramon some cigarettes. Talk about paranoid, that was Ramon. He was afraid to go anywhere. That's what Francie said. He thought the police would get him.

The day had warmed into the eighties by then, and the heat made the neighborhood slower. Only a few people were in the park. I was on my way back and had reached the oleanders on the sidewalk when I heard Ramon moaning in Spanish. It sounded like a song, a wailing.

I sprinted to the gate. Ramon was on his knees beside a shallow depression in the earth. Beside him was an orange tree whose roots were wrapped in a gunny sack filled with dirt. Ramon was holding up something—bones, they looked like, bones joined together, the upper arm and forearm of a human being. Ramon was crying what sounded like, "Los huesos, los huesos. Mia madre, los huesos."

Francie rushed out of the house just as I reached the broken gate.

Ramon didn't want us to call the police. That was the gist of what Francie got from him. They'd ask questions, he said, and he'd be sent back to Honduras. He didn't want to go back. "Ese sera mi fin," he said. "Este sera el final."

"But we have to call the police."

"He says they'll kill him if he goes back," Francie said.

I explored the shallow pit where Ramon had been digging. Tilghman had marked the spot with an iridescent orange flag. I didn't find anything else. The earth was crusted from heat and rain and heat again. I pickaxed a few spots around the pit, shoveled deeper in the hard earth. No other bones, no clothes, no skull. Zapata sniffed around but wasn't interested.

Francie took the bones inside and put them on the kitchen table. There was no question the bones were human. The fingers were all intact. The ulna was fractured where it joined the wrist, but the humerus was solid. From the delicateness of the fingers, I thought the bones must have been a child's. It was impossible to judge how long they'd been buried, but I guessed a long time. They were grayish, pitted as if with acid, fragile, dry as bird bones. When I picked up the hand to look at it, the little finger broke off and fell to the floor.

"We have to call someone," I said. "That's our obligation. If Ramon hasn't done anything wrong, he hasn't got anything to be afraid of."

"Don't be so stupid, Scott. We're talking police here, not law. Not ethics. Do you think the police care if he hasn't done anything wrong? He's illegal. They'll ship him back."

"What about the people whose bones they are? What about the family?"

"Why don't you tell the police you found the bones?"

"Me?"

"That solves Ramon's problem."

"But that's not what happened."

"Life is lie with an f," Francie said. "All right, I'll tell them I found the bones. The police won't care about that, either. Whose bones these are doesn't care. Actually I was thinking about Tilghman. If I get involved, they'll connect me to Tilghman."

"It's Tilghman's yard," I said.

Francie was angry. That was clear. She picked up the telephone and punched in some numbers. I thought she was calling the police, but she wasn't. "DuPlooy?"

There was a pause.

"DuPlooy, listen, it's me, Frank. No, something's come up. It's not Tilghman. Not that, either. I won't be able to make it for a while. I'll give a call."

After she hung up, she glared at me. "This is costing me money," she said. "Why don't you do us all a favor, you and your goddamn honesty, and go back to New Hampshire, or wherever you crawled out from?"

The dust settled. Ramon, still moaning about the bones, got into his wired-together truck and disappeared down the street. Francie called the police. She went outside to wait for them and played with Zapata.

With the bones in front of me on the table, I played Widow's Dance. I laid out cards in fifteen sets of three cards each, which couldn't be replaced, and three sets of two each in the crib. These you could build on up to three, or replace with any other card if you were able to create a vacuum on the board. There was one extra card, which, in this game, was the seven of hearts. That was the signal card, and I put it out in front to build on in sequence. There were two other sevens showing on the board, one of them in the crib, and two eights, so I had an excellent start. The object was to build from the sevens upward and around the deck—queen, king, ace, two, and up to six.

From time to time I looked at the bones and wondered whose they were. I stretched out my own hand beside the finger bones, watched my own sinewy fingers flex, contract, dance beside the dry phalanges. I touched the fragile, ossified hand. Then I picked up the little finger that had fallen on the floor and tucked it into my pocket.

I finished my game of solitaire and got up to see where Francie was. She was circling her hand over Zapata's mouth. Zapata was trying to catch her fingers.

"Should we call Tilghman?" I asked.

Francie stopped her hand in midair. "What's wrong with you, Scott?"

"Maybe he should know what's going on?"

"He'd come back."

"I thought you wanted him to come back."

"Not *mad*. I don't want that. That's another reason for you to say you found the bones. He won't be mad at you. What's the difference if you lie, or you let me lie?"

"There's a difference."

"Do you always think you're right?"

"I'm right some of the time. Not very often." I paused, smiled faintly. "I can tell you what birds are singing."

We listened, but in the heat of the day, there weren't any songs. Francie patted Zapata, and he rolled over in the dust.

Chapter fourteen

Squad cars with their lights flashing blocked off the area around the back gate, and the police kept traffic moving on Second Street. But the ruckus had drawn a crowd. People craned over the bushes. Children climbed on the new wall and dislodged a few of the cinder blocks. I suppose everyone was waiting for someone to be arrested or shot. The sergeant finally cordoned off the entire street so the police could do their work.

The forensics people took photographs of the yard and removed the bones, except for the finger I had kept, in plastic bags. These were sent to the lab for examination and analysis. Investigators combed the area for whatever they could find around the shallow hole Ramon had started and Francie later had said she was digging.

The sergeant who questioned Francie had the annoying habit of squinting, as if he distrusted even the most ordinary information. "You were digging?" he asked Francie.

"We're building a wall and planting some trees. We have a permit."

"Why isn't your boyfriend doing the work?" He squinted toward me.

Francie didn't look at me. "He wasn't here."

"You own the house?" he asked me.

"No."

"But you live here. You're a renter."

"Of sorts."

The sergeant looked at me more closely. "Employed?"

"Is that relevant?"

"Everything is relevant."

"I'm a visiting professor of biology at the university," I said. "She's not my girlfriend. And what makes you think she couldn't own the house?"

The sergeant mopped the back of his neck with a paper towel from the roll the forensics people had left on the patio table. "Do you own the house, ma'am?"

"No."

"Who is the owner?"

"Tilghman Myre."

"All this mess his?"

"All of it," Francie said. "I just work here."

"You wouldn't happen to know where Tilghman Myre is?"

"Phoenix," Francie said.

"Or when he's coming back?"

"I don't live here," Francie said.

Television crews from the four local stations arrived and set up lights so they could film the yard. With the wall half done and the ground dug up, the yard looked like the scene of an explosion. Reporters had got in with the TV people, and when the sergeant was done with us, he made a brief statement. No, there were no suspects. The police would get a warrant and do some digging in the ground. When the forensics people had gone over what had been found, they'd all know more. Without a positive identification, there was no direction for the investigation to take. It was pointless to speculate on the cause of death. In any event it looked to him as if the bones had been there a long time, maybe twenty years, maybe from the Ice Age.

The forensics crew returned with a warrant and spent the afternoon with pick and shovel and jackhammer. They hammered the ground long after Francie had left, long after dark. The flashers of the squad cars turned the air raspberry. A spotlight was set up in the grapefruit tree.

I watched the earth cut into chunks, broken apart with shovels, and sieved in a big screen. Now and then, through my binoculars, I measured their progress, but nothing of substance ever appeared in the screen except a few stringy yucca leaves or an occasional shard of twisted metal or glass.

Toward eleven that night the sergeant knocked on the glass door. I was playing solitaire. "A long day," he said.

"It's nearly morning."

"You said the owner's in Phoenix, this Tilghman Myre?"

"I didn't say he was in Phoenix."

"No, right. The woman said that. The one who's not your girlfriend." The sergeant paused and squinted through the open door into the backyard. "Where is Mr. Myre if he's not in Phoenix?"

"I didn't say he wasn't in Phoenix."

"No, you didn't. That's right, too. Where is he?"

"I don't know where he is exactly. He could be in Phoenix."

"And you don't have a phone number?"

I looked straight at the sergeant. "No."

The sergeant squinted at me. "We haven't found much in the yard. We may have to tear up the sidewalk, maybe the street."

"I'll tell Tilghman when I see him."

"If you talk to him, have him give us a call."

In the morning passersby came right through the broken gate. Zapata sat on the patio watching them. They milled around the yard, touched the shovel, grabbed handfuls of dirt which they sifted through their fingers. One man stuffed some dirt in his pocket. I could imagine him saying a year from then, as he drove by, "That's where the guy buried his mother in the backyard."

Finally, to discourage people from prying, I sat out by the gate in the sun and read *Carte Blanche*. I didn't care whether or not the people thought I'd buried the bones.

Carte Blanche was about two college students, the daughter of a doctor and the son of an air force colonel, who, in the sixties, had set up a cadre to overthrow the government of the United States. I'd been born in the fifties, and had missed most of the sixties except for the music. I liked the idea, not new, that the government was the enemy. In these days the notion had a jaded aspect to it because no one trusted the government anyway after Nixon. We put up with it. We knew it was there. We lived with it.

Every once in a while, I glanced up through the gate at the cars passing or the people looking in over the wall. Once I thought I saw Tilghman's Land Rover go by, and I got up and peered down the street. The car had turned left. I went around on the sidewalk to the front of the house.

Tilghman came around again and slowed when he saw me. "What have you been doing, Scott, selling ten-cent beers in the yard?"

"You've been in Phoenix," I said.

"How'd you know that?"

"That's what Francie told the police. In case they ask, which they will."

"I *was* in Phoenix," Tilghman said. "What's going on?"

"Ramon found some bones in the yard," I said. "Nothing Zapata put there."

"What kind of bones?"

"An arm and a hand. Not a whole person. We thought it better to leave Ramon out of it."

"Who's this 'we'?"

"Francie and I."

He looked at me as if he didn't understand, as if he was slow in getting the gist of the words. He looked exhausted, as if he hadn't slept since he'd left. "Bones?" he said. "The police were here?"

Chapter fifteen

The newspapers and television stations barely made a ripple of the story. It was not a case really. There was a small mention in each of the papers, but nothing on the TV news. Tilghman cooperated with the police, if not cheerfully, then politely. He said he'd been in Phoenix, watching the Suns beat the Bucks. Tom Chambers had had thirty-two points, including six straight free throws down the stretch. The Bucks had made it close with a twenty-two-to-four run in the fourth quarter, mostly from Sidney Moncrief, then their star guard, but the Suns were tenacious enough at home to hang on.

"You could have listened to the game on the radio," the sergeant said.

"I could have read about it in the newspaper," Tilghman said. "Do I need an alibi for something?"

"What kind of work do you do, Mr. Myre?"

"I'm retired."

"At your age?"

"I did well in real estate and southwestern art."

"You own this house?"

Tilghman nodded. "Not that long. Less than two years."

"The woman who called us said she was your employee. She's building the wall?"

"Which woman is this?" Tilghman asked.

"She's not your girlfriend, either? Tall, brown hair, the one who wasn't wearing any gloves when she was digging in hard earth. She must be somebody's girlfriend."

"Why must she?" I asked.

Tilghman quieted me with a grin. "You mean Frances Slocum," he said. "Sometimes she helps me out around here."

The sergeant squinted. "If she's nobody's girlfriend, what's her telephone number?"

Tilghman did his own digging in the yard. He took it as some omen that he had marked the spot on the ground where Ramon had dug up the bones. He had me out there digging, too. "Here," he said. "Dig here, Scott."

I swung the pick to the hard earth.

"Deeper."

"Tilghman, there's nothing here."

One night Tilghman dreamed. He yelled in his sleep, and when I ran into his room, he was sitting up in bed in the dark. The streetlight from the outside illuminated a streak of bare wall.

"What was it?" I asked.

"I had a dream about the woman."

"What woman?"

"The woman whose bones we don't have." Tilghman was dazed. His eyes were open, but he spoke slowly, as if he were still asleep and seeing the dream.

"What about her? What did you dream?"

Tilghman closed his eyes. "I was holding her arm. We were walking in a place I didn't know, on a wide path. Her arm was looped in mine, and she held me tightly." He opened his eyes again. "She was only bones, and then she fleshed out. She was Hispanic, Guatemalan, beautiful. She lay down on the grassy path, pulled me down." He stopped and pulled his sheet back and showed me the wet spot where he'd come. He lay back down and turned away from the light.

In the morning he had nothing to say. He acted as though his dream had never happened.

I still had my classes during these weeks. I was busy. The mist-net project was under way, and I had worked out a routine for setting the nets, and leaving them under the bridge at Florida Wash so I didn't have to take them back and forth from the university. My friendship with Harriet was unsettled, but taking shape slowly. Perhaps it wasn't destined to be what she wanted, but neither was it limited by my own diffidence. We saw each other at the university, and sometimes we went out for dinner at a restaurant she liked downtown. I didn't take her to help with the mist nets anymore, and I stayed away from her place on nights when "Mystery" was on. And I decided I couldn't go to the conference on the oceans out in California. I would get over Demer, but I wasn't in any hurry.

By this time I'd given up looking for apartments. The ones I could afford, mostly in the barrio, were too dangerous—Demer would have given me a hard time about that. Besides, Tilghman wanted me to stay on. He liked company, he said. He liked the sounds I made in the house, and he was glad someone else was there to answer the telephone. I worked in the yard with him or with Ramon. Zapata liked me.

I hadn't found out much about Demer. Tilghman was close-mouthed about her. Whenever I edged toward the topic, he was sardonic, evasive, jocose. Francie said he was crazy, but I took her judgment with the grain of salt one puts on wounds. So what if Tilghman had kept a few photographs he shouldn't have? So what if he built an eight-foot wall around his backyard?

But Tilghman's dream troubled me. Dreams were labyrinthine excursions through a fragmented past, random synapses in the brain which connected unrelated data, so in the beginning I put no stock in Tilghman's ranting. But later I thought of the dream as a turning point, a sign. The forensics lab had identified the bones as those of a woman in her early twenties. There was no evidence to show how the woman had died or who she was. The bones had been in the ground for thirty-to-fifty years.

Tilghman assimilated this information calmly, asked a few questions about methods of dating bones. Then he said, "Can I get them back?"

"Get them back?" asked the forensics woman.

"I'm the closest relative."

"Mr. Myre, I don't think so." The forensics woman smiled patiently.

"The bones were in my backyard," Tilghman said. "They're mine."

"Our procedure is laid out for these cases," the woman said.

"I don't give three turds about your procedure," Tilghman said. "I want the bones."

"We keep them in case other evidence is discovered. That's our policy."

"Policy can be changed. You said yourself they'd been in the ground over thirty years."

"I can ask," the forensics woman said. "Why do you want the bones?"

"Inez Montera," Tilghman said.

"I beg your pardon?"

"Inez Montera. She deserves a decent burial."

What did Tilghman know about Inez Montera? Inez Montera was Demer's childhood friend in Guatemala. I assumed Demer had told Tilghman about her. But I didn't get the connection.

Tilghman spent hours trying to get the bones. He talked to politicians and the police commissioner, and whenever he spoke of the bones, he called them Inez Montera.

"How do they know I'm not related?" he asked me. "How do they know? Maybe she's a great aunt."

"You grew up in Minnesota."

"You think I'm joking," Tilghman said.

"What's the connection to Inez Montera?" I asked. "She's Demer's friend."

Tilghman looked at me. "She's disappeared," he said. "Demer thinks she's dead."

"When did you find that out?"

Tilghman shook his head as if he wasn't listening to me anymore. "These people vanish," he said softly. "One day they're going about their business, and the next, no one knows where they are."

"This happened to Inez?"

Tilghman turned away. "She was abducted from a taxicab when she was taking her little girl to a birthday party. A black car cut them off. Four men got out and pulled Inez from the taxi and pushed her into their car. They sent the daughter on to the birthday party."

"Where was this?"

"Downtown Guatemala City. Broad daylight. The car had tinted windows and no license plate so no one knows who kidnapped her. At the same time, everyone knows."

"Demer told you this?"

"You can read the letter if you want."

"You have it here?"

"No. You think I'd leave Demer's letters for Francie to find? I want the bones back, Scott. I want to bury Inez Montera in a real grave."

I dug into my pocket. "We have this," I said. And I held out my open palm, which had in it the little-finger bone which I'd picked up from the floor.

Chapter sixteen

After Tilghman's dream there was a subtle shift in things. Tilghman became more moody. Sometimes he worked feverishly in the yard planting trees and cactus. He bought more lumber than he could possibly use—four-by-fours, two-by-fours, two-by-eights. He ordered sheetrock, insulation, wiring. He planted bamboo in front of the garage door where he said light would filter through the leaves into the windows, when the garage door was windows. He dug postholes for a trellis he wanted to cover with bougainvillea.

Then for days he would do nothing. He wouldn't swim at the university. He didn't eat much. He'd sit in the yard amidst the materials as if he were overwhelmed by the projects he'd started. Sometimes he'd figure on a pad of paper or draw designs. I thought he was laying out the yard or sketching the apartment in the garage, but when I saw the pad, it had on it drawings of shrines, elaborate shrines with crosses and candles, mausoleums.

One night I was in bed and I heard Tilghman moan. He was having another dream, I thought, but when I got to his room, he wasn't there. He was in the living room holding his knees, which were folded into his chest.

"Now what?" I asked.

Tilghman didn't look at me. "You're lucky, Scott. Lucky."

"How am I lucky?"

"No father."

"I had a father."

"No one who lied to you. My father lied."

I sat down on the floor on the rug that Demer had sent. All I had on was the underwear I slept in.

"My father had a stroke," Tilghman said. "I went back to St. Cloud twice."

"Francie told me."

"I was there a few days each time." He paused, thinking. "When you're born, you start in the middle of someone else's life. You learn little pieces. I knew my father had cheated on my mother. He was exactly what I never wanted to be."

"He loved you," I said.

"I didn't love him. He had no loyalty to anyone else."

"Then why did you go home?"

"My mother asked me to. And then, I didn't want regrets. I didn't want my father to punish me with guilt if he died and I wasn't there." Tilghman rocked back and forth, holding his arms around his knees.

"You talked to him?"

"A stroke is a little death in the brain. Cells lose oxygen. Sometimes there are a series of strokes, one feeding the others. After the first one he was all right. He got back to driving a car, walking around, all of that. The second one, though, was more serious. When I got there, he was in the hospital in a private room. He was alert. I asked him how he was feeling, what had happened, and so on. He was cordial. He wanted to know how I was doing. Fine, I said, which meant nothing to him or to me.

"The longer I sat with him, though, the more I thought about his life—whether he'd ever loved my mother at all, how many affairs he'd had, why he'd ever in a million years thought I could be an insurance man. So I asked him. I asked those questions and a few more. He answered in a slow voice, as if he remembered clearly, but not quickly. Every day I asked more questions. Sometimes he'd start to answer and fall asleep. I asked once about his childhood. When he was little, his father had chained him to a tree in their front yard. When he was eighteen, he'd had a girlfriend who'd drowned. She'd fallen out of a boat at some lake, and he hadn't been there. He told me about that. And he had met my mother at a picnic. They'd thrown horseshoes and eaten marble cake." Tilghman paused, looked toward the kitchen where a dim light shone from the clock on the stove. The refrigerator came on, and the cricket chirped. "That was all. Questions, trickles of answers, more or less the way it is with everything. He was telling about meeting my mother when he died."

"Died? You told Francie . . ."

Tilghman stopped rocking and lapsed into silence. I put my arm around him.

For my part things changed, too. I liked the teaching more than I'd expected to. I liked entertaining the class. I liked their questions and their jokes. We had a good time in the field, and we told stories in the van going out and coming home.

One evening after I'd brought the van back, I was grading some essays in my office. I'd assigned a paper on avian navigation, and I'd left the students to seek out the various theories to see how many different ones they could come up with. Some experts believed the stars aided the birds' flight, but what did they do on cloudy nights? Others thought birds possessed gyroscopic brain tissue and could perceive level ground as well as true north. Still others posited instinctual learning: birds were coded from birth and needed no guidance. Another idea was that each species had leaders who'd already traversed the territory from wintering ground to breeding area. The others were followers. I liked the essays. They presented enough theories to show that human beings still had a lot to learn.

As I marked the papers, I drank a beer which I'd kept in my drawer. Now and then there would be rumblings in the halls. The language classes used the biology amphitheaters for films, and between the films, there were voices, footsteps, then as the students left, dissipation into quiet. It was on the edge of one of these disturbances that a knock came on the door. "Yes?" I put the beer under my desk.

The door opened. I expected to see one of my students—maybe Janet, the woman with the buzzed haircut, whom I'd come to like. She had shown up several times during office hours to talk. But it was Harriet who appeared. "I saw the light on," she said. "Are you working?"

"I was grading papers. What are you doing here?"

"I saw *Le Déjeuner sur l'Herbe*," she said. "Do you know Renoir?"

"Not personally."

"You speak some French though."

"I used to," I said. "Il y a plus années."

The hall was quiet. Harriet gazed around Fred's office. She hadn't moved from the doorway.

"You can come in," I said. I didn't pick up the beer.

"Isn't it astonishing what animals build?" She closed the door and looked around the room at the nests. "What would whales build if they had a medium in which to create?"

"They'd build weapons," I said.

"Maybe they would. Sea-to-land missiles." Harriet strolled slowly to the window. "Have you ever been to France?"

"Once with Tilghman."

"You and Tilghman," she said. "Tilghman and you." She chanted the names.

"We traveled," I said. "Tilghman spoke French. One time in Toulouse he posed as a Frenchman. He'd been in Europe for a year and had those pointy shoes and the haircut. I was the translator."

"Scott and Tilghman."

"We met two Americans. Women. We drank wine in a café and afterward ended up in their hotel room. One of the women wanted to get Tilghman into bed. She wanted to sleep with a Frenchman. That's what her friend told me. We sat in the dark corner of the room. Tilghman ranted in French. 'What's he saying?' my friend asked. 'You can imagine,' I told her. Tilghman was talking about the lakes in Minnesota, about paintings in Yugoslavia, about the wine we'd just drunk in the café. All of a sudden the woman with me put her arms around my neck and kissed me. 'Talk to me like that,' she said."

Harriet smiled. She walked across toward the door again and touched a hummingbird's nest on the wall. "And did you?"

I was aware suddenly of how quiet it had become in the building. The clock tower outside struck muffled bells. All the movies were over, and Jaime must have locked up and gone home.

Then I stood up from my chair and stretched. That simple movement, no more than tossing a pebble into a still pond, broke the tension in the room. I walked over to the window, and for a minute I watched the palm trees swirl in the soundless breeze. Shadows of the trees slithered along the pavement. Someone crossed the street farther up and got into a red sports car. The ripples of the stone radiated outward and outward.

"Do you remember that night in Monterey?" Harriet asked.

"Of course I do."

"We had that wine."

"Chardonnay."

Harriet held her long, loose hair over one shoulder, braided it idly. She didn't look at me. "I wanted to ask you to my room that night."

"You didn't though."

"You were married. I didn't want to deceive anyone, even someone I didn't know. And I didn't want you to, either. Was that wrong?"

"No."

Harriet moved to the door and turned off the light. For a moment the room was completely dark. Then, as if by magic, a new light from the street formed discernible patterns—the shadows from the mullions in the window, silhouettes of blowing palm fronds on the walls, the smooth white rectangles of the essays on my desk. Harriet didn't wait for me to speak, nor did she ask what I wanted. She came over to me, knelt down, and untied the shoelaces of the boots I'd worn that day in the desert. Consent was lifting first one foot and then the other, so she could pull the boots off.

Chapter seventeen

Tilghman swam in long, effortless strokes. He bubbled his feet underwater, breathed every other time his right arm jettisoned from the surface of the pool. He had on small goggles that looked like aviator glasses and a maroon swimming suit. He swam ten laps, eleven, twelve, ducked under in the deep end, twisted his lean frame, and pushed away from the tile.

For reasons of hygiene I had already dipped myself in the shallow end. I wasn't a swimmer but a stone. It was hot, midday, and I sat on the edge of the pool and dabbled my feet. The water reflecting the sun appeared like moving sheets of mirrors through which Tilghman eased like a dolphin.

The weather report had said clouds in the afternoon, a chance of a thunderstorm, and I thought vaguely of setting the mist nets. If there was a storm, we might have lots of birds driven to earth.

Tilghman flip-flopped again in the shallow end, swam three or four strokes, and stood up. Water shimmered from his body like light. He pulled up his goggles. "You could try, Scott. You could get into the water and try."

"I get my exercise lifting cement blocks."

"It's not the same."

"You can't say I'm fat. I'm not fat."

"You're soft though. You need stamina."

"For what?"

"You know what. You shouldn't shit where you eat." He shook water from his ears, then lowered his goggles and began swimming again. He swam more lengths than I could count. He could have swum forever up and back, his long arms rising and falling through the water.

Tilghman meant I should be careful about Harriet. I knew that. There had been only that one time in my office, but Tilghman knew about it. Harriet was the first woman I'd been with since Demer.

I don't exactly remember what I felt then. I was confused. Romance: that was the word on Demer's card, but she'd meant sex. Was that what Harriet and I had had? There were a dozen expressions for what we'd done: fucking, making love, screwing, sleeping with, having carnal knowledge of, having sex, making it, copulating, balling, knowing. Therapy. Each of these had a different connotation. Couldn't one person be screwing and the other making love? Screwing implied a mechanical act. Carnal knowledge was secretive, maybe perverse, a pact between two people who never spoke to each other. Having sex was more human than screwing, but still devoid of attachment or emotion. Copulating: two newts, two elk, two entwining snakes. Balling: crude, lacking even a tinge of tenderness, blatantly chauvinistic from either side of the bed. "Sleeping with" amused me. Who was sleeping? Fucking. I liked fucking for its candor, and the word had a long history to recommend it. It was crass, but it implied passion. Making love: absurd. It suggested that love was in some way created out of thin air. It gave the act a blurry, sentimental, and mindless affect.

I was tempted to call what we'd done "learning." Learning suggested a progression toward knowledge, and the word was absent a human object. You couldn't learn someone else. You might learn *it* or learn *from* someone else. Learning conjured for me the idea of Platonic goodness. It was open-ended. You could go on learning until your brain cells collapsed and died.

The sun emerged from the clouds—the clouds moved—and heat swarmed into my skin. I stood up from the edge of the pool and looped my blue towel around my shoulders. I'd had enough sun.

Tilghman saw me and stopped swimming in the middle of the deep end. "Wait a minute," he called. "I want to talk to you." He submerged, undulated toward the side of the pool, and rose for air. "What about Mexico?"

"It's a big country."

"I'm going down to see Ellis again. Do you want to go?"

"When?"

"Pretty soon. Don't you have a spring break? You can bring the cetacean."

"She's a cetologist."

"I'll bring Francie. She likes to fish."

"Have you asked her?"

"No."

"Harriet would have to deal with her mother," I said. "It would give her some incentive if she knew Francie was coming along."

Tilghman pushed himself up and out of the water. "Let's go ask right now. We'll go visit her at work."

In ten minutes we'd showered, dressed, and were on our way into the maze of streets. It was stop-and-go through town, but after a few lights, we coasted along serpentine avenues with tall trees and immense lawns, hedges immaculately pruned, flower gardens. The houses were pink adobe mansions with red-tiled roofs, or white stucco palaces with pillars guarding the verandas. Each estate had a view of the mountains and enough water to turn the desert into the tropics.

"The heart of the artichoke," Tilghman said. "El Encanto Estates. The good life."

"This is where Francie works?"

"DuPlooy is a fascist," Tilghman said. "Remember what's at stake here. Frank is a dancer. She's a model in her spare time."

"She said you have photographs of her."

"I do," Tilghman said. "So what?"

"Why don't you give them back to her?"

"They're mine. They're in the safety-deposit vault with Demer's letters. Francie might be famous someday. Did you know she's from South Dakota?"

"What does that have to do with it?"

"She came down here to study dance. Can you imagine that? If you want to study dance, go to New York. She should have known better than to come to Tucson to dance. She went to Oberlin or one of those hotshot schools in Ohio."

"Why did you kick her out?"

"She moved out," Tilghman said. "I couldn't stop her."

Tilghman slowed and pulled into a long driveway. We descended through a tunnel of overhanging trees toward a fountain in the distance. The lawn spread out beyond the drive. Here and there were clumps of flowering shrubs. A white gazebo near the house guarded a small pond. We pulled up beside Francie's yellow-green VW parked at the fountain. I opened the door of the Rover. A Hermit Warbler was singing somewhere in one of the tall pines, and a Townsend's was across the lawn, also high up. Clouds were building in the west, though the sun was still shining where we were.

"The makeup," DuPlooy said. "Please do not ruin it." He came out from behind his camera, hobbled past us as if we weren't there, and hoisted his heavy butt onto a stool near the staging area. He took a puff from a cigarette that he'd picked up from the edge of the table. He was perspiring freely. His forehead and thick arms were glazed with sweat, and he wiped his face with a handkerchief. Strands of nearly white hair matted his arms and the back of his head. I guessed he was in his midforties and had been sick.

Francie touched her eye. That was what had brought DuPlooy from his camera. She was sitting with her legs under her on a white sofa. Her dark blue sheath dress was so short that the hem rode above her knees. The dress was plain, but elegantly low on one shoulder, puffy in the midlength sleeves. Her hair looked frosted, curled, meticulously arranged. She didn't look as though she could dance or liked to fish. She held a long-stemmed wineglass in which a scallop of red liquid wavered.

All of this was happening under a panel of bright white lights. I thought of my uncle, who wanted to invent the real arctic light.

"Just take the goddamn pictures," Francie said. "If you take the pictures, we can drink some of this stuff."

"You'll leave lipstick on the glass," DuPlooy said.

"What am I doing this for?" Francie asked Tilghman.

"Money," DuPlooy said.

Tilghman hadn't said much, but I could tell he didn't like DuPlooy. "The question is whether you're going to Mexico with us," Tilghman said. "Scott needs to know."

"And inform your friends we have a deadline," DuPlooy said. "We can't have interference like this."

"Call me," Francie said.

"Scott wants an answer now. He wants to ask Harriet."

"Who's Harriet?" Francie broke her pose and got up from the sofa.

"No, no, no! What are you doing?" DuPlooy tried to grab

Francie's arm, but Francie eluded him and strode out of the light toward Tilghman. "Why are you bothering me at work?" she asked.

"This is work?"

"It's not a sideshow," DuPlooy said.

"It looks like a sideshow."

"Get out," DuPlooy said. "You and your friend both."

I thought Tilghman might punch DuPlooy then, but instead he shrugged. "Let's go, Scott. Or do you want to stay and watch? Frank can give you a ride back. He can watch, can't he, DuPlooy? He won't bother you. It's just taking some photographs of a trained seal."

I hadn't thought about staying, but the idea appealed to me. It was a world I'd never seen before.

"It'll be another hour," Francie said.

"Two hours," DuPlooy said, "if we don't get started."

"Maybe you can get an answer from her," Tilghman said to me. "Be my guest, Scott."

Tilghman left. I sat down against the back wall. I could see why Tilghman was so hard on DuPlooy. There were only so many poses which could enhance a glass of wine, and most of them involved pouting lips and a flash of leg. It was apparent DuPlooy knew the variations of Francie's face. He had her turn by quarter inches so her eyes had differing shadows.

DuPlooy ran through three rolls of film. "Think of sex," he said. "Think of orgasm."

"What's that?" Francie asked.

"Don't smile."

Francie moved, thinking of orgasm.

"Good. That's good. Yes. Turn a little." DuPlooy urged her on, snapping away. "Head higher. Turn. Pull the dress down a little. Dip the shoulder. Good. Chin up. Look across at the ambassador from Britain. Yes. Yes. Good."

I was mesmerized.

It was a little after four when Francie and I started on the bottle of pinot noir. She had changed her clothes and was back to herself— jean cutoffs, a short-sleeved blouse, and clogs. She had scaled away her lipstick, too, and washed her face. The frost was gone from her hair.

She combed it; it was still wet.

DuPlooy was in the darkroom developing pictures, so we took the bottle out to the car. We sat on the fender and passed the bottle back and forth. The clouds had rolled in tightly from the northwest, and a gray sky lowered over us. Thunder cymbaled over the Catalinas.

"What about going to Madera Canyon?" I asked. "It's a perfect time to set the mist nets."

"For your birds?"

"Research," I said.

"Then I'll get to watch you work," she said. "I'll buy the gas, if you'll buy the next bottle of wine."

We got into the car and headed west to the interstate. She had apparently recovered from her anger over calling the police about the bones. She held no grudge anyway. It struck me as odd, though, driving to Madera with her. She was Tilghman's friend. But when I thought about it, it wasn't any different from working with her in the backyard. We were acquaintances with Tilghman in the middle. She was only doing me a favor. "You don't care about seeing the photographs DuPlooy just took?" I asked.

"Not really. That's his business."

"But Tilghman's matter."

"Tilghman's are different." She passed the wine bottle. "How are you finding Tilghman now? What's this about Mexico?"

"You tell me."

"I'd like to go. I know Ellis. He has a wonderful place."

"Tilghman said you like to fish."

"I hate to fish. Tilghman took me once when we were down there, and I hooked a marlin. He made me reel it in for two hours. I was so sunburned I couldn't work for a week. I was waitressing then. That's how I met DuPlooy. He saw me in the restaurant and said he needed someone with a sunburn."

"You caught a marlin?"

"I never landed it. It got off the hook when it came in to the boat."

I handed the wine back. Francie held the bottle right at the top and drank two long swallows. "What's so funny?"

"The way you drink. Did you learn that in South Dakota?"

"I'm from Illinois," Francie said. "My family's from a small town in southern Illinois. My father's a repairman. He can fix

---

almost anything—clocks, tractors, cars, stereos. He taught me a little so I wouldn't be another woman walking around ignorant. That's how he put it. But southern Illinois is prime country for boredom. I went to school in Carbondale and came out here because I had asthma."

"Tilghman said you went to Oberlin."

"Tilghman says anything. I went two years to Southern Illinois and took some dancing classes. I'd always liked ballet, but we lived on a farm so I never had lessons. Then I came to Tucson to study. My dance professor here was a friend of Ellis's."

"That's how you met Ellis?"

She nodded. "And that's how Tilghman met Ellis. My dance teacher Elena Valdez knew Ellis from California years ago. She took Tilghman and me down to Puerto Peñasco one time. Tilghman and Ellis became friends."

"And where is Elena Valdez now?"

"L.A. She runs the dance company at UCLA. She's said I should come out there and she'd try to get me into some shows."

"Why don't you?"

"I'm thinking about it. Until recently there was Tilghman. He encouraged me to dance, but then I hurt my leg and had to drop training for a while. I'm just getting back to it. Anyway now I'm making good money with DuPlooy."

"Was Tilghman normal then, when you met him?"

"He was dealing in paintings and had his hand in real estate. I thought he was normal. He took me to movies, out to dinner, to plays. He was good to be with. He liked being with me. That's what I felt. He talked about ideas and liked my dancing. He wasn't playing games. I liked that. We moved in together, or, rather, I moved in with him."

"And then things went downhill."

"I *thought* he wasn't playing games. A few weeks after I moved in, he said he had made as much money as he wanted to and he quit working. He'd sold two buildings and all his paintings. So he was around a lot. Then all of a sudden, he wasn't around so much. He'd disappear for days at a time. When he got back, I'd ask where he'd been, and he wouldn't tell me. What was I supposed to think?"

"What did you think?"

"I thought he was fucking someone else. How was I supposed to know he was going to Mexico?"

"You found out?"

"He was going down to Ellis's. That's how I found out. Elena wrote me from L.A. Somehow Tilghman got involved in some deal with Demer."

I motioned right, and Francie slowed for the exit at Continental. We descended to the stop sign. To the right were the Safeway, the mall stores, layers of condominiums. "We need more wine," Francie said.

"Go left. There's a store in Continental."

We turned left under the freeway, then made a right onto the narrow road through the pecan grove toward Madera Canyon. We stopped at the little store with bars on the windows, and I bought a ten-dollar bottle of cabernet sauvignon and a corkscrew for Harriet.

"It's safe to bring Harriet to Mexico?" I asked.

"Safe? You mean is Puerto Peñasco safe? Or being with Tilghman?"

"Both."

Francie laughed. "Tell her not to drink the water."

My taste in wines ran to quantity not quality. Once you drank enough it didn't matter what the year was. I cradled the bottle in the front seat while Francie drove. "Trione. Cabernet sauvignon. 1987. Did I tell you Tilghman's father died?" I peeled the metal from the cork and got the corkscrew started.

"He told me he was recovering. You mean he died during the last couple of days?"

"No, I guess the second stroke killed him."

"Why would he lie?"

"I don't know. Maybe he didn't want the sympathy." I thought of that for a moment. It seemed plausible. Then I remembered something else. "He wants to bury Inez Montera."

"Who?"

"The woman Ramon found. I saved the finger bone."

"Oh, that Inez Montera."

"Inez Montera is Demer's friend in Guatemala. Tilghman says she's disappeared."

"And you believe him?"

"He says he'll show me the letter from Demer."

I pulled the cork and handed the bottle to Francie. "We should let it breathe," she said, and she took a taste. "He wants to bury a finger bone?"

I nodded. "The police won't give him back the other bones. Tilghman says the finger bone is enough."

"I told you Tilghman's crazy," Francie said. "I told you, didn't I? But I like that. I do. The finger bone." She laughed and drank again. "I get to help bury her. I was the one who said I found her."

Thunder from the north chased us. Clouds had rolled in over Mount Wrightson. I smelled a change in the air, the dampness that gave the sage and mesquite and cholla blossoms a wet scent, as if they were already preparing for rain. I rolled down my window.

We stopped first at Florida Wash. Francie wasn't dressed for cactus and hackberry, or for rattlesnakes, either, so I set the nets myself while she waited on the bridge. It took me five minutes to get downstream around the bend to where the nets were, and another ten minutes to get them tied in place. Lightning flickered down into the Sierritas while I worked.

Then I climbed back by a different way—off to the south into the grass, where I met up with a road I'd never seen before, an old ranch track with two wheel ruts, overgrown with tall grass. The road circled around the hackberry trees and paloverde toward the highway.

At the edge of the trees, I paused. Francie had taken off her clogs and was dancing on the bridge. She held the bridge rail, lifted her leg high, stretched her other arm to the sky. Then she turned, leaped across the pavement, landed gently, knelt. She lifted slowly from kneeling, and curved her body as if she knew that behind her the hills tapered gently to the north, where the dark clouds lay. Lightning spread over the gray air. Francie arched toward the thunder that followed, pressed her hands to her ankles, ran her hands up her bare legs in a caress, then over her thighs, stomach, breasts, neck, cheeks. She lifted her hands toward the bottle of wine on the corner of the bridge, moved across the bridge again in an ess, swayed, curved her body as if she were wind. Then she stopped and went to the railing. "Scott?"

"Over here," I said.

She picked up the wine bottle and drank. "Here's to Tilghman," she said.

Thunder unraveled along the canyons beneath Mount Wrightson, and a few raindrops sang in the grass. Francie retrieved her shoes and ran for the car. I scrambled down under the bridge and fetched the other nets. Francie backed the car down.

The danger was flash flood. If it rained hard, it was possible to have four or five feet of water pour down from the mountains in a few minutes. The gullies would fill. The dry creeks would be torrents. We might be trapped high in the hills.

But the rain held off. We got up to Proctor Road, and the sun even came out for a minute or two, slicing under the clouds. But it was still raining hard to the north of us. I fixed the nets, slipping the poles through the loops I'd left in the bushes. I tied down the bottoms of the poles. The light waned again, and thunder ricocheted from the rocky walls above us.

We coasted back down across the bajada in front of the lowering clouds. A few drops splattered the windshield. A Western Kingbird rose from a fence post, skittered after an insect, and flew to the top of a telephone pole. A little farther on I pointed out a Roadrunner, then a kestrel—slate blue wings and back, orange tail. We passed the wine back and forth.

"So what do you get out of watching birds?" Francie asked.

"Tilghman asked me that once," I said, "the one time he went birding with me."

"And what did you say?"

"I couldn't answer."

"You had no idea?"

"Remind me to tell you sometime. Anyway it was something I learned young."

"Want to know what I learned young? That men aren't reliable." She laughed, drank again, steered with one hand.

I didn't laugh. "Did Tilghman sleep with Demer?"

"I don't know. Was Demer the kind of woman who'd do that?"

"Yes. Is Tilghman the kind of friend who would?"

Francie looked at me. "He's your friend. What do you think?"

I wasn't thinking. The wine roiled in my blood. "I loved Demer," I said, "if that's a crime."

"Do you love you?"

I smiled grimly. "I've tried, but it's like filling the sea with stones."

The rain started in earnest in the pecan groves at Continental. The leaves tattered in the air. The rain made a tinny sound on the roof of the VW, soaked the black highway. Francie slowed on the bridge over the Santa Cruz River, which was still a trickle, then veered right onto the ramp of the interstate. I hadn't been aware until then how much we'd drunk. The second bottle of wine was nearly gone.

Doctors say our powers of observation are markedly diminished by alcohol. Reaction time slows. Speech slurs. The amount of light reaching the retina is so reduced that vision is impaired. The brain scrambles. Motor neurons are numbed. We stagger, lose balance, can't steer a car in a straight line. We lose inhibitions, can't remember. All this must be true. These are facts corroborated by coroners' reports.

It's my experience, though, that my own power of observation is enhanced. Perhaps I wouldn't distinguish so quickly a Couch's Kingbird from the more numerous Western Kingbirds that perch on fence posts and wires. I might miss a Zone-tailed Hawk soaring among a swirl of Turkey Vultures. But I see myself more clearly. I see the outer world less exactly, but the inner world more vividly. The murky shapes, fluttering images, vague experiences—I see these precisely, more lucidly.

And so it was then. The beauty of the inner landscape startled me. It left me weak with promise. I stared out the windshield of the VW moving through rain. A thin misty gray washed from the air and over the highway. The rain covered the gray-green hills, slid right at us. Lightning drifted though the air in slow motion. Cars coming toward us on the divided highway blinded me with their headlights.

It rained harder. We were in the midst of it—the gray slick highway reflected clouds, the countryside closed around us. Francie didn't slow down. She couldn't have seen more than a few feet ahead, but she kept up her speed. I imagined the rain collecting beneath Mount Wrightson, gathering in small crevices, pouring down gullies into side canyons, flowing down the bajadas, rushing always to the lowest places.

Then over a rise there was a break in the storm. For an instant the land opened outward like one brief glimpse into a dream, and the sudden, gold sunlight knifed through the misty air. A Mourning Dove sailed toward shelter in the shiny, wet-leafed cottonwoods along the river. Francie accelerated on the downslope.

Within a mile we hit new rain. A buffet of wind knocked Francie's foot from the gas, and she leaned toward the windshield. She had to be drunker than I was. Red lights zoomed up in front of us. She braked. By rights we should have skidded, but at that moment we were traveling uphill, and gravity slowed us. She swerved left, missed the corner of a semitrailer truck by inches, then passed two other cars which had caused the truck to brake. Francie honked and careened past in a shower of rain sparks.

I gripped the dash. Francie laughed, slapped my arm. "What's the matter, Scott? Haven't you ever died before?"

I laughed, too.

The clouds had swept east before we reached Tucson, and the smooth edge of the sky and land and sun emerged from the mountains. I imagined birds, thousands of them, fallen from the sky. That was the world I knew, the one which had a natural order to it, even in chaos. Or maybe it was the near accident which gave me pause. What did Francie mean, hadn't I ever died? But the darkness in the wake of the storm felt like silk, and as we were coming over the last hills into the city, the lights spread out like a blanket of stars. The houses shone. The highway glistened. The last frail rays of the sun slanted through from the west.

PART TWO

Chapter one

Highway 86 ran west from Tucson through the Baboqui-
vari Mountains and across the Tohono O'odham Reservation.
The white dome of Kitt Peak Observatory shone like a Greek
temple against the jagged, pale brown cliffs. I imagined the stars
one could see from there, the nights visible within our own night.
But in daylight the land was different. The road dipped and curved
through saguaros, cholla, prickly pear, past shacks and adobe
houses, along telephone wires. It was clear, cooler than it had been
in quite a while, and greener since the rain. Ocotillo unfurled its
leaves. The creosote and the grasses lightened. Flowers had ex-
ploded from nowhere like red and orange and violet firecrackers.

It was spring break, but Harriet hadn't come with us. At the
last minute she'd felt guilty about leaving her mother—she could
justify it for whales, she said, but not for pleasure. I'd protested.
I'd called her mother, who seemed perfectly agreeable to having
Harriet go along. Harriet had said no.

I was both disappointed and not. I'd miss the company, but at
the same time, I was uncertain what might have evolved in four
days together, now that we had embarked on "learning."

Ramon was going to feed Zapata while we were gone, but
Tilghman had had to get dog food. He had also had new tires put
on the Land Rover. He wanted to bring back plants for his back-
yard—some organ-pipe cactus which grew only in the Sonoran
Desert west and south of Tucson, and bougainvillea for the trellis.
To get these plants, he said, we might have to do some rough
driving cross-country.

The Land Rover made noise. Air roared through the open

windows and the engine knocked. The far back was filled with shovels and buckets which clattered, along with our suitcases and duffels. Francie rode shotgun, and I sat in the backseat with the cooler. We had just passed through the collection of goverment houses at Sells on the reservation.

"What about a Dr. Pepper?" Tilghman asked. "You awake, Scott?"

"Who could sleep?" I asked. I peeled the lid from the cooler and fished among the ice chips for a dark red can.

"Francie could sleep," Tilghman said. "She could sleep through a good fuck."

"Not a good one," Francie said. "But lately there hasn't been any kind. You know what I mean? Is there a beer in there, Scott?"

I handed up the Dr. Pepper and a Schlitz. I took a beer for myself. "How long has the engine made that noise?"

"Months," Tilghman said. "A friend of mine in Puerto Peñasco worked on it and said it was okay."

"What kind of friend?"

Tilghman smiled. "Worry, worry. That's Scott. No sense in being idle when you can imagine the worst."

"If you imagine the worst," I said, "then you're never disappointed."

"Why don't you get it fixed?" Francie asked. "That's what most people do when their cars bum out. You have the money."

"Don't you have faith?" Tilghman asked.

Heat shimmered from the pavement. We ascended a gentle hill and looked out across nothing as far as we could see to the undulating blue horizon. A Loggerhead Shrike skimmed the sparse grass at the side of the road and landed on a strand of barbed wire. Robin-sized, gray, black-and-white wing markings. The shrike was called the butcher bird because of its habit of impaling its prey of grasshoppers and small birds on thorns and barbed-wire cleats before tearing them apart. Family Laniidae.

We passed a wide white sandy wash. A truck passed us—a blue Royal Crown Cola delivery truck with thousands of bottles stacked in cases. Tilghman slowed as we came to a roadside cross. "The soul departs the earth from a single point," he said. "That's the launching pad for someone." He glanced over at Francie. "Did I ever tell you the story of Ellis?"

"You never tell me anything."

"You never ask. Anyway Ellis was teaching writing at San

Diego State a few years ago, sometime after *Carte Blanche*, when he was famous. He was driving up to L.A. on one of the farm roads, going a little too fast maybe, but not reckless. There was a line of trucks and cars parked along the berm where pickers were at work in the fields. In Ramona, this was. A little boy ran out from behind one of the trucks."

Tilghman paused, and Francie looked out the side window.

"The boy's parents were right there. Ellis had to stay in Ramona for a few days while the police looked into his record. He'd had a ticket once for careless driving and one DUI."

"But it wasn't his fault."

"Nobody cared about fault. The parents didn't speak English. They didn't know enough to call Ellis's insurance company or to sue him."

"What did Ellis do?"

"He got their names and told his insurance people what had happened. The company refused to volunteer a payment, so Ellis hired his own lawyer and got a settlement for the family."

"Good for Ellis."

"Except you know the rest of the story. They couldn't find the family. They'd moved on somewhere, to some other crop. No address. Forget forwarding. Ellis never got over that. He gave the settlement money to César Chavez. And then he took Spanish lessons."

Tilghman lurched the Land Rover to the side of the road, braked hard, and stopped. Francie fended off the dash. I grabbed the cooler, which slid forward. We had stopped beside another shrine.

We got out into thistles and weeds. Without moving air it was warmer, almost hot. The cross wasn't far off the pavement on a little uplift of bare ground. It was maybe two feet tall, of rough wood, the top pounded into the earth by a hammer whose marks were still visible in the grain. A low, rectangular adobe wall enclosed the small plot. In front of the cross was a small glass enclosure which held a burning candle. An empty quart of Budweiser had been propped against the wood. Tilghman picked up the bottle and tossed it into a clump of prickly pear.

"Someone must light a candle every day," Francie said.

"A lot of candles," Tilghman said.

"A lot of gasoline," I said, looking around. Two barren buttes lifted on either side of the rail-straight highway. There wasn't a house in sight.

Then Tilghman knelt down in front of the cross and bowed his head. Francie and I looked at one another. I had never seen Tilghman do anything like that, had never witnessed in him any reverence for anything. Where had that emotion come from? Tilghman stayed on his knees for a minute or more. I turned away finally. It made me nervous.

I walked away toward the fence, where papers and bottles littered the side of the highway. Out in the yuccas and cholla I heard the cooing of a Roadrunner in the still air.

Chapter two

We stopped at the Standard station at the intersection of highways at Why. That was all there was there—a station and a trailer parked a few hundred yards behind it in the weeds. The garage was a square cinder-block building painted white. There were junked cars around it, and two tow trucks, one for big rigs, parked at the edge of a wide gravel turnout. A faded blue van with a weathered star on the side sat with a flat tire beside the trailer. Tilghman nearly hit the metal sign propped by the gas pump: FULL SERVICE STATION.

We all got out. An older man, an Indian wearing a beaten-up cowboy hat, sauntered out of the open bay of the garage. "Going to Mexico?" he asked.

Tilghman nodded. "I stop here every time."

"People want American gas," the man said. "They all fill up here." He pulled the nozzle from the pump.

"Any new horror stories out of Rocky Point?" Tilghman asked.

The Indian smiled a tough smile full of creases. "Just the usual ones."

Francie went to the bathroom. I leaned against the fender of the Rover and watched Francie's sliding gait, the way she held her shoulders straight, as if she'd spent years practicing good posture. She had her pocketbook slung on a strap at her side.

"Looks good, doesn't she?" Tilghman said.

"Okay."

"Looks aren't everything."

I smiled. "She's hardly a ticket on a doomed flight," I said. "Why did you tell me she was from South Dakota?"

"Isn't she?"

"Or that she went to Oberlin?"

Tilghman grinned and stared away into the sun toward the huge white scar of a mine sizzling on the horizon. "There used to be gold around here, but never very much. Over near Quijotoa they found a fair-sized pocket once, and naturally they thought there was more. A dozen men spent their whole lives digging for something that wasn't there."

"What do they mine here?" I asked, pointing toward the horizon.

"Copper," Tilghman said. "The mine pretty much supports the town of Ajo a few miles north of here."

"Lots of copper down around Bisbee and Douglas," I said. I gazed into the heat waves that blurred the white scar.

"Too little water, too much sun." Tilghman turned to the old man pumping gas. "Isn't that right, Lorry?"

The Indian nodded. "That's what this country is like. Deadly."

"Except for Quitobaquito."

The man topped off the tank and propped the nozzle back in the pump. "Eighteen forty-five," he said.

Tilghman pulled a wad of bills from his pocket and peeled off a twenty.

"What's at Quitobaquito?" I asked.

"Same as here," Tilghman said. "Only there's water."

Francie came out from the station swinging her purse. A camper trailer pulled in from the north, and I thought that the old man was probably glad to see an empty tank on one of those big campers.

After Why the land changed from mesquite barrens to rugged mountains. The horizon closed in around us—rocky outcroppings, jagged ridges. I asked Tilghman for a map.

Francie found one in the glove compartment and handed it back to me. I folded it out and found the Organ Pipe Cactus National Monument. There was a road that ran west from the headquarters to a little blue spot at Quitobaquito and back to Lukeville on the border. "This is the northern tip of the Sonoran Desert," I said. "We've studied this in class. Organ pipes can't tolerate frost. The monument is really the only place this cactus grows in the U.S."

"No water," Tilghman said. "A few deep wells are all. There's the spring at Quitobaquito and the Sonoita River, but the river's dry now. This used to be part of the old Camino del Diablo up to Yuma."

"And the mountains?"

"Growlers to the west, Ajos and Puerto Blancos to the east. How would you like to be lost in those hills?"

I scanned out the window. The mountains were barren rock bleached by sun, serrated, forbidding. I imagined being lost in them, having to kill snakes and lizards for food, cutting open saguaros to suck the pulp. Tilghman might have liked the challenge, but I'd prefer to watch birds at the spring at Quitobaquito.

We drove miles in silence. Francie sipped another beer. She tucked a few loose strands of hair under a bandanna she wore. Tilghman looked serene. His elbow was cocked out the window, and he watched the pale highway, held the wheel loosely. In the old days he would have been thinking, hatching some plot. Maybe he still was.

I remembered the time we were staying at his parents' cabin near Detroit Lakes in Minnesota. It was a rainy night, but warm, and we'd been in town at a bar. Tilghman had drunk too much Yukon Jack, so I was driving home. We'd just climbed into the open Jeep when Tilghman gave the finger to a passing Cadillac.

The Cadillac stopped and waited for us at a red light. Its window was down. "What's the big idea?" the driver asked. "You a faggot or someone?"

"Want to race?" Tilghman asked. "This man driving is Mario Andretti's nephew. A C-note says we beat you to the next light."

"Up your ass," the man said.

Tilghman grinned and took out a .22 pistol from the glove compartment. The light changed, and Tilghman shot out the front tire of the Cadillac. "We take MasterCard or Visa," he said. "Drive, Scott." In the old days Tilghman had done a lot of things like that.

I leaned forward between the two front seats of the Rover. "Here's something I want to know," I said.

"We have answers," Francie said. "Everything right here."

"I want to know about Demer."

"Well, Scott," Tilghman said, "I'm not sure you do." He glanced in the rearview mirror at me. "You're talking memory, not answers."

"She went to see you," I said. "A few months later she left me and went to Costa Rica."

"She came to Colorado to ski," Tilghman said. "She didn't come to see me."

"Small difference."

"Look, people do things, Scott. Afterward the other people involved get over them, or they don't. What's the point in carrying around all that bitterness?"

"I'm not bitter. I want to understand it."

"Why shouldn't he be bitter?" Francie asked. "His wife left him."

"Now we're getting expert testimony," Tilghman said.

"It's a legitimate question," Francie said.

"What makes you think Scott didn't beat her?"

"He's not the type."

"There's a type?" Tilghman's voice flashed, then relented. "Let me tell you what type Scott is. I've known him a long time. He's a very honest man. He doesn't want to hurt anybody. He doesn't want to get involved. One time in college there was a demonstration in Harvard Square—world hunger, U.S. policy in Angola—I can't remember what it was about. I think Gerald Ford was president. We were carrying signs and shouting, and I looked up at the iron fence around the Yard, and there was Scott perched up high, watching."

"I was taking photographs for *The Crimson*."

"You weren't down there marching. Or bashing heads with those of us who were."

"What does that have to do with his wife?" Francie asked.

"I don't know. Something."

"I worked, I came home, and I was faithful to her."

"Oh Jesus, now he's a saint."

"I'm not a saint."

"You deserted her," Tilghman said. "You moved out."

"My uncle's place was nearby. I wanted to give Demer space."

"Space?"

"Yes."

I remembered one time Demer had come home just when I was packing to leave on a bird tour. I was in the alcove by the front door, organizing guidebooks. I was surprised to see her.

"What are you doing?" she asked.

"I've got a trip to Florida."

"I don't want you to go."

"You gave me the impression last night you couldn't wait for me to leave."

She took what I was holding—a box of maps—and dropped it on the floor. She unbuttoned the front of her white uniform slowly. I watched her eyes, then her fingers. The white cloth separated in a vee of darker skin, and the thin lacy edge of her slip appeared beneath the heavier white. The white fell away. She pulled her arms from the sleeves of the blouse and dropped the white to the floor. The pale slip floated over her head. She shrugged off her bra, slid her hands over her breasts hard, let one hand descend to the white panties. Her legs parted, her eyes closed. She pushed her hand deeper under the white.

Tilghman, on a hill, downshifted to third. The Land Rover rumbled.

"So who really left whom?" Francie asked.

"We split amicably."

"Bullshit. One of you didn't. You, Scott."

"I agreed to it," I said. "If she didn't want to stay, I didn't want her to."

"I rest my case," Tilghman said.

"Did you leave Clarice?" I asked.

"Yes, I left Clarice." Tilghman looked at me in the rearview. "At the end I would come home to this immense house of wood and glass which I had no part or interest in, and Clarice would be praying to some drawing on the wall. I used to wonder how I'd got there. Oh yes, in the beginning—we all know how beginnings are. We'd had that hellfire—crashing down the mountain on skis, late nights in bars, heavy sex, some toot. It was wonderful. The next thing I knew she was praying to the wall."

"Demer didn't pray to the wall."

"You see what I mean though. Clarice had time, money, and a husband—all those problems solved."

"Getting a husband is a problem to solve?" Francie asked.

"She didn't need me anymore except as an accomplice."

"You're saying Demer didn't need me?" I asked.

Tilghman shifted back to fourth on the downslope. He shook his head. "I don't know what Demer needs."

Chapter three

The border between Lukeville and Sonoita was called Gringo Pass. BORDER CLOSED 12 MIDNIGHT TO 8 A.M., the sign said. A modern, soaring, concrete customs building guarded the U.S. side, and a little wooden house watched over the Mexican side. We stopped at the little house for our tourist visas.

We waited in line to fill out forms for an official who sat at a table in the center of a bare room with paneless windows. There was no breeze. The man was explaining to an American couple how perfectly safe it was to travel the coast road to Mazatlán. He was sweating and wiped his face with a white handkerchief.

"You couldn't pay me to drive to Mazatlán," Tilghman told the wife, who was in front of us in the line.

"Max, listen to this young man." The woman tapped her husband on the back.

"Maybe during the week you'd be okay," Tilghman went on. "But don't drive at night or on weekends. Do you have super-big tanks of American gasoline?"

The man had turned around to listen. "We have two extra five-gallon canisters," he said. "I planned for tough driving."

"You might get hijacked for the gasoline," Tilghman said.

"Have you been to Mazatlán?" the man asked.

Tilghman nodded gravely. "And once was enough."

Francie and I took the couple's place at the table and filled out our forms. The couple left. Tilghman took his turn. When we went outside, the couple was scrutinizing their atlas, which was draped over the hood of a Ford Taurus station wagon.

"Don't listen to him," Francie said, motioning toward

Kent Nelson

Tilghman. "The road to Mazatlán is fine. The couple that got murdered was going to Guaymas."

"Where's Guaymas?" the woman asked. "Isn't Guaymas on the way?"

"Don't listen to her, either," I said. "She's from Cleveland."

When we got to the Land Rover, three little boys snapped to attention at the front bumper. They had washed the windows and the headlights without being asked, but now they were anxious to be paid. Tilghman gave them each five dollars.

We drove into Sonoita, steered right along the main road, slid past a huge billboard for Fanta orange. The street was hot. A few scraggly eucalyptus trees and some dusty palms bordered the highway.

At a stop sign a half-dozen children besieged us with white cans with red crosses painted on them. Tilghman gave more money. "It's not the Red Cross," he said, "but they know what works. Americans have heard of the Red Cross even if they haven't heard of poverty."

A little farther on we exchanged dollars for pesos and bought Ellis a bottle of tequila as a house present.

Beyond Sonoita the road narrowed. The two-lane pavement dipped and curved over the rocky hills. Trucks passed us from the other direction, whining their gears on the grades or hurtling down the hills and compressing the air between us. Around one bend we came upon a man rolling a tire in the middle of the highway. We had no idea where the man was going. There were no houses nearby, and for several miles afterward, no cars on the shoulder and no side roads.

According to Tilghman the road had been built in 1945 by the U.S. Army Corps of Engineers. Puerto Peñasco had been an alternate site for the Yalta Conference, and for security reasons, a land-supply and access route was required to and from the United States. It was still a good road. In a desert without frost, things didn't crumble away.

Twenty miles into Mexico, the saguaros and organ pipes gave way to salt flats covered with sparse mesquite. We passed a few adobe huts surrounded by stick pens for goats. Chickens browsed the bare yards and along the highway. Stacks of twigs leaned precariously against the houses—firewood for cooking and heat. By each hut three or four mongrels plagued with flies stretched out near the open doorway.

The mountains fell away into the distance where, I supposed, the sea lay. We eased across mirages. The Land Rover clanked loudly, but there was no escalation of damage. Several times I thought I smelled salt air.

Through the milky hot haze, a rocky outcropping appeared— a volcanic plug left when the land had boiled and slanted skyward. Graffiti covered the rocks now, and on top of the eroding stones was a small cross.

A mile beyond, Francie wanted to use the bathroom, but there wasn't one. "It's the vibrations," she said. "How far are we from Rocky Point?"

"Another thirty miles."

"Then stop. I've got to go."

Tilghman pulled over on the shoulder. Francie got out, and Tilghman opened his door, too, to let whatever breeze there was slide through the interior of the car.

"You'll like Ellis," Tilghman said. "Floundering writer. Floundering is a profitable industry in Puerto Peñasco. *Platijas*, they're called. They cut the fillets right in the market, and what they don't sell, they freeze." He turned sideways in the seat and for a moment stared across the flats. Then without warning he leaped from the seat and ducked around the hood to the other side of the Rover. "You're under arrest," he yelled.

Francie jumped, struggled with her shorts. "You scared me, Tilghman."

"Indecent exposure and littering," he said. "Do I take you peaceably, or do I draw my weapon?"

"Draw your weapon," Francie said. "But you won't take me without a fight."

Tilghman unzipped his shorts and dropped them. Francie laughed. He wrestled with her, and when she broke away, he chased her around the car onto the highway, still with his shorts around his ankles.

I scooped another beer from the cooler and got out and walked a few paces away to urinate. Francie and Tilghman were still laughing. I snapped open the beer, drank two long swallows, and zipped up. I pressed the cold can to my forehead.

Then I started running. I jogged along the dusty flat ground, slowly at first, holding the beer can in my hand, finding a rhythm. I wobbled in the heat, drank awkwardly, tossed the can to the ground beside a broken tequila bottle. Slap, slap. My shoes padded on the dusty earth. Sweat rose quickly on my back and under my arms. My breath echoed in my ears.

I veered to the pavement, felt the soft, hot asphalt ooze under my weight. Heat swirled up around me like a dust devil spinning into air. Two steps, a breath of hot air, exhale quickly, another two steps. My shirt stuck to my back.

The land descended imperceptibly toward the sandy horizon, and I wished I could have run like that all the way to the sea, without looking back at Francie and Tilghman. I resolved to learn to run far. As Tilghman said, I needed stamina.

Tilghman's steps came up fast, tick-tack, tick-tack, gaining on me. For a few seconds I increased the pace, but I slowed again, knowing I couldn't outrun him. He caught me and loped alongside like a shadow tight on my shoulder. We ran in silence for maybe a mile.

"What do you want to do?" Tilghman asked.

I didn't understand the choices.

"You want to ditch her? We could leave her at Ellis's and drive to Mexico City."

"You mean Francie?"

Tilghman turned around and ran backward, gliding as fast as I was running forward. "She's coming up in the car."

I glanced over my shoulder. The Land Rover wavered in the hot air. "Drive to Mexico City in that?"

"Why not?"

"I'm all right," I said. "I don't mind Francie."

Tilghman turned around, and we ran a good fifty paces without speaking. "I have some work to do here," Tilghman said finally. "This won't be all pleasure for me."

"What kind of work?"

Tilghman didn't answer. He sprinted ahead, as if I had to keep pace to get an answer. I couldn't have kept up with him if I'd wanted to. My legs were heavy. It was too hot. Beer sweat dropped from my chin to the asphalt and evaporated. I stopped running and felt the larger heat rise in me.

Francie stopped the car. "Where did Tilghman go?"

I got in on the passenger side.

"You didn't have to leave, Scott. He was just playing around."

"I know."

We came up to Tilghman in a mile or so. He still ran as I remembered him from track, without a hitch in his stride, a smooth flow of arms and legs. The white soles of his shoes popped up from the pavement, his arms circled close to his sides. He waved us past, and Francie drove on. I watched Tilghman recede behind us, still running easily.

"You ran track together?" Francie asked. "Is that much true?"

"Tilghman was good. I was average. He could have made the national team if he'd wanted to."

"But he didn't."

"He wanted to do other things more."

"Such as?"

"Fulbright to Yugoslavia. He studied art. His father was willing to finance two years of training, but Tilghman turned him down. Maybe if his father hadn't offered, he would have done it. At the time Tilghman said he didn't want to waste the energy doing something he knew he could do."

"Maybe he didn't want to try."

We drove into the sea-hazy air, and after a couple of miles, Francie pulled over to wait. The terrain was sand and fierce light, a light without depth or color. Even the road seemed to disappear in the near distance. I couldn't see ahead or behind. Everything was light—heavy and hot.

Tilghman finally appeared far away in the haze. His legs, large at the thigh, churned toward us as if he weren't touching the ground. He had taken off his shirt and, as he ran, waved it in his hand. His red shorts blurred through the mirage.

He ran on that mirage of slick water. He closed the gap, arms pumping, head held straight in the long stride. About two hundred yards away, he began jumping hurdles. Three steps, leap, three more, another leap, his right leg tucked underneath his body, left hand extended forward, elbows akimbo, white shirt making circles in the air. His head was low, but always in the perfect plane of the jump. Leap, sprint, leap. He sprinted the last thirty yards right at the Rover, gaining speed. He jumped, caught one foot on the base of the back window, CLUNK, another on the roof, POCK, then another on the hood, PUCK, and off. He stopped ten yards past us and raised his arms above his head in mock triumph.

Chapter four

The stench of fish was everywhere, emanating from the fish stalls along the road, from the exposed tidal flats, from the shrimp trawlers drawn up to the piers in the harbor. We curled up the rocky hill, leaving the harbor on our right. Along the water a long gray warehouse with painted letters—*Los Pescadores* (in black) *Samuel* (green) *y Fernando* (pink)—eroded in the salt air. Behind this warehouse was a newer cement building where a loud hammering was muffled by the humid air. "Frozen-fish factory," Tilghman said. "Mariscos congelados de Peñasco. They make their own ice."

We skirted another pier. Out in the water a dredger floated on a metal raft. The water was calm.

"Where are the tourists?" I asked.

"Swimming with the sharks," Tilghman said. "Who said there were tourists here?"

The headland swept around the bay, and far down the coast on the other side of the harbor, a few seedy-looking pastel houses shone in the sun.

"That's Bahía Choyo across the water," Tilghman said. "That's the American slum. Ellis lives in the other direction, behind us. The town is more lively in the morning when the boats come in for the markets."

We angled left along a row of empty fish stalls made of cement. A little girl was hosing one of them down. On the other side of the street were souvenir shops with vases, blankets, T-shirts, trinkets made from shells. Obviously some tourists came, at least on weekends.

Behind the fish market a welter of houses sidestepped up the hill—painted cinder blocks of pink, turquoise, and pale blue. At the end of the street, the Hotel Miramar overlooked the breakwater and the entrance to the harbor. Beyond the breakwater was the open Gulf of California.

We circled past the Miramar and back down through town. That was the tour. Along the Boulevard Benito Juárez, someone had painted a wall with SANGRE DE LOS GRINGOS. Even I didn't need a translation.

"*Sangre*," Tilghman said. "Sangre-de-dragon is a flower. Sangría is a red wine. Don't worry, Scott. Puerto Peñasco is a friendly town."

The avenue was laced with potholes and lined on one side with ragged palm trees whose dead fronds dangled from the crowns. There was not a single new car parked along the street. No sidewalk. Pedestrians, lots of them children, walked among the cars at the side of the road. We passed a school and two billboards for Tecate. We turned right at a small store onto a paved velvet road.

"You took political science," Tilghman said. "This road is a textbook."

We floated along the smooth asphalt. We couldn't see the Gulf anymore, behind a ridge of sand on our right, but the evening breeze came from that direction. Spare, rainless clouds scudded above the dunes.

Then, abruptly, the pavement stopped, and we bounced along on hard-packed, washboard sand. "This is where the bribes ran out," Tilghman said.

A little farther on we veered right from the main road and followed a narrower sandy track into a swale, then accelerated up and over a couple of dunes to the ridge, which offered a fuller view—a treeless waste of agave and sand and a line of immaculate white houses at the edge of the blue Gulf.

Tilghman let gravity speed the car, and we dipped into another trough and came up a steeper hill to the bluff. We passed houses tangled with magenta and red bougainvillea and other houses in various stages of construction. All the finished houses were whitewashed. Some had turrets and towers, others verandas, gates, ornate ironwork. All of the roofs were red tile.

Then a motorcycle came out of one of the side streets, slid toward us, and righted itself. Tilghman steered away, leaned on the horn. The motorcycle raced past us as if we were barely moving. "Asshole," Tilghman said.

"That's Ellis," said Francie.

The bike slowed, drifted left, then swung in front of us into a driveway on the right. I grabbed the back of the front seat and threw an arm around Francie in front. Tilghman braked and just made the turn into the driveway on the other side of the semicircle. By the time we stopped, Ellis had his helmet off and was grinning at us, his bald head gleaming with sun and sweat.

Later. I stood on the terrace with a Tecate and watched the shrimp boats on the water, their winch booms stretched like the blessing Christ as they plied the strait between us and the offshore islands maybe two miles away. The sky had paled to lighter than the sea, to the blue-white of dusk.

"What are the islands?" I asked Ellis, who was sitting drinking a margarita.

"Las Cabras," he said. "The Goat Islands. There's a myth that there are goats on them left by the Spanish conquistadors."

"Ever been there?"

"I've been close. I've never seen any goats."

"What about whales?"

"I've never seen any whales, either. If you want to look for whales, we can rent a boat."

There were cats in the dunes—a gray one hunched behind a yucca and a yellow-striped one near the neighboring house under construction. Ellis pointed to a dark one, not quite black, near the low wall around the terrace. "The cats have taken over," he said. "They've proliferated with the people."

"Like starlings," I said.

Ellis picked up some stones from a bucket beside his chair and hurled a volley at the dark cat nearby. The stones made no impression on the cat, except it moved two steps back.

I had always liked islands. These were rough rock that looked in that light like sleek porpoises. But I could see the cliffs, too, and the birds circling.

Francie came out with another pitcher of margaritas and filled Ellis's glass. "You want one, Scott? I brought an extra glass."

"All right."

"Tilghman wants to know about dinner," Francie said.

"We have to head the shrimp," Ellis said. "That's the main

---

work. I'll get them."

Ellis got up. He didn't look anything like his dust-jacket photograph. He was short and bald. A ridge of long gray hair rimmed his ears, and a paunch rolled over his belt. His thin bowed legs made him look like a motorcycle cowboy. And compared to the jacket photograph, he looked sad. I wanted to forget he'd killed a child, but every time I looked at him, it was in his eyes.

We headed the shrimp on the veranda. The cats crowded in toward us, and now and then Ellis threw stones at them. Gulls wheeled overhead. We drank margaritas.

Ellis told us a story about Adelita, who owned a fish stall in town. He had been a customer of hers and Miguel's for a long time. "I'm a year-round customer," Ellis said. "I'm an American who speaks Spanish, so they give me the freshest shrimp and the best red snapper, see? We're friends. When I go to the States, I bring them presents—you know, a radio, a decent broom, nothing too expensive. But a couple of weeks ago, I brought back some steaks and a bottle of perfume for Adelita. Adelita is no little Adele. She's five feet and one-eighty. So I stop to get scallops . . ."

Tilghman appeared then at the side of the house and walked along the dune trail toward the edge of the bluff. Francie and Ellis had their backs to him. He stood for a moment listening to Ellis's story, I assumed, and gazing out toward the islands. Then he looked toward me with an odd glance, as if he was impatient with the story, with our leisurely work, with something we were doing. He passed behind the dune and went down the hill toward the beach.

". . . so Adelita is in the stall by herself. I give her the steaks and the perfume. She opens the perfume right away—that's for her, right? So she starts shouting to her friends to look. 'Hey, hey!' she says. I'm nodding politely. She splashes the perfume on her neck. She drowns herself in it. The fish stall smells like a boutique. I laugh, a little nervous. She gives me this smelly hug. Finally I start to give her instructions, what to tell Miguel about cooking the steaks. 'This is prime American beef,' I tell her. 'You can't cook it too much. That's the mistake too many husbands make.' She stops all of a sudden and looks at me. 'Miguel?' she says. 'No tengo esposo.' And she hugs me again."

Francie laughed. Ellis laughed.

"'*No tengo esposo*,'" Francie said to me. "'I don't have a husband.'"

"Now Adelita thinks I'm in love with her, bringing her perfume."

I smiled and nodded. But having it explained made it not so funny.

We finished shelling the shrimp, and Francie took them inside. Ellis split the last of the margaritas in the pitcher. "We can start dinner," he said. "Do you want to find Tilghman?"

"All right."

"He's probably gone to the beach."

I walked out the path to the edge of the bluff. From there the trail zigzagged down the steep slope, but I didn't see anyone there. It was nearly dark, and the lights of the shrimp boats moved across the water. But I could see well enough in both directions down the beach, far down into the sea haze. No one was there. Toward town the sand curved outward in a hump and then receded, I assumed, toward the rocky hill which gave the town its name. The tide was out, so the beach was wider. Pools clotted with seaweed patterned the sand. I didn't see Tilghman anywhere. He'd have had to run to get so far away.

Chapter five

Tilghman didn't show up for dinner. Ellis, Francie, and I ate shrimp and spaghetti and drank wine by candlelight in the living room beneath the huge glass chandelier. Ellis, who'd drunk straight tequila as he'd cooked the shrimp, recounted for us an incomplete history of the American presence in Puerto Peñasco. Apparently an American developer had wanted to build a resort there for people from Tucson and Phoenix, and he'd succeeded in getting some houses built along the bluff at Las Conchas where we were. "What did he care if it's the desert?" Ellis said, waving his hand in the air. "When money's invested, the obstacles can be overcome later—like where to get fresh water. Of course I got in cheap, before the madness, even before electricity and plumbing. For a long time I had a propane refrigerator so I could have cold beer."

"When was this?" I asked.

"Nineteen seventy-seven. A few years after *Carte Blanche*. I wanted a place to get away."

Some drinkers, like me, make phone calls when they drink too much. Some get morose. Some talk loudly and tell stories. That was Ellis. He started raving. Why had the goddamn developers put in electricity? How could people want a second home when most people in the world had no home at all? Politicians didn't give a rat's ass about the poor. Laws were designed for the rich, and no one protested because we were all taught in grade school that's how it's supposed to be. He went on like that for half an hour, and then he hit the wall. He paused, put his head down on the table, and passed out.

114

After a moment of silence, I looked at Francie. "Where do you think Tilghman went?" I asked.

"He went to town. Where else is there? This is what he used to do to me, Scott. He'd be gone like this, sometimes for days, and then he'd come back."

"Doing his work?"

"I know he comes here sometimes. And he goes to Guaymas."

I cleared the table, and Francie heated water for coffee. We did the dishes together. Then we put Ellis in his room, played chess, and waited for Tilghman.

That night I didn't sleep. A long time after the house was dark, I was still awake, curled up on one of the window seats in the living room. Maybe I was still dazed by the margaritas and the wine. That happened sometimes. Booze made me think too much. My eyes were open. The breeze had picked up a little and drifted over me like moonlight.

Then I heard someone in the room. I thought it must be Francie, come out to get a drink of water, or maybe to see whether Tilghman had come back. Whoever it was lurked in the hall, opened and closed a door softly. Then a whispered voice: "Scott."

It was Tilghman.

"Yes?"

"I thought you'd be sleeping in a bedroom."

"I liked it out here."

"I need your help," Tilghman said.

I sat up. Tilghman's silhouette moved in front of the open screen door to the terrace. He sat down close to me. "Are you hurt?" I asked.

"No."

"To do what then?"

"Get up. Quiet though. Francie's a light sleeper. Let's not talk here."

"We drank a lot of wine," I said, as if that explained something. I got up and got dressed.

Tilghman slid open the screen door to the terrace, and we went outside. A rippled half-moon shone across the water, bathing the white houses along the bluff in cool light. The islands off the coast were black shapes separated from the moonlit sea. I was surprised how chilly the night was, and how easy the moon made it to see in the dark.

Tilghman led the way around the house. "We have to push the Land Rover," he said. "It won't start."

"And you wanted to drive to Mexico City?"

Another man came around from the dark side of the Land Rover—a dark-skinned man in light-colored clothes. He wore a bandanna around his forehead to keep his long hair from his face. No words were exchanged. Tilghman opened the driver's door and planted his feet on the crushed stone of Ellis's driveway. The other man and I each took a headlight and pushed from the front, rocking the corners. The Rover inched backward over the crackling pebbles and up the drive.

With a little momentum, it was easier to keep the car rolling. My feet slipped once, and I banged my elbow hard, but I got purchase again and kept going before we lost the roll. When we got the car to the sandy roadway, Tilghman backed it around heading downhill and jumped in. We pushed from the back until gravity took over into the swale. Near the bottom Tilghman popped the clutch, and the engine caught.

The other man and I ran down the hill. Tilghman spoke a few words in Spanish to the other man, and we got in. I wasn't introduced, but Tilghman had called the man Raul. Raul sat in the middle, while Tilghman drove fast toward town. Tilghman concentrated on the road, but he was thinking of something else, too. The Land Rover fishtailed in the sand.

Distance elapsed. The cold revived me, and the speed. We cornered past the last house and over the hills. The town appeared like sparkling lava flowing into the dark night beyond.

We cruised the stretch of smooth asphalt to the Boulevard Benito Juárez. The main street was empty now, and we raced by the windblown husks of the palm trees. Then Tilghman turned left onto an unmarked sandy street.

I thought we were heading toward Bahía Choyo, but warehouses appeared, storage depots piled with pipes and iron. Yards full of heavy equipment idled under arc lights. The smell of fish ebbed and flowed according to the breeze, though after a few minutes, I ceased to notice it. Above and toward the sea, the orange water tower loomed in the lights around the harbor.

We came out at the end of the street at a rickety pier which spider-legged into the channel. Shrimp boats were tied up three abreast, their arms pulled upward and tight on cables. A single pole light at the end of the pier cast a semicircle of light over the planking and the boats and turned the water to sheet metal. The tide had gone out again, and in the light, the exposed mud flats were littered with oil drums, tires, the rusted shell of an old shrimp boat canted at an angle to the moon.

Tilghman pulled the Land Rover into a shadow behind a small concrete shed where a half-ton pickup was parked. He let the engine idle and got out. The pounding from the frozen-fish factory echoed across the water.

Tilghman gave Raul instructions, then nodded for me to get out. "We have to move," he said.

I stepped down. Raul had already got out Tilghman's side and was hurrying down the broken planks of the pier.

"Now what?"

"Now I need you," Tilghman said.

Tilghman had cleaned out the shovels and buckets back at Ellis's that afternoon, and now, when he flipped down the backseat, he had a good-sized cargo space. Then he motioned me over to the half-ton.

A canvas tarp was drawn over the bed, and we lifted it back, one of us on either side. "This should have been done already," Tilghman said. "But things don't always go right. We didn't know there would be this many."

He swung himself up onto the bed of the truck and found the wooden posts and crosspieces that fit into the notches on the sides. The crosspieces were about five feet long and were connected to one another with slats so the bed could carry more. Tilghman lifted these up, and I guided the bottoms of the posts into the notches. There was no piece for the tailgate, so we stretched the canvas over it and tied one corner down.

By this time Raul was bringing the men and women across the stern decks of the shrimp trawlers at the end of the pier. The people carried satchels, cloth bags, old suitcases. One woman had a child in her arms. Another dragged a little boy by the hand, dangling him in the air between steps as she hurried over the loose planks.

"Open up the back of the Rover," Tilghman said. "I need you to drive."

Tilghman threw back the tarp on the half-ton, so that as the people arrived, they could climb in. I opened the back of the Rover. Raul climbed up into the truck and helped people up.

The women and children got into the Rover. The woman

with the baby cradled it and stepped up in one movement, as if she was practiced at maneuvering into small spaces. She lay down on the floor, knowing she had to hide. The other woman with the little boy was short and squat. She struggled with a net bag in one hand and tried to lift the boy with the other. But the boy was scared, and I finally put my hands under his arms and lifted him in. That was my first criminal act.

Chapter six

We started out of Puerto Peñasco at two in the morning. There was only one road. The smell of fish gave way to the smell of unwashed bodies—offal, sweat, a dampness that lingered in clothes. After a while I got used to that smell, too, the way one gets used to dim light. I followed the taillights of the truck ahead, watched the corner of the canvas fly loose from its mooring and lash back and forth in the wind. Tilghman didn't stop to tie it down. Occasionally one of the men in the back of the truck would poke his head out and grab for the flailing rope, but then he would withdraw again. I tried to think of other things than the moment— of Harriet, for instance, the night she'd come so brazenly to my office, or of Francie that afternoon of the storm when we'd got drunk together. But always I came back to where I was, to the desert and the realization that Demer was behind this somehow.

Once I tried to speak to Raul, who rode with me. "Who are these people?" I asked. "Where do they come from?"

He shook his head.

"What's going to happen when we get to Sonoita?"

He smiled and nodded and stared out the windshield.

I already knew who the people were and where they'd come from. Demer had told me. They were like Ramon, and they were all riding in the Land Rover with Raul and me.

No other cars passed us heading to Sonoita. No one came against us, either. We drove past Ejido Cornelio, a shack surrounded by coarse brush and closed up for the night. A dog's eyes shone in the headlights. We drove across the barren salt flats. I thought every junked car at the periphery of the headlights was the police.

119

In the hills near Sonoita the truck lurched and slowed. Tilghman had to shift down. Somewhere along this stretch, we had seen the man rolling the tire in the center of the road, but he was not there now. We inched up the long grades at ten-to-fifteen miles an hour. The canvas over the back of the truck was slack.

Once the woman with the little boy lifted her head from behind the seat and asked something of me, but I couldn't understand her. Raul answered for me. I caught the word *frontera*, but that was all. The woman put her head back down.

In the middle of the night, Sonoita looked bombed out and deserted. I cast an eye out for the police, who must have been the only survivors in the rubble, but there weren't any. At first I thought we would deliver these people to someone in Sonoita who was more knowledgeable about the border, maybe to an official bribed and placed significantly in an office on the U.S. side at Lukeville. Then I thought perhaps we'd leave them off at the border to be met by someone on the other side. Gringo Pass, I knew, was closed at that hour.

But Tilghman took the back streets, weaving among the darkened shacks and cinder-block houses. We ended up on Highway 2, going west. I saw a sign for San Luis Rio Colorado.

Outside of town were more hills. Raul and I drove in slow pursuit, following the truck as it labored on the upslopes. To drive at night through territory I didn't know made me uncomfortable. Tilghman was right: when there wasn't anything else to do, I worried. That night not seeing was a blessing. Distance didn't exist. My panorama was red taillights, the spray of the Land Rover's headlights into the brush along the road. And there were stars. I picked out the Big Dipper from the vast circle of the speckled sky, then followed the two stars of the Dipper toward north. North was the one thing I knew for certain.

We reached the top of a ridge, and Tilghman let the truck coast down. We passed one lonely truck coming from the opposite direction, a beat-up pickup with four men in the cab and two in the bed. At the bottom of the hill, we crossed the outwash plain, rose again, passed on the left a silent house with a sign out front I couldn't read. A little farther on Tilghman pulled over to the shoulder.

I snapped off my headlights, but kept the motor running. Tilghman spoke to the people in the back of the truck, then came up to my window. The woman behind me sat up. "We're leaving the road," he said. "If I turn off my headlights, you do the same. Keep in my tracks."

"Where are we?"

"Just follow."

Not far ahead we made a right onto a hard-packed gravel turnout stained with oil and littered with oil drums and bottles and papers. We crossed this expanse and picked our way up an incline onto a rocky track through cactus and brush. The truck jumped and pitched, and the canvas flap jerked around. We traversed the ridge, then some looser talus. The truck yawed once, and I thought it might topple sideways into the gully, but Tilghman gunned the engine, and the tires peeled over the loose stones and the truck righted itself. I kept the Rover a little higher on the slope and maintained speed.

After a quarter mile, no more, we came up onto a plateau above the highway where the land flattened out. We didn't stop. We turned northward through a patch of grass and cactus—habitat for quail and lizards and snakes. The truck drew dust from the dry land, and I rolled up my window.

The grassland petered out into rocky scree. At six-tenths of a mile, Tilghman turned west again. We wound around more hills, and it occurred to me his intention was to leave no tracks. We bounced over holes and rocks until we came to the border, not all that far from the highway.

The border was a barbed-wire fence. Tilghman drove right through a spot which had been cut, and once both vehicles were on the other side, we stopped. Raul got out and went back to the fence with a flashlight and a pair of pliers.

Tilghman came back to me and leaned toward the window. "In another two-tenths, we hit the road to Quitobaquito. It parallels the border, and we'll head west to the spring. It's a little farther that way, but there's less chance of being spotted." He tilted his watch into the dashboard light. "We have two hours to daylight. We should be able to make it to the gas station."

"You need gas?"

"No. The old man, Lorry, knows we're coming. That's where we'll split up."

Chapter seven

We rested at the spring at Quitobaquito. The moon had veered past the zenith, and the pond was rich with moonlight. A single black cottonwood knelt in reflection in the calm line made by the moon. Except for those two shards of light, one in the sky and one on the water, the night closed around us.

But the cool air was alive with sounds: frogs calling for mates or luring other frogs as prey, the eerie squawk and splashing of a heron in the desert, and the insects. The insects sounded every-where: chirping, clicking, humming. Not far away, on a hogback ridge, a coyote bayed and yapped to its comrades.

We parked at the gravel turnout and doused the headlights. All of us got out except the mother and the sleeping baby. We stretched, walked around, nursed our wounds. One man had a saltwater burn on his leg that Tilghman washed with water from a canteen and rebandaged. The man had been lying in bilge water for two days on the trip from Costa Rica to a fishing village on the coast of Honduras. Another man had been cut with a machete and could not walk upright because of damage to the nerves in his legs. One of the women, whose children had been killed by death squads, could utter only incomprehensible words which, even to the others, were no more than the sounds of an animal.

Tilghman had brought a little food and drink in the truck—bread, dried fish, olives, cheese, Fanta orange, milk. The mother riding with me gave most of her portion to her little boy named Rodolfo.

I had begun to relax a little by then. We'd come all the way from the sea without encountering the police. We'd crossed the border easily. I could already see we would meet the old man at the Standard station, where, I gathered, he would take over. Of course there were still risks. The truck could break down. Or the Land Rover. A broken radiator hose or fan belt or a flat tire could leave us stranded. Or someone might be patrolling these back roads of the monument. But I had confidence we'd make it.

After a few minutes Tilghman called everyone together again. Most of the men gathered at the back of the truck and talked in low voices. A few people came over from the pond or from the Rover. They assembled slowly because everyone was tired. I was tired, too, but my fatigue wasn't the same—an instant's loss of sleep compared to their numbing exhaustion of years.

Then the woman screamed in the darkness. She yelled something in Spanish and screamed again from the swarthy tangle of saltbrush behind the Land Rover. Standing by the front fender, I was the closest one to her. I grabbed the flashlight from the seat and ran toward the sound of her struggling in the dark. She was moving, lashing out at something. In the light I saw Rodolfo. He was clinging to his mother, moaning, too, as if he was fending off her fury. He had his trousers down around his ankles. What had he done?

I aimed the light into the brush. Rodolfo was going to the bathroom. Then I saw the snake. It was half in the air, half caught on the thorns of a bush, twisting, skewered with its fangs in the woman's thigh. I ducked into the tangle, pulled Rodolfo away, and gave him over to Raul, who had come up behind me. I steadied the light. The woman stopped flailing, as if the light soothed her.

Tilghman got there. He pushed away the branches, held the woman's arm. The snake was a thick diamondback, five feet long. It's fangs had hooked into the woman's skin, and its jaws were open so wide it couldn't get its fangs free. I kept the light in the snake's eyes. Tilghman spoke to the woman and held her close.

I reached down and placed a finger on either side of the snake's head, and squeezed tightly, extricating one pair of fangs and then the other. I lifted the snake away. It spiraled in my hand, and I scraped back through the thorns to the edge of the gravel, where I heaved the snake as far as I could away from the road.

Tilghman helped the woman from the thicket. Someone had brought a blanket and spread it on the ground. Tilghman lay the woman down. Rodolfo cried.

"There's a clinic in Ajo," Tilghman said. "It's two hours from here if we're lucky and don't have trouble along the way. Or we could go back to Sonoita."

Already I had stripped a shoelace from my sneaker and tied it securely around the woman's leg above the fang marks. I took out my knife, opened the blade. "Does anyone have a match?" I asked.

"¿Fosforo?" Tilghman called. Raul struck a match and held it under the knife blade.

"Hold onto her," I said. I patted Rodolfo's arm while the knife blade was cooling in the air. Then I cut X's over each of the fang marks, pretty deeply into the skin. I wiped the blood away with the bottom part of my shirt, peeled back the skin, sopped more blood.

Tilghman was speaking to the woman the whole time.

I pressed my mouth to the incisions like a kiss and sucked warm blood.

"Silencio," Tilghman said softly. "Calmate."

I repeated the kiss and spat blood and venom onto the ground.

Tilghman had a first-aid kit with alcohol in it, and I daubed alcohol on with a piece of cotton and affixed a bandage lightly so the wounds could bleed. Then we carried the woman to the Land Rover.

"You go ahead," Tilghman said. "Don't wait for us. The truck's too slow. Lorry will know where the clinic is and the doctor. He knows the people up in Ajo."

I nodded and got into the driver's seat.

"I told Rodolfo you knew what you were doing," Tilghman said. "I said you were the doctor of birds at the university. I'd do this myself, Scott, if I didn't have the others."

"I understand."

"At the clinic . . ."

"I know."

"Say nothing," Tilghman said. "Now listen, when you go out this way, you'll pass through the monument rangers' housing compound. Go slowly. Turn off your headlights."

"All right."

"I'll meet you in Tucson later, or back at Ellis's."

The rangers' houses were dark, and we had no trouble getting past. The frontage road circled in front of the visitor center and back out to the highway.

At the Standard station, Lorry called the clinic and told the doctor I was coming. Lorry had to wait for Tilghman, so everyone else stayed at the station while I drove the woman and Rodolfo up to Ajo.

I told the doctor the woman had been bitten while we were camped out in the desert. I'd treated her as best I could. He said I'd made good incisions in the wounds. He gave her an antivenom shot and instructed the woman in Spanish what precautions to take. He didn't ask why she had been walking around in the desert at night, or why a woman and child who spoke no English were with a man who spoke no Spanish. I liked the doctor a great deal. He knew his work.

It was five in the morning when we headed south from Ajo to Why. Stars were still out, but pink light seeped up into the sky from behind the eastern hills. Rodolfo slept in back. The woman sat beside me in the shotgun seat, eyes open, but half asleep, too. I wanted to talk to her, to know where she was going next, what she expected, whether she had friends to help her, what she *knew*. Such things seemed to matter so early in the morning. But she couldn't answer questions I couldn't ask.

The Standard station was dark when we got there. I swung the headlights across the two trucks and the blue van, and the lights glanced from the office windows. I pulled up to the door and waited a minute before I let the engine die.

A woman came out from the trailer in back. She walked slowly, bent over from the waist.

"I have the woman and the boy," I said.

The old woman stopped as if to hear my voice more clearly. She looked past the Land Rover to the empty highway. "The others went on," she said. "Couldn't wait. They didn't know when you'd be back."

"So what do we do?"

"Tilghman said for you to drive to Casa Grande."

"Where is that?"

"Let me get a map," she said.

While we waited, Rodolfo's mother slept. I watched the land turn blue and the highway lengthen through the cactus and mesquite into the dawn.

We drove toward Casa Grande on back roads through the Tohono O'odham Reservation, through a country whose signs had no meaning at all to me: Ali Ak Chin, Anegam, Kohatk. The Land

Rover clanked and groaned, but I was inured then to worry, too tired to care. Rodolfo's mother slept, but Rodolfo woke and stared over my shoulder through the windshield. He talked to me. Maybe he talked of his father or his friends. Maybe he talked of the country we passed through—the eroded ravines and the government-issue houses and the saguaros and the pale desert grass. He could have been saying anything.

The address in Casa Grande was an unobtrusive square adobe with a new frame garage attached. A woman came out of the house as soon as I pulled into the drive. She was a slender Anglo woman about my age, with a slight limp to her walk and a toothy smile. With her hand she brushed her long, straight, black hair from her face. "We thank you," she said. Those were her first words. "We have already heard the story of what you did."

"I drove a few extra miles in a busted car," I said. "I think the woman's okay, but she needs rest."

"We'll take care of her," the woman said. "How do you feel?"

"I'm all right."

"You can sleep here," she said. "We always have an extra room."

I was tempted, but I shook my head. I felt then I'd earned my weariness, but at the same time, I was afraid to stay. I wanted to get away.

So I left Rodolfo and his mother with the woman. I turned the Land Rover around and got onto the interstate to Tucson. Sad: that's what I felt then. It hit me as I was driving. I don't know why I felt such sadness. It was the fatigue maybe. That was all. I had done something. I always cried when I was tired.

Chapter eight

At Tilghman's I slept. I went to bed at 7:30 that morning and woke up at 5:00 in the afternoon. A smooth, shadowy light spilled over into the backyard, and I sat outside and listened to the mockingbird whose territory was the resurrected yard. What had happened the previous night seemed already distant from me. I hadn't driven the Land Rover across the border or rescued a woman from a snake or delivered two people to Casa Grande. Yet the images were there, and I thought the dream of what had happened, with only a slight skew, could turn into a nightmare if I let it.

But the sadness I'd felt was gone. I felt as exhilarated as a man who'd escaped death. To celebrate, I walked down to Speedway and bought a bottle of Tanqueray and some tonic and a lime. For the next hour I sat in the yard. Gin worked wonders. It struck the right chords in my brain. The backyard, the wall rising before my eyes, the smooth air, the mockingbird's song all had a supernatural aura, as if imbued with a light of their own. Gin was magic.

I stayed outside until dusk. Then I went in and sat in the fluorescent light in the kitchen. That light wasn't the same. The gin chemistry was altered. I turned on the answering machine and listened to the messages—two in Spanish for Tilghman and a call about a delivery of topsoil. Then I was surprised to hear Jack Watkins's voice. A White-collared Swift had been reported from South Padre Island. Did I want to go for it? And someone had called in about a Green Violet-ear, a tropical hummingbird, that was frequenting a feeder near Wimberly. "I know you don't chase birds anymore," he said. "But I wanted you to know what you were missing." He didn't leave a number, but I knew where to call.

Harriet had called, too. She'd changed her mind at the last minute and had tried to catch us before we left. She said she was sorry she'd missed us. I thought Tilghman might have called, but he hadn't. I didn't return the calls. I played some solitaire.

At nine I turned on the radio for news. There was no report of illegal aliens caught on the Tohono O'odham Reservation or in Casa Grande, so I assumed Tilghman and Raul and the others had made it through. It was eerie listening for a friend's name on the news.

I drank more gin. I remembered the night Tilghman and I had drunk gin. It was our last spring in Cambridge, and his father had just driven from Minnesota to see him. We'd had our last dual meet with Yale, the track season was over, and graduation loomed, not to mention the future. Tilghman's father was waiting for us at the Charles Hotel, but Tilghman and I stayed at the bar drinking.

"If it were good news," Tilghman said, "he would have called me."

"Crap," I said. "Give him a chance to explain."

"It's what I told you before," Tilghman said. "Remember?"

"I remember, but you have no reason to think that."

"Drink," Tilghman said, "it's on me."

And it was bad news. It was what Tilghman had predicted the summer before: his father was leaving his mother.

I was pretty drunk when I called Jack Watkins about the White-collared Swift. Jack's wife Megan answered. "This is Scott," I said.

"Scott, you sound funny."

"I'm in Arizona."

"Jack went to South Padre Island, Scott. He thought you might call."

"I called."

"Is something wrong?"

"No, I just wanted to talk. How are you, Meg? How are the children?"

"Growing up. I have my greenhouse. You should see the tomatoes I got this year."

"It's April and you have tomatoes?"

"In the greenhouse. Are you drunk?"

"Gin," I said. "I'm having memories of people I once drank gin with. Do you remember Santa Margarita Ranch?"

"Of course I do. We were looking for the Hook-billed Kite."

We had been looking for the Hook-billed Kite on the back roads of a ranch on the Rio Grande River. We hadn't had any luck. The thickets and live oaks festooned with Spanish moss had given us only the common birds—sparrows, Green Jays, cardinals. Demer had been along, too, and there was that tension I often felt with her: we weren't doing anything productive. For a while we sat by the river and watched a Green Kingfisher and some kiskadees work the shallows. Jack had brought along gin in the cooler.

By the time the sun fell into the web of trees, we were all pretty happy. I was happiest. We went to look for the kite again, and I stood in the back of Jack's truck to get a better view of the canopy and the sky where the kite was most likely to show itself. The road we were on was just a track through the undergrowth.

We scraped along at ten miles an hour, not seeing much of anything. For some reason—motivation at such moments is sketchy—I got it into my head to play a trick on the ones riding in the cab. I was going to jump out of the bed of the truck like Tarzan onto a low, overhanging limb. The truck would of course continue onward, and somewhere ahead they'd discover I was missing.

We approached a likely looking branch, and I jumped deftly from the truck. "Deftly" is my memory. I got hold of the branch all right, and pulled myself up. But what I hadn't thought of was that the limb might give. With my weight on it, the limb sagged, and I landed back in the bed of the truck. The truck, as predicted, kept on moving. I smacked into the tailgate so hard it sounded as if we'd run over a land mine. I flipped over the tailgate and landed on my feet in the middle of the road, still holding onto the branch. I smiled and tried not to cry. I was black and blue from shoulder to butt for two months. Except for the gin I might have been killed.

"Do you remember how furious Demer was?" I asked Megan.

"She wasn't happy," Megan said, "but it was a pretty stupid thing to do."

"So Jack's got hold of a White-collared Swift?"

"I don't know that he's got hold of it. He's gone down on a stakeout."

Megan and I talked a little while longer about vegetables and children and Demer. She said she hoped I was all right.

"Shit," I said, "I have a *job*."

"Jack didn't want to fire you, Scott. It was business, not friendship."

"I know."

"I won't tell him you were drinking tonight."

"Thanks," I said. "I may be calling him for a job again someday."

"I know he'd like you back. Good-bye, Scott."

When I hung up, I called my uncle. He was watching the videotape he'd made of a Celtics game earlier in the evening. "I had a meeting," he said, "and couldn't watch it live."

"Who's winning?"

"Bird has nineteen, and eight assists. The Pistons are up by three."

"Do you want me to tell you who won? I heard the news."

"Don't dare."

"How are they in the standings?"

"They're in second," my uncle said. "K.C. is a good coach."

"Did you get the money I sent?"

"I did. Thank you. I was surprised." My uncle paused, probably to watch a big play on the TV. "Are you behaving yourself?" he asked.

"Trying."

"You got a letter from Demer," he said. "You want me to send it?"

"Of course you should send it. When did it come?"

"A couple of days ago."

"Read it to me."

"You want me to read it to you?"

"Is there an echo?" I asked. "Are you that busy?"

He left the telephone for a minute. I could hear the Celtics game in the background. I poured more gin into my glass.

"Okay," he said. "You're sure? It's from somewhere called Cayo District, Belize. You know where that is?"

"Just read it."

He tore open the envelope. "It's not very long," he said. He paused.

Dear Scott,

I've moved to Belize. We stopped in Guatemala City for a month, which was how long our visas lasted. Then we flew here. We had a night flight over the Pacaya volcano. That's where the Guatemalan government has dumped many of the disappeared. It was frightening to see the lava twisting down from the crater, fading out at the bottom into the darkness. My friend Inez may be in the ashes. She was kidnapped several

weeks ago. I hope her soul haunts those who are responsible.
My uncle stopped. "Who's Inez?"
"Inez was a friend of Demer's."
"You want me to read the rest of it?"
"Go ahead."

I'm with a man named Will Terborg. He's from Tennessee, studying for the ministry, twenty-three years old. He came down as part of a two-week church mission and has been here six months. He's quiet, what I would call devout. I know he's put off by my irreverence. (The Catholic church is part of the problem here—that whole turn-the-other-cheek mentality.) I tell Will he's full of shit three or four times a day, but we work together well as a team. He's tall, maybe six-three, and thin as a stick, with glasses. He has a fiancée in Chattanooga who doesn't understand what he's doing in a place she can't find on a map.

My uncle stopped again. "What is she doing down there?"
"Read," I said.

The countryside here is a patchwork of small farms cut from the jungle. We're not far from the ruins at Tikal—two-and-a-half hours by truck. We've been there once and another time to Yaxja off the Flores road. Mostly, though, we're waiting. It's very hot. And it rains. When it rains, it can be demoralizing. We're cooped up in the pension, and the rain hisses on the banana leaves and roars on the tin roof. Nothing is simple here, and yet everything is simple. You have to wait for things to happen. We want to meet the nuns at the Mission San Xavier. They're helping some friends of ours. We think it will work out. I'll let you know. You can write me at San Ignacio. Everyone knows me here.

Demer.

"That's it?"
"That's all."
"No love?"
"So you want me to send it to you? I can put it in the mail at work."
"Yes." I was thinking of all the letter didn't say.
"When are you coming back?" my uncle asked. "Isn't the term about over?"
"May," I said. "I'm thinking of staying for the summer."

"In the desert?"

"I'll wait and see. What's the Celtics' score? Do you think they can go all the way this year?"

"They're up by one. Start of the fourth quarter." My uncle went on about Bird and Parish, and McHale's not trying hard enough. He thought they could make a run at the Lakers in the finals. I drank my gin to the bottom of the glass.

When I hung up, I was dazed. I tried to picture Central America, where the countries were. Panama, Nicaragua, Guatemala: I knew where they were. I couldn't place Belize.

Then I dialed Ellis's number in Mexico, which Tilghman had left by the phone. Francie answered in static.

"Is Tilghman there?"

"I can't hear you. Is this Scott?"

"Tilghman. Yes, it's me."

"You don't have to yell. Tilghman's asleep, Scott."

The line smoothed out. "I wanted to find out what happened," I said.

"He got back around noon. He's been asleep since then."

"Don't wake him," I said.

"Are you drinking?"

"I'm with Madame Tanqueray."

"Tilghman told us about the woman. Did she make it all right?"

"She's all right."

Static zoomed in and out and then quieted again. "You could have taken me along," Francie said. "Instead of leaving me."

"Next time you go, and I'll stay home."

"Are you bringing the Land Rover back?"

"Tomorrow," I said. "Harriet wants to come."

"I'll bet she does," Francie said.

"It's not like that." I paused and thought about telling her about Demer's letter, but then, thinking of Harriet again, I forgot. "I'll see you tomorrow."

"Drive carefully," Francie said through more static. Then she hung up, and the line was quiet.

Chapter nine

It's hard to tell why, after that telephone call to Francie, I went out and got into the Land Rover. Maybe Tilghman's recklessness was infectious. Or the gin let me loose. I knew where I was going, of course, but the decision wasn't wrought of due deliberation. It was fueled by some upheaval in my interior landscape, a tremor which rolled rocks. If I was going to get past Demer and Tilghman, I owed allegiance to impulse.

I headed north on the interstate. I imagined the Land Rover was a speedy tank. I could plow over anything and everybody. I was in a Supermobile, a car of steel. I yelled out the open window. The roar and clank of the engine only encouraged me to drive faster, weaving across the lanes.

"What do men want?" Demer had asked me once. This was after her fling with Rafael, when I had had to accept the unacceptable. "What are men like?"

"What are women like?" I had asked back.

Men wanted sex, women wanted love: that was how it was usually phrased. The sentence was old as history. Priests and politicians had been trying to legislate against the idea for centuries: Thou shalt not covet thy neighbor's wife. Thou shalt not commit adultery. Pay up for the children. It was always the men who did in the women. I didn't know what men wanted. I didn't know what I wanted. Sex without love: that was what Demer wanted.

"Sex without love," I shouted out the window of the Rover. "Sex without love."

Harriet liked to pass herself off as the pristine biology

133

teacher, caring only about whales. Bullshit. She'd come to me in my office, of all places, had knelt down and untied my shoes, slid down the canvas pants I'd had on, unbuttoned my shirt. But she wouldn't undress herself. She had stood in the center of the room with her clothes on, expecting me to undress her. "Undress me, Scott." That's what she hadn't said. I said the words aloud, driving seventy-five down the interstate.

I exited at Orange Grove Road, made a running stop at the end of the ramp, and wended my way through neon for the next couple of blocks looking for El Camino. Somehow I missed the turn and had to backtrack. I made a U-turn at the green arrow, right in front of an invisible police cruiser sitting next to a Dr. Photo in the nearby mall.

That was the error, the least of many, but the most noticeable. The flashing blue light dipped behind me out of the mall parking lot into the street. I pulled over, tried to think sobering thoughts. *Jail* occurred to me. *Chains.* Tilghman. Rodolfo.

The policewoman got out and took down the license number, then came around to my window. I stared straight ahead so she wouldn't see my eyes.

"'Chew more Skoal and fuck goats,'" she said. "Is that a message for humanity?"

"No, sir," I said. "It's not my car."

"Driver's license and registration."

I fumbled through the glove compartment, hoping Tilghman had put the registration back after we'd crossed the border into Mexico. He had, and there was no pistol, either. I extracted my license from among the leftover Mexican bills in my wallet.

"Massachusetts," the police officer said. "Are you Talmadge?"

"Yes, sir. Yes, ma'am."

"Not your car though." She compared the names on the registration and the license. "Employed out here, Mr. Talmadge?"

"I'm a visiting professor."

"You been drinking, professor?"

"No, ma'am. Well, a little bit."

"How little?"

"I'm on my way to meet a friend. I missed the turn. She doesn't live far from here."

The woman wrote on her pad, copying numbers. She tore off the stub and handed the ticket through the window. "If I were you,

Mr. Talmadge, I'd leave my vehicle here and call my friend."

"Yes, ma'am. Thank you."

"I'll wait."

I got out on the shotgun side. There was a phone booth at the Exxon station. The blue flashing light made me dizzy as I walked, made the pavement under my feet rise and fall like surf. I tried to negotiate a straight line, but there wasn't one in me. I aimed for the phone booth without looking down.

I called Harriet collect. I let the phone ring a dozen times while I stared at the police cruiser. The officer at least had turned off her blue light. Finally Harriet answered.

"Thank God," I said.

"I was asleep," Harriet said. "Scott?"

"Let's go to Mexico," I said.

Harriet picked me up in fifteen minutes. The policewoman had gone. I considered driving the Land Rover to Harriet's or back to Tilghman's, but Harriet instructed me on the faulty thought. "You're a fool,"she said.

I was in time-release drunkenness, more wasted now than ever. All the gin had hit the fan. I stared at the wild array of lights which blitzed past as Harriet drove the freeway. Her car was a silver Buick, a midsize, equipped with a special seat so her mother could swing in and out in her wheelchair. Compared to the Land Rover, it was like riding in a vacuum tube.

"What were you doing at the corner of Orange Grove and El Camino?"

"Making an illegal U-turn."

"At midnight?"

"I didn't know it was midnight. I was coming to see you."

"It's hardly the hour for a social call."

"There are only so many chances we have," I said. "How could I know there'd be a policewoman there?"

Harriet looked at me. I looked away. "You'll have to tell me where you live," Harriet said.

Zapata barked in the house when we drove up. For a minute Harriet and I sat at the curb. The air smelled of oleander and burnt fuel. In the distance on the bank building downtown, time and temperature were blurry numbers.

"Thank you," I said finally. I opened the door. "There's a

Green Violet-ear in Texas." That was the stupidest thing I could think of to say.

"I thought we were going to Mexico."

"Mexico, yes." I got out and leaned against the open door, held onto the side mirror. I felt myself sliding.

Harriet had to help me. She pulled me up, looped her arm around my waist. I was nearly a foot taller, but she was stronger. We steered through the gate, weaved through the obstacle course of tools and bricks and concrete, and climbed the porch steps. I fished for the key.

"It's not locked," Harriet said. She opened the door and pushed it gently.

Zapata nuzzled us. I went for the gin bottle, but Harriet maneuvered me past it into the living room. Then we were in my bedroom. She unbuttoned my shirt and pulled it over my head. I unbuckled my own belt and flopped onto the bed so Harriet could pull off my jeans. The worst thing is the swirls, when the room spins like a dryer cycle, but fortunately that didn't happen. There was just darkness, darkness and cool air from the window.

I remember the bed moved once. The mattress depressed at the edge and, though I couldn't move, I felt my body lean toward the weight. I couldn't open my eyes. I felt Harriet touch my face, my forehead, trace a line down my cheek. Then she lay down beside me. She settled her head on my bare shoulder and put her arm across my chest. I drifted in sleep toward the White-collared Swift and the Green Violet-ear.

Chapter ten

Harriet figured we'd take the Land Rover to Mexico, so when she left Tilghman's in the middle of the night, she'd taken my car keys. "You were comatose," she said. "I didn't think you'd mind."

"You could have stayed."

"What would my mother think?" she asked.

"What's your mother going to think now?" We were driving the Ajo road toward Why, passing the Kitt Peak Observatory. It was a clear day and sweet.

"We'll have separate bedrooms," Harriet said. "That's what she'll think."

We rode through the midmorning heat. The deterrent to most people's drinking is the hangover the next morning, but I have the curse of not getting one. My worst consequence was my telephone bill. When I drank, I paid for it through AT&T.

It was easy traveling with Harriet. We shared the joys of exotic places, and I liked listening to her stories about whales. She told me about the time she'd been kayaking in Prince William Sound, before Exxon had fouled it, and had had a humpback surface so gently beside her there was barely a ripple in the water. "It was as if the whale knew how fragile my boat was," she said. "The whale's tail was longer than three kayaks end to end, and I swear to this day that he sang to me."

I counted as we passed the crosses at the side of the road. There were more than I remembered. I slowed at the one we'd stopped at before to see whether the candle was still burning. It was, and someone had put back the Budweiser bottle, too.

"Someone you know?" Harriet asked.

"No one specific."

"Why did you come back from Mexico?" Harriet asked. "It wasn't to get me."

"Tilghman wanted me to."

"That's not much of a reason."

I shrugged and changed the subject. There was a Phainopepla perched in the chaparral. "Red eye," I said. "White wing linings. It's a silky flycatcher called Phainopepla. In late spring they raise a second brood in wetter habitat."

We drove for an hour into the heat. Harriet dozed for a while. I studied her full lower lip, the bowed upper one, the long eyelashes. She wore a T-shirt that said SAVE THE WHALES.

I wondered whether I could love her, whether she could love me, what the effect would be of our first lesson of "learning." What had she meant by lying down next to me when I was passed out? What did that paragraph signify to the story?

We stopped for gas at Why. Lorry came out of the office, pulled his cowboy hat low against the sun. He went to the rear of the Land Rover and took off the gas cap. "Going to Mexico?" he asked me.

"Right," I said.

He fit the hose nozzle into the tank and gazed out at the highway. "American gas," he said. "They all fill up here."

I nodded. "Any new horror stories from Rocky Point?"

"No, just the usual ones."

I paid for the gas with cash.

PART THREE

Chapter one

A frigatebird swooped down on black wings toward the water, rose again, and sailed on the warm southerly wind. It crossed from blue to streaming white clouds and back again to blue. I handed the binoculars to Harriet, standing beside me at the rail. For a moment the bird held itself nearly motionless in the air, its forked tail weaving the wind. Then it broke its still flight and peeled away toward the headland. The boat drove onward.

Tilghman had been quiet all that morning. He'd barely spoken to Ellis or to Ellis's friend Leonidas, who'd gone forward to the bow where Tilghman was. Normally Tilghman would have helped coil the lines, but a greeting from Leonidas drew only a stare.

The boat rolled in the shallow chop of the channel. Out past the breakwater, whitecaps tossed beneath a line of low clouds, which I thought might bring rain. The boat was called the *Estrella de Belen*. It was a faded blue shrimp trawler, forty feet, with doors and nets slung on winches out over the wide afterdeck. Ellis had commandeered it for us with what he said was minor cash and a bottle of mescal. The engine vibrated the rail I clung to. Ellis, hung over, lay wrapped in an army jacket in the windless lee of the cabin, his eyes closed to the sun. I watched the stream of gulls above the churning wake.

Francie veered across the afterdeck toward us and caught the rail. "The town's not so pretty, is it?" she said. "This is one of those places you win in a sweepstakes. You get a fifty-foot lot and pay a yearly management fee. They claim you own oceanfront property."

She was right; it wasn't pretty. Along the harbor the silver oil tanks and the single orange water tank gleamed in the sun. Cranes angled crazily along the skyline of the harbor. The town, with all its square cinder-block buildings, including the Miramar, made the rocky hill look heavy.

"Look the other way," I said.

Harriet hadn't turned from the sea. We got past the breakwater, and the blue and gray opened outward, bounded by some shore we couldn't see. The surface took on the shades of the sky or the character of the bottom—blue, gray, turquoise. The Gulf hid its creatures in deep water.

Las Cabras lay off to starboard through the bright haze.

The previous night hadn't turned out as I'd expected. I'd wanted a quiet evening with Harriet, perhaps some wine, scallops, an early night in bed for recovery. But Tilghman thought we should take Harriet out on the town and treat Ellis to a good time. We were guests who owed the host. Francie was for it.

We went to a cantina not far from the Hotel Miramar, a divy place with a jukebox and a linoleum-topped bar. Francie and I drank Coronas, though I was determined not to drink too much. Harriet and Ellis had wine; Tilghman had a Fanta. There was dancing. Tilghman got Harriet to dance once, and Francie coerced Ellis. I watched and listened to the music. I had had no idea Harriet was so graceful or so good a dancer.

We ate fish paella, tamales, beef burritos, enchiladas. It was a festive meal, full of goodwill. Tilghman was charming. He joked, sang with the music, talked about Americans living in Mexico.

Then Ellis started drinking mescal. That was when the trouble started. Tilghman had been talking to Harriet about her work, and Harriet, as usual, was expounding about whales—the footprints they left on the sea when they sounded, how their families were organized, their songs. I'd been watching the TV above the bar. The news was on, but I couldn't tell from the film clips whether something had happened or was about to happen. Harriet went on about the Russians and the Japanese hunting whales to extinction. The right whale had been so named because it was the right whale to kill. There were only a couple hundred left, I heard her say, and the gene pool was probably too small to ensure their survival.

"But don't you think," Ellis said, holding his glass of mescal in the air, "that what you're saying is a bunch of crap?"

Harriet fixed Ellis with a sudden stare. "I happen not to."

"Money is what matters, *honey*," Ellis said. "Not whales. Not fucking rain forests or rhinoceroses or goddamn birds."

"Money is the cause of the world's decline," Harriet said. "To that extent I'd agree with you. Money makes men hunt whales."

"And women don't hunt whales?" Ellis asked, leering. "Who wears the perfume? Come on, lady, give me a break. What is more important, animals or people?"

"Animals are more important than people like you." Harriet stood up, and I thought she was going to let Ellis have a fist in the mouth.

Francie got up, too. "He's drunk," she said. "Let's go home."

That had been the end of the evening. We paid and got into the Land Rover and had a cold ride home with everyone staring out a different window.

Tilghman made a beeline across the stern deck unzipping his fly. "Call of the wild," he said. "Gangway."

"What is it?" Francie asked.

"You'd hardly know," Tilghman said.

"*Hardly*, that's good," Francie said. "It looks like a penis, only smaller."

"Envy," Tilghman said, "is a dead end." He leaned off the stern, holding a cable.

When the boat hit the deeper swells beyond the jetty, Leonidas came aft, too. He wore loose beige trousers, a white T-shirt, and slip-on sneakers. He balanced himself by the cabin and rolled a cigarette with frail fingers. Ellis had told us Leonidas had worked on the highway after the war and had learned English from the engineers. He finished making the cigarette and shielded a match behind his bony shoulders. A plume of smoke curled around his white head and was swept away in the wind.

"Are there any goats?" I asked him.

"Oh yes, there are goats."

"On the islands? You've seen them?"

"No, I have not seen them."

"You've been to the islands?"

"Never." He shook his head. We jerked into a trough and the drone of the diesel deepened against the swells.

"What about the States?" Francie asked. "Have you ever been to Phoenix?"

Leonidas widened his stance on the deck, but he didn't hold the rail. He pulled on his cigarette. "What is Phoenix?"

"A city north of Tucson."

"I have been to Sonoita," Leonidas said.

The boat dived into another trough, and spray billowed over the bow and across the rail where we stood. Ellis stirred from his protected spot behind the cabin, sat up, squinted. "Keep the boat straight," he said.

"That's what you get for drinking mescal," Francie said.

"Never again," Ellis said. "I promised Harriet, and I mean it. This is penance."

The *Estrella* curved around the headland where the white houses at Las Conchas shone alabaster against the brown bluff. We diverged from the coastline, though, and made for the islands—bare rocks with the white specks of gulls and terns hovering above them. They now presented a different face from the one we'd seen from Ellis's house. They looked like prehistoric creatures rising from a slab of gray. Farther on, the perspective changed again. Distance opened between them, a sea channel cutting between two high cliffs. I took the glasses back from Harriet and scanned the birds' nests on the sheer walls—gulls, terns, cormorants, a few alcid burrows. The islands were steeper than I'd thought. The cliffs were a hundred feet high.

The larger island, where we were headed, had a collar of white sand at the base of an arroyo where trees grew. A saddle joined two humps at the top, and the island tapered down toward the strait.

It began to rain. The rain seemed to come from nowhere, singing on the surface of the sea. Warm. There was no reason to seek shelter from it. And it couldn't last. Out behind the gray clouds was more blue sky.

When we neared the larger island, Leonidas went to the bow again to guide us in closer. The water was different colors according to the way the bottom changed. Where there was sand, it was bluish white to turquoise, and over rocks it was a darker green. Leonidas motioned with one arm, then the other, when he saw submerged rocks.

"Okay, chief," he called. "¡Basta!" The captain slipped the engine into neutral. We coasted. Then Ellis let the anchor out on a winch.

"Now what do we do?" Harriet asked.

"Now we swim," Tilghman said.

Ellis was the first one in. He took off his shirt and dived from the railing in his shorts and tennis shoes. He looked like a puffin in awkward flight. His bald head came up in a circle of bubbles. "Water's fine," he called.

Harriet hadn't brought a bathing suit, but her clothes were wet from the rain. "What's to wait for?" she asked. She jumped overboard without even emptying her pockets.

Francie had worn a sweatshirt over her suit, but she had on sandals instead of tennis shoes. She took them off and buckled them together. Then she climbed onto the rail and dived. Despite the sandals she barely made a splash.

Tilghman and I lowered the cooler to Ellis alongside in the water. We'd brought beer, soft drinks, sandwiches. I thought we were going to wade the cooler ashore, but instead Ellis floated it in front of him and pushed it as he swam in.

Then Tilghman went. He ran across the afterdeck and dived straight out, smacking the water fully extended. He came up swimming and laughing, then rolled onto his back and watched me. "Come on, Scott. I want to see this."

My idea had been to step off on the rocks at the edge of the island, but that's the way my ideas often turned out: wrong. Harriet and Francie had already reached shallow water and were watching me. I peeled off my pants. Harriet waved to me.

"Come on, Scott," Francie called. "Don't be a dink."

I climbed over the railing and held on for a minute. At such moments your life is supposed to flash before you in rapid sequence. But I saw nothing. I jumped.

Chapter two

The island was rocky, hot. The rain had moved off. Ellis, still hurting, slept in the shade at the crown of the beach, while Tilghman and Francie climbed the arroyo to look for goats higher up. I lay in the sun on a boulder at the edge of the water where Harriet was snorkeling, exploring the sealife. Even in the heat I felt an odd tension, as if something from the night before was left over. Harriet had forgiven Ellis his slander, but there was some lingering emotion, ill-defined, but palpable, which I would only grasp later, when events had played themselves out.

Across the water Puerto Peñasco melted into the hillside, though I could still make out through the haze the white houses on the bluff. The *Estrella* rolled in the sea halfway between us and the mainland, its arms spread now with the nets out. An easy breeze from the sea cooled me.

Harriet dived, disappeared, came up again in a new place among the rocks. Her long hair swept back and forth with the sea tide. I turned my head, closed my eyes to the orange darkness. I dozed and dreamed of fish—yellow fish, bass, sea trout, schools of silver minnows flashing in filtered light. Bluefish, sharks whose unerring easy glide meant they were moving oxygen through their gills, tarpon, amberjack, marlin. I dreamed of myself underwater, having to breathe from the warm currents.

I woke to Harriet's cool hand on my back, to her soft voice, to drops of water falling from her hair. "You're getting burned," she said.

I opened my eyes. Her face was shaded, but a rim of silver outlined her smooth head and her wet hair, which was draped around her neck. Her shirt clung to her shoulders and breasts. I took hold of her hair without thinking and pulled her head down gently and kissed her. She slid close in beside me on the stone.

For a few minutes we lay together in silence. Where was Ellis? Where were Francie and Tilghman? I edged my hand under Harriet's shirt and across her back. I felt beneath her the hot stone, heard gulls cry above us in the air. There ought to be many words for 'love', I thought. The Inuits of Alaska had nine words for 'snow'. We had several for 'lie'. We named the species of birds according to the way they appeared to the eye, and if they looked nearly the same, as do Alder and Willow flycatchers, then we distinguished them by song and gave them different names. Why were there no other words for the vagaries of emotion? All our disparate feelings were coalesced into that one word: 'love'.

And what was love? Love for our brothers? Love for whales? Love for a man or a woman? Love for pleasure, love for money, love for air? If there were more words, I would have been able to speak to Harriet, to make sense of the shortcomings I felt, to be honest with her. But failing such words, what could I say? I kissed her again without saying anything.

Then a voice saved me. It wasn't Harriet's, but one more distant. Harriet rolled away from me, and I sat up and saw Francie above us on a crag, waving her shirt in her hand.

"What's she saying?" Harriet asked. "Did they find the goats?"

Ellis called over. "Something about Tilghman," he said. "She wants help."

I pulled on my sneakers and got up. Ellis started up the loose stones at the bottom of the arroyo. But I was quicker. I climbed past him in no time. I held scruffy trees, scrabbled over gravel and stones. Ellis turned back. In minutes I was high above the wreath of sand.

The scree toward the top was more treacherous, like climbing on ball bearings. I fell back sometimes farther than I moved forward. My breath came in gulps. My legs wearied. But I didn't stop until I came out onto a ragged grassy slope that canted upward.

There I caught my breath. Harriet and Ellis were far below, watching me. Viewed from so high up, the sea lost its glitter. The *Estrella* toiled across it, barely moving.

The grassy slope was steep, but at least the footing was solid. I ran again, jumped from tuft to tuft to hard ground, climbed toward the crest. But the crest was only a false summit. The island was higher and deeper seaward than it had appeared, extending into another basin and to a farther rocky headland. I skirted the basin in the direction where Francie had been. The grass, ungrazed, rippled in the gusts of wind that swept up the cliff from the sea.

Francie had to be lower down than I was, and along the cliff edge. I made my way around that way. Finally she called to me from the rocks not far ahead.

"Tilghman," I said. "Where is he?"

"Over there." She pointed toward the far end of the island.

"Is he hurt?"

"He says he's going to swim to the next island to look for the goats."

"There aren't any goats," I said. "It's a myth."

"Tell that to Tilghman."

I didn't see Tilghman. From where we were, there was only sky, a thin whitish blue punctuated by gulls and graceful terns which lifted from the headland. "Where is he now?"

"I couldn't keep up with him with sandals on."

The next island was a good half mile beyond the headland. It was rockier than the one we were on, not so green. I knew it was a trick Tilghman was pulling. A bluff. Maybe a myth like the goats on the island. It was the kind of thing Tilghman used to do to unsettle me. But I'd been with him often enough when he wasn't bluffing.

"I'll talk to him," I said. "See if you can signal the boat."

I took off running. It was easier going down into the swale. I skipped over hummocks of grass, put no weight in my step. My knees absorbed the jumps. For the first few hundred yards, I followed Tilghman's tracks—a stone overturned, a slash in the gravel, an indentation where grass had been stepped on. From the distance between his steps, it appeared he wasn't running.

Finally, from a high point on the headland, I spotted him. He was below me, climbing down toward the water. The slope there was not so steep as the arroyo, but it was strewn with boulders washed out and rolled from above. Tilghman was edging down a big boulder, one hand giving balance.

"Wait up, Tilghman."

Tilghman fled. He scrambled down the rock and behind another boulder, where I couldn't see him. The only thing for me to do was follow.

That was how it went—Tilghman leading, appearing once in a while lower down, then hiding again, while I aimed for where he'd been. The footing made the going slow. I didn't know where he was headed except down.

He got to the water first. When I came out from behind the last few boulders, he was already twenty yards out on a rocky shoal. We stared at each other across the water.

"What are you trying to prove?" I asked.

"I can't prove anything," Tilghman said. "I don't try."

"What do you want then?"

"I want you to swim across with me."

I smiled and looked across the blue channel between the islands. I imagined the currents and the sharks and the deep water.

"I'll be right beside you," Tilghman said. "Don't you trust me?"

"No."

"Will you go if I tell you about Demer?"

"I know about Demer."

"You think you know." He motioned for me to come out to the shoal. I shook my head.

"You trusted me the other night," he said. "You did something you didn't think you could do."

"That was once."

"You have to practice, Scott. If you practice, you get accustomed to it. You can't do things just once."

He took a few steps backward to the far side of the shoal.

"What about Demer?" I asked.

Tilghman's eyes held mine across the air. I didn't understand his confidence, his arrogance, whichever it was. And I felt sorry for him. He was lonely. He stood on that rock with the tide surging around him as if he were a heroic figure, but he was alone. He didn't say anything more. He stepped off the rock and waded out and started swimming away from me. I called to him, but he didn't stop, and in a few minutes he was in the rough water where the tide was strong through the strait.

Chapter three

The boat had to pass me on the way to Tilghman, and once it had picked me up—I had to swim out to it—Tilghman was already far out in the channel. The dark cliff of the other island was a shadowy veil beyond him. I stood shivering in the bow and tried to measure how the current ran by picking out a gull and following its progress against the sea. But the bird floated and dipped and swerved, and its whereabouts told me nothing about the water.

Leonidas was cleaning the stern deck, pushing the trash fish and debris of shells and sea plants back into the water. Some of the fish were dead, but some still flapped and sprawled across the wood. Blue crabs crawled into the corners of the stern, where Leonidas rousted them out with his rake. He picked up the big horseshoe crabs by their tails and heaved them overboard. The blues he trapped and saved in a plastic cooler. The rest—seaweed, dead fish, a few stones—he jammed through the openings at deck level. Each time he did this, the gulls above the wake screeched and dived to the water.

Once, as I was watching Tilghman, he went under. All I saw were waves. Cormorants whirred across the water where he'd been. Gulls strove toward us, hearing the cries of other gulls feeding behind the boat. My eyes tested the glare. I tried to remember where I'd last seen Tilghman, where against the cliff he'd been swimming, but it was as though he'd never been there at all. How could he vanish into the sea?

My heart whispered "no." He had taken this risk for no reason, at the expense of the rest of us. We counted on him, I thought, for something we could not even know about, something as fragile as light on water and just as easily lost. But then he appeared again, as I knew he would, in the shadow the island cliff made on the water.

By the time the boat got close, Tilghman had reached the rocks at the base of the cliff. He climbed from the water and began to pick his way upward, not waiting for us. He sorted through the boulders and sea stacks, progressing to the lower cliff. He inched his way up.

There was nothing we could do but watch. The captain spoke to Ellis, and Ellis consulted the rest of us. "He wants to know whether we should pull in or give him room."

"What do we gain by going closer?" I asked.

"We could talk to him."

I shook my head. "Give him room."

We watched Tilghman climb. Birds whirled around him. Higher up, he reached the birds' nests, and they took wing, crossing and recrossing the air so the cliff looked besieged by gulls and terns moving in and out of the shadow. The boat idled in the choppy water in the lee of the cliff.

The last few yards to the top, where wind and rain had eroded the ridge, were not so steep. Tilghman pulled himself up and over the sparse grass, then ran a few paces to the crest. He turned a circle under the sky.

I had him in the binoculars. His skin was wet, and on his face was a look of stunned joy. He ran in place for a few seconds, then stopped. There was nowhere to go. He edged down again over the hummocks of grass and rocks to the rim of the cliff. He stood there only a moment, as if he already knew what to do, and with all the seabirds circling beneath and around him, he dived.

Chapter four

That evening we were all back at Ellis's. Francie's face was swollen with sunburn. Squinting had drawn tiny white lines which extended out from the corners of her eyes. Her face was puffed like a grape. She was lying face down on the sofa while Tilghman bathed her with Solarcaine. He was waiting for his friend to come and look at the Land Rover.

"How does that feel?" he asked.

"Ouch."

"Turn over."

Francie rolled over, braced herself with one hand on the floor. "What a shitty way to spend your honeymoon."

"DuPlooy will be angry," Tilghman said.

"I don't care about DuPlooy. I care about skin cancer."

The room settled. A wren sang from the bougainvillea next to the door to the terrace, its lilting song filling the room.

"Ouch," Francie said. "Where is justice? This bastard swims a shark-infested strait, then dives from a cliff, and doesn't get a scratch. I loll on a boat and do nothing and suffer first-degree burns."

"The life of action," Tilghman said, "versus the life of art."

"Fuck you," Francie said.

"Promise?"

The wren flew from the bougainvillea to the wall of the terrace and sang again. "I haven't heard a wren for months," Ellis said. "I thought the cats had got them all."

I looked out. A hazy twilight fell over the sea. The islands were distant, hovering in mist. The wren flew back to the bougainvillea.

Harriet had taken *Carte Blanche* from the bookshelf—Ellis had a dozen copies—and was reading outside on the terrace. Now and then she looked in through the open door, and when Ellis came to watch the wren, she asked, "Did you know these people?"

"Oh yes, I was there. Down and dirty in San Francisco. I was in Chicago, too, during the riots. I had a friend, a photographer for the *Tribune* . . ."

"Ellis knew everyone," Tilghman said. "And then, after the book, for a while everyone knew him. I keep telling Francie that fame won't make her feel better."

"Who wants fame?" Francie asked. "I want to dance."

"You want fame."

I liked thinking of Ellis in Chicago. That history fleshed him out, balanced, somehow, the life he led now in this house with the chandelier and the windows looking out to sea. I'd read most of his book back at Tilghman's, and I marveled at the optimism Ellis had had in those days. Where had it gone?

We drifted from beer to beer—Bohemia, we were drinking, except for Tilghman. Harriet didn't care so much for beer so I had finished hers, and Ellis had made her a tequila sunrise. Francie, after a while, drank them, too. "Tequila's better for sunburn," Francie said.

"Tequila mockingbird," Ellis said. "Do you see? By Harper Lee. She wrote that one book."

No one said anything.

Tilghman's friend Jésus arrived, a tiny man in oil-soaked slacks. He took a Bohemia from the cooler and opened it with his teeth.

"Have a beer," Ellis said.

The wren sang its wild, slurry song which echoed and re-echoed. Then suddenly the bougainvillea snapped and red blossoms fell across the veranda. A table went over, along with Harriet's drink. Harriet jumped. A big gray cat had dropped on the wren from the eave above, and the vine had collapsed. In the fall the wren had escaped, but the cat had got tangled in the vine. It clawed for purchase among the leaves and stems.

"Son of a bitch," Ellis said. He nearly tore off the screen door and caught the cat before it could get untangled. "You fucking lousy cat. You goddamn cat." Ellis had the cat by the throat. The cat squirmed and scratched, but Ellis held it. In a minute the cat's legs stretched out, and Ellis shook its body out of the vine, raining down more red blossoms on the stones. "Damn cats," he said, but the anger was gone from his voice.

"See what fame will do?" Tilghman said.

I went out with Jésus and Tilghman, hoping to get a word with Tilghman before he took off somewhere else. I'd given up on evolution. I wanted answers. But he and Jésus had their heads together under the hood and were speaking to one another in Spanish. I handed them tools, and once Tilghman asked me to get in and start the engine, which I did. When it got darker, I held the flashlight for a while.

Then I went back inside. Harriet was reading on the sofa then, under the light. Ellis was preparing squid. "Where's Francie?" I asked.

"Shower," Ellis said. "She thought cold water would help her sunburn. You want to cut some squid?"

"I've never done it," I said.

Ellis washed them and then grappled with the slimy bodies in the bowl. He pulled one apart with his finger, felt for the cuttlebone in back, pinched it out, splashed the squid in fresh water, and laid it on the cutting board. "Slipperier than cats," he said. "All you have to do is cut the tentacles just behind the eyes. Don't throw them away. We'll eat them. Then cut the body into sections."

In the shower Francie had started singing. She had a sweet voice, but with the water running, I couldn't make out the song. Maybe there wasn't a song.

"Squid goes well with tequila," Ellis said. "Harriet, how are you fixed with that mockingbird?"

"It's just orange juice and grenadine, isn't it? I'm doing wonderfully well." She held up her glass nearly empty.

The shower went off but Francie's voice continued behind the door. Words now:

> C'est le soleil, il est si chaud, il est si fort
> Mais l'ombre de nous . . .

The French surprised me. It brought back to me a verse I had no reason to recall, the way I sometimes remembered dreams.

> Des visages, les visages de tout le monde
> Je les vois
> Ils passent comme je me promene
> Je n'ai pas une ombre

Comme si mon corps serait invisible
Et le monde n'existe plus que dans mes yeux
En dehors de moi-même.

The singing stopped abruptly, as if Francie was suddenly aware we were listening. *Ombre:* shadow. That was the common word. I liked that she was self-conscious about her singing.

When the squid was cut up and frying in batter, I took another Bohemia into the living room and found my deck of cards. I laid out solitaire on the floor. Solitaire was a terrible exercise, but it kept me from thinking of the sun's last frail light over the water, the apparent changes in the distance between the islands and the shore, the sound of the Land Rover starting up. I didn't think of Demer or Inez Montera or the woman in Casa Grande. I saw only the numbers on the cards and what went where.

Francie came out of the bathroom with a towel wrapped around her. Ellis was drinking at the stove, poking the squid in the frying pan with a fork. Harriet was intent on her reading. Francie looked at me, and I rendered her look at that moment into a dream. Water dripped through her hair onto the floor. Her face looked less swollen, but her shoulders were red, beaded with water. She peeled the towel down over her front a few inches to show me the line where the red became white above her breasts. Then she took two steps and came around the corner into the kitchen, and the dream was broken.

Ellis brought in a plate of fried squid. "Have some," he said to Francie. "Squid has great healing powers. And it's an aphrodisiac." He passed the plate to Harriet, then set the plate down. "Help yourself, Scott."

Harriet looked up. "This is an excellent book."

Ellis had his mouth full of squid. "That's what the critics said."

"Are you writing something new?"

"A new book," Ellis said. "Always. I'm always writing a new book."

A superficial calm took hold of us. I say superficial because we could hear the Land Rover revving in the background. But for that moment we were all wearied to quiet. I, for one, was played out by the day's events, scorched by the sun and glare, arm-tired, bending to alcohol. I ate squid and collected the cards of my unfinished game. Even my desire for Harriet had ebbed to benign passion. When she looked up again at Ellis, I got up and went out to see whether Tilghman needed any more help.

Chapter five

By nine o'clock we'd eaten, and the booze had laid us low. We sorted ourselves into various rooms. Ellis had his own bedroom, of course. Francie took the guest room near the front door, and because of her sunburn, asked Tilghman to sleep somewhere else. Tilghman opted for a window seat in the living room and lay down with a blanket over him. I had thought Harriet in these circumstances might have had the courage to ask me to share the other guest room, but when the time came, she was too tired or too dazed from orange juice and grenadine to think of it. There was only a single bed anyway.

I curled in my sleeping bag on a pad on the window seat on the other side of the door from Tilghman. I settled in, but I knew Tilghman was awake. A bright sea light flowed through the window. "What made you do it?" I asked.

"Do what?"

"The swim. The dive."

"It wasn't so dangerous as it looked."

"It was more dangerous than it looked."

He breathed a deep breath. "You're too cautious, Scott. You even see Harriet as dangerous."

"I don't take foolish risks. I don't dive from cliffs or smuggle people into the country."

"You did once."

"You think you're not going to get caught?"

"I think we'll get caught."

"Then why?"

Tilghman turned over. "Let me tell you something, Scott. You think I did something to change Demer. But it was the other way around. Demer changed me."

"How do you mean?"

"When she came out to Colorado, she'd reached an impasse. She liked nursing, but she wanted to do more."

"I knew that."

"More than just helping one or two people at a time."

"Why didn't she talk to me?"

"She couldn't talk to you. She knew whatever she said, you'd disapprove."

"I thought she could make some concessions."

"There weren't concessions. That's what she was trying to tell you. What she wanted to do required a choice. You were never much good at choices."

"Is that why she was unfaithful?"

"I don't know. But so what if she was?"

"You don't think that matters?"

"Not compared to her work."

"Did you sleep with her?"

Tilghman smiled. "If I had, would it make a difference to you?"

"Yes."

"Then I didn't."

"What a bastard you are," I said.

Tilghman was quiet for a minute, but my anger didn't cool. I thought he was lying, but I had no way to know.

Finally he said, "What Demer has accomplished already is more than she hoped for—all the people we've brought across. When I think back to Steamboat, married to Clarice and living in that big house . . . I didn't understand what I was doing then. Demer showed me. It wasn't just her ski visit, either. When she'd write me from Costa Rica, you know what I'd do? I'd take her letter to a bar and order a Heineken. That was my life compared to hers. I'd drink the Heineken and read her letter and have another Heineken. That's what my life was like then, and now it isn't."

"She put together this lifeline?"

"She came as far as Manzanillo. She wanted Guaymas—Guaymas to Nogales overland by truck. She made contacts. One time the border patrol caught a truck at Nogales —twenty-two Salvadorans trying to get out of that hole the U.S. has been digging for years. The Salvadorans were deported. We don't know what happened to them, but as with Inez Montera, we know. They are more of the *desaparecidos*."

"You can't know that."

"I talked Ellis into buying the *Estrella*. He knew the shrimpers down here. It's the perfect cover—sturdy, not too big a boat, but big enough. And there are a million shrimp trawlers between here and Guaymas."

"Ellis owns the *Estrella?*"

"It's in Leonidas's name. It's the only thing Leonidas has ever owned."

"What about Raul?"

"Raul is Leonidas's son. He used to be a fisherman. Then he left here and went to a technical school in Manzanillo."

"How did you meet him?"

"Ellis. Raul came back here about a year ago to work in the frozen-fish factory. He got involved in the union. There was a strike. Raul understands why people want to leave where they are. He's seen his own brothers go north. From here it's easy though. They walk across, and if they're caught and sent back, they try again. But from there—Guatemala, El Salvador, Honduras—not so easy."

"Why didn't you tell me this before?"

"We have to be careful. Francie doesn't know as much as I've just told you. She's never been with us. I thought it would do you good to go along and see for yourself. Maybe you would understand. Demer never wrote you because she was afraid of what you might write back. All it would take is for the government to get hold of one letter."

"I just heard from her," I said. "She's in Belize now."

"I know. She's trying to set up a network on the other coast. I've known that for a month."

"Who's Will Terborg?"

"Will's got connections in Belize City and Belmopan. He knows the church people in Guatemala near Benque Viejo del Carmen."

"Have you talked to her?"

"On the phone? No."

My anger dissipated a little, and fatigue took over. I supposed I was relieved somewhat to know a few details of Tilghman's mission.

What I thought then was that there existed a kind of self-knowledge you possessed, a vision of yourself, ill formed and hazy, perhaps, but nevertheless essential to your own well-being. It was a blend of honesty and corruption, performance and deceit, truth and trickery. You allowed a good margin for error and a healthy dose of forgiveness for your own sins. What Tilghman had said of his time with Demer hadn't convinced me. I wasn't reassured. I knew Tilghman was testing this self-knowledge which I imagined I had. Testing: that's what Tilghman did best.

The next day Tilghman and Raul took the *Estrella* to Guaymas. I wasn't asked to go, and I didn't volunteer. They'd be gone four or five days if things went well, and I had to be back in class after the vacation. Tilghman said we could take the Land Rover if we wanted to go back early. There wasn't any need to wait for him.

Ellis offered to charter a boat for deep-sea fishing, and he knew by then Harriet wanted to look for whales. I was surprised that Francie agreed to go. She hated fishing. But if Tilghman wasn't there, she said, she wouldn't have to fish. Harriet was delighted of course, but I begged off.

"There's nothing else to do," Harriet said. "You might as well see what birds there are in the Gulf of California."

"Another time," I said. I wanted to be alone. I didn't want to have to make conversation or be polite. The information that Tilghman had given me was disturbing me again after a fitful night's sleep.

I rode with them to the harbor. The charter dock was near the fish market, not where the shrimp boats were unloaded to the factories. Ellis had already called for a boat and mentioned Leonidas's name to get a break on the cost. The captain was a friend.

When we arrived, all the others had to do was step aboard. I waved to them from the quay as they motored out the channel. The powerboat was more streamlined than the trawler, and it cut easily through the water. Francie waved back from the stern. She looked comical in a fishing hat, a long-sleeved shirt, and a jacket with a high collar to keep the sun from her neck. I held my hand high.

I watched till they were gone, and then I ascended the hill away from the quay, past the cinder-block houses and broken walls. I gauged how high I climbed against the sea. Once I stopped to look into a garden of flowers: roses, hibiscus, bougainvillea, azaleas. Across the street on the side of a store, someone had written *¡VENCEREMOS!* It was a beautiful word, though I didn't know what it meant. The sound was beautiful. I whispered it to myself over and over: *venceremos, venceremos.*

I continued up the hill to the plaza. That was where the church was, where two bell towers lifted gracefully skyward. Only one of the towers had a bell in it. Swallows came and went, already working the morning breeze for insects.

The door to the church was open, and I went into the cool, motionless air. I had never prayed much, had never had the occasion to think God cared one way or the other what I did or didn't do. God was an artifact, and religions were riddled with so much that was gaudy, macabre, and cruel I'd long ago ceased to consider them useful except to others who needed to believe, or to governments which wanted their people to believe. I believed in birds and weather and the husks of saguaros, whose fibrous cores desiccated and spilled out onto the ground.

But that morning I prayed. I knelt at the altar near the jagged light which poured down from a broken window, and I prayed to the awkward carving of Christ. I prayed that Demer was still alive, and for Inez Montera. I prayed for the people Demer was trying to help. I prayed for her to forgive me, and for the forgiveness of my weaknesses. I prayed for Tilghman, too. It was an incoherent prayer, not directed particularly to the figure trapped in wood. It was an insane prayer, selfish and blasphemous and painful.

Afterward, outside, the sun was bright in my eyes. Some of the fishing boats that had been out at night were coming in toward the breakwater. A few were already in the harbor. I walked down the hill toward the quay along a different street, past a school where a man was swinging a little girl on the swing. The girl was chubby and dark haired and wore a stained dress. The man didn't swing her very high, and he kept speaking to her as if he were saying something beautiful, like *venceremos, venceremos.* The arc of the swing passed in front of the sea, back and forth, and the man kept saying what I believed was *venceremos,* but it must have been "hold on tight."

The girl laughed, but her laugh was tinged with fear, or something not quite right or normal. Her face looked happy, but her eyes had in them a certain sadness. I cried. I couldn't help it. The tears caught the sunlight, and I could see through them the little girl, who was watching me from the swing.

———

Then another couple came into the playground, and the little girl spoke to them as she swung, a little higher then, and her eyes were different seeing these people. I thought they must have been her mother and father, and the other man was a friend who'd brought the girl to the playground for a while. But I didn't know. The girl stopped swinging, and the woman lifted her from the board and held her.

I went down to the quay. Two of the fish stalls were opening. Men and women were carrying baskets of fish and seafood from trucks. One stall was occupied by a short fat woman who matched the description of Adelita, but I didn't go close enough to smell her perfume. Near me was a boy filleting flounder. He laid the fish eye-up on a board and stuck the point of a long knife into its head to hold it steady. He wiped the body with a sponge, released the knife, and sliced a straight line horizontally across the fish's tail. Then just behind the gills, he cut a vee, and with two lightning strokes slit the back and the belly and lifted away a perfect slab of white meat. He turned the fish over, wiped that side with the sponge, and made the same incisions. He lifted the fillets onto a stack and tossed the bones into a can on the ground beside him.

I watched him do this for half an hour until he had a big stack. I bought four and walked back along the beach to Ellis's house.

They had caught snapper and bonita and had taken the sun. I had taken tequila. "I bought some flounder," I said, "in case you got shut out."

"Ellis is a master fisherman," Francie said.

"The boat captain gets the credit," Ellis said. "We even got Francie to take a turn."

"It wasn't so bad without Tilghman," Francie said. "You should have been there, Scott. We saw all kinds of birds."

"What birds?"

"Gulls and terns, mostly," Harriet said. "And storm-petrels and shearwaters."

"And one bird—it was so graceful . . ."

"Grace is not a field mark," I said, pronouncing the words carefully.

"White wings," Harriet said. "Red bill. Long red tail."

"Like a streamer," Francie said. "It sailed with the boat for a while, not with the other birds, but above them, as if it needed more air than they did."

"Red tail?" I asked.

"Do you know what it was?"

"Long slender tail, maybe a couple of feathers?"

"Graceful," Francie said.

Of course I knew its name. I conjured the bird in my head from pictures in books, from all I knew. Red bill, slight barring of black on the trailing edge of the tertial feathers of the white wings. I had never seen one, but I knew what it was. "Red-tailed Tropicbird," I said. "Rare, very rare, off the California coast."

"You should have come," Francie said.

We had a feast of fish. Ellis cooked half the flounder and some snapper and made a white-wine sauce. We drank wine and laughed and talked about the fishing and the friend of Leonidas's who'd guided the boat, and what we were going to do the next day. We were all different people without Tilghman there.

I went to bed early, right after dinner. Tequila. I slept right away.

But in the middle of the night, I woke. That happened sometimes when I drank—I'd sleep and then sit bolt upright in the middle of the night. My heart pounded, my eyes wouldn't close. I thought of Demer's writing to Tilghman all those letters she had not written me. He had known a month before I had she was in Belize. What else had she said to him?

I tried praying again, even for sleep, but nothing happened.

After I'd been awake a while, I heard the toilet flush. I turned over on the window seat in my sleeping bag, and saw Ellis holding a flashlight. He had on the same shorts and dark T-shirt he'd worn at dinner. The flashlight glanced around the living room, caught shards of the chandelier, moved over me and then away. He turned the light off. Then he walked barefooted down the hall past his own room. I knew by the distance he walked. I thought he must be going to the front door, maybe to look for something. Had someone knocked at that hour? But he turned into Harriet's room halfway down the hall.

PART FOUR

Chapter one

In history you see the inevitability of certain events. You say, "War was bound to come," or "They'll be divorced," or "It was only a matter of time." Chronologies press to particular conclusions and when they arrive, you're not surprised. I remember seeing an English movie once, a black-and-white film shown late at night on television. The movie was set in Africa in a country ruled by a cruel and evil enemy of the Crown. The colonel who'd seized power in this country had done terrible things, and the British were trying to assert moral right against him. A small corps of specially trained, well-instructed British counterinsurgents had made their way back into the country to wrest control from the colonel and his army. There was some complicated plan, and in its unfolding, the Brits were found out. Battles ensued, and, in the end, the counterinsurgents were chased across the beautiful landscape by the government troops loyal to the colonel. The Brits wanted to make it to the border. They were outnumbered and poorly armed. Reinforcements were supposedly coming, but the border was safe haven.

The government troops gained. Land cruisers and all-terrain vehicles skidded through mud holes and across the great grasslands. Skirmishes were fought. Then the colonel himself joined the pursuit in one of the open Jeeps. At the last minute, as expected, the frontier came into view. The Brits escaped across the border into friendly territory.

They stopped in a grassy clearing, and the camera panned across the hills to where the colonel's troops had come up short. The colonel, with a few henchmen, came across the frontier for the

165

obligatory conversation about the future, about intentions and the renewal of the fight the next time the two forces encountered one another. The tough, leathery British commander promised he'd be back. The colonel nodded and smiled. Then he gave orders for his soldiers to shoot everyone. And they did. That was how the movie ended.

I had this premonition I couldn't shake. Every day I expected to hear some terrible news about Demer. It was mid-April then; spring break was over. I hadn't seen Harriet for two weeks, ever since that morning I'd left Puerto Peñasco alone, when Tilghman was on his way to Guaymas on the *Estrella*.

That morning Harriet and I had had a singular exchange, more noteworthy for its avoidance of issues than for what we'd said to one another. I'd awakened to the light of the sea, the curtains open and fluttering. The sun was on me, doubling the warmth of my sleeping bag. I smelled coffee.

"Sleep all right?" Ellis asked cheerfully. "Want some coffee?"

I sat up, remembered Ellis in the dark T-shirt the night before in the hallway. "Coffee smells good," I said. I shielded my eyes from the sun and looked out at the islands. The sea was calm.

Ellis brought over a cup, along with the pot, and I held my cup while he poured. "Say when."

"When," I said. He stopped pouring. "Where is everyone?"

"Francie's walking on the beach. Harriet's still asleep." He took a look at me. "Be glad it wasn't mescal," he said. "You want breakfast? I have some fresh melon."

"Maybe some toast."

I sipped the coffee—strong and bitter—and pushed the sleeping bag away. I pulled on jeans and went to the bathroom. In the toothpaste-speckled mirror, the person opposite was a man with no known ties to anyone, a man who in that stage of life (thirty-two seemed late and getting later) could slide from then on. Sliding had much to recommend it, too, gravity being the only requirement, and it was free. But I couldn't slide.

I washed my face and brushed my teeth, and when I went out the door, I met Harriet. She had a towel over her shoulder, her robe on. Her hair was loose down her back.

"I'm going back to Tucson," I said.

"I'd like to stay, Scott. It's my vacation."

"I understand."

That was the sum of our conversation that morning. We passed one another. She went into the bathroom to shower. I had a leisurely breakfast with Ellis at which Harriet didn't appear. Ellis said he'd be happy to bring Harriet and Francie up to Tucson. He had to get some supplies anyway, and Tilghman could use the motorcycle if he came back and needed transportation.

I was gone before Francie came back from her walk.

Migration was well under way by then. Cassin's Sparrows had returned singing to the grasslands. Brewer's Sparrows, so numerous in the nets in March and early April, had virtually disappeared. Warblers trilled in the dry thickets—Lucy's, Orange-crowned—along with some gnatcatchers. Thrashers perched boldly in the open, staking territory. The vireos—Bell's in the wash, and Warbling Vireo higher up in the canyon—gave their staccato variations. Swallows skimmed the ravines. There were kingbirds and doves everywhere.

The indigenous birds of the higher canyons—Painted Redstarts, and Grace's, Red-faced, and Olive warblers—had returned, along with the Band-tailed Pigeons, flycatchers, grosbeaks, tanagers, and the myriad of hummingbirds of the Southwest. Every day we waited for the Elegant Trogon to appear.

The days were hotter. The class was out in the field by seven in the morning, and we spent more time in the canyons, where the breezes and shadows and the stream-cooled air gave a respite from the heat. Every time out I gave field quizzes.

"What song is that?" We listened to the melodious ringing from the top of a pine. *Black-headed Grosbeak.*

"Name the bird on the sycamore branch." A drab, upright bird, small, without wing bars or an eye ring. *Western Wood-Pewee.*

"What field characteristics best separate Broad-tailed Hummingbird from Broad-billed?" *The Broad-tailed has an iridescent red throat and makes a high-pitched buzzing with its wings, while the Broad-billed has a blue gorget, a conspicuous orange bill, and is silent when it flies.*

"Were we to see Aztec Thrush, what would it look like? *Robin-sized and shaped, dark head and belly, black-and-white wings.*

I swore to the students I graded these quizzes and entered their marks into the computer in my office, but I didn't have the heart to. My own impression was that any class learned as much as they wanted to. The most to hope for was that they took with them to other aspects of their lives a sense that something else existed in the world besides football and television, cars and romance.

But for a while, then, I even dreaded the classes. Dread wasn't the precise word. The classes were what I had to do while I waited for the bad news. I woke early, drove the van to wherever we were scheduled to go. But the country wasn't the same. What had excited me a month before—the smells of ocotillo blossoms and prickly-pear flowers, the changes in the grasses when it rained— now made me conscious of how the landscape could be altered by one's own fears. I didn't know what I was afraid of. Demer. Tilghman. Myself.

I wasn't in my office much. I avoided the department. Except for taking a shower, I stayed clear of the university. I went running. I began with fifteen minutes' jogging around the neighborhood twice a day, added a few minutes each day, leveled out at the end of the first week at forty minutes total. I was as out of shape as I'd ever been. I ran to the university and back, ran the track, the sidewalks. I'd done nothing since college except look for birds.

In the evenings I ran out Speedway, past the interstate, up the Gates Pass Road, turned right on Indigo Drive. Somewhere in there I'd pass from the light into the shadow of the hills. In the shadow where it was cooler, I was more comfortable. All around me were houses and saguaros and the dark outline of the Tucson Mountains against the orange-and-blue sky. I'd touch a silver mailbox with no name on it and turn around.

Gradually I felt the muscles revive, stretch, strengthen. My breathing, so labored during the first week of running, eased. If I didn't try too hard, I could run my course in an hour. If I pushed, I could do it in fifty-two minutes. Every so often I tried for a new record to the mailbox and back.

Harriet called me several times at Tilghman's and left messages on the machine: "Scott, please let me hear from you," and so on. I didn't answer the phone or return the calls. There was an occasional note in my pigeonhole at the department: "Where are you? You weren't at your office hours." As she had told me, it was easy to avoid someone in a city the size of Tucson.

If the students wanted to see me, I met them at Greasy Tony's on Speedway. I spent a fair amount of time there, and I got to be friends with several of the students—Lucie Cates from Flagstaff and Darryl "Blade" Davis, who came to class on roller skates.

We'd have dinner, drink beer, and talk about birding. I'd some-
times tell them birding stories about ticks, chiggers, mosquitoes,
mud slides, moose attacks, rainstorms, faulty equipment, poor
health, lack of money—those were the trials that I'd endured at
one time or another. Once I'd watched a Snowy Egret drown in
salt water at Fort Jefferson on the Dry Tortugas because it was too
weak from dehydration to climb out of the water. Another time, in
Alaska, looking for the nest of the Wandering Tattler, I'd run into
a grizzly sow and cubs. In Chino Canyon, not far from where we'd
set the first mist nets, a bull snake had jumped me from a tree while
I was scouting around for a rare Black-capped Gnatcatcher that
had been reported there. In the Everglades Jack Watkins and I had
walked two miles in ninety-degree heat along a mosquito-infested
canal road, wearing towels over our heads and gloves on our hands,
to reach the opening to the bay, where, instead of finding the
hoped-for Greater Flamingo, we glimpsed the spectacle of hun-
dreds of Roseate Spoonbills and herons and egrets and their reflec-
tions in the still, gray, dawn-lit water.

I felt bad about avoiding Harriet, but in a way I was glad her
attention had turned to Ellis. I liked Harriet; I admired her. But
I couldn't keep up with her. So I chose to keep silent. Silence was
a way of saving face. It allowed nothing to take the place of some-
thing. That's what I hoped for anyway. Silence corroborates no
truth. That wasn't cruelty, was it?

The days passed and scars formed over wounds. I wanted to
give Harriet, to whom I owed a lot, time to find out what Ellis
could offer her. I wanted to give myself more time to forget.

Chapter two

Tilghman and Ellis brought back from Mexico eight bougainvilleas, which Ramon and I planted at the base of the trellis. We'd already laid the bricks for the new patio. Bamboo flourished under the windows of the gutted garage. Ramon had already spread out a load of topsoil on the old dirt driveway and had seeded grass. We had another pile to put in the flower beds. The new orange trees, tiny sprigs in the bare earth, smelled so sweet the air was toxic.

But the wall dominated everything else. We had built it week by week, a layer at a time. I had carried hundreds of cinder blocks. Ramon had mixed tons of cement. He had measured, remeasured, reinforced and engineered the archway. The three-hundred-pound gate was on order.

But the wall was so high the backyard barely got any sun. No sun reached the doorway of the porch. The patio got sun only from eleven till two. "What about claustrophobia?" I asked. "What about darkness?"

"What about the police?" Tilghman asked.

"They'll think you have something to hide."

"I do."

The wall was there, a physical force. Ramon's next task was to plaster it pink.

It was right around this time that Tilghman one day brought home the contents of his safety-deposit box. He came into the kitchen when I was eating a ham sandwich and set the cardboard carton on the floor. "Here's what Demer has sent me," he said, "if you're interested."

170

There were manila envelopes with sheafs of pages in them—journals, letters; postcards of seashore and jungle, of quetzals, temples, vases, marketplaces, palaces, flowers. Tilghman pulled some of these out to show me. The letters, most of different-sized pages, were in chronology, so that when Demer came back she'd have a logical sequence to reread. Whether she intended someday to do something with all of this—put what she'd written into a book, maybe—I didn't know, but I doubted she meant for me to see them.

Yet here was an opportunity few people get: the chance to hear, without the subterfuges of everyday conversation, in the vernacular of someone you once loved and who once loved you, the truth about yourself. This was her record of what she thought and felt. She had no reason to lie to Tilghman. Whatever she wrote about me would be free of the mask of marriage. And not only would I hear the truth, but it might help me. The words could make a difference. I could change.

"No, thanks," I said.

"I'm not going to argue with you," Tilghman said, nudging the box on the floor. "They're here if you reconsider."

Then he took a large envelope from the box. "Come here," he said.

I left my sandwich and followed him into the living room.

"Close your eyes."

I closed my eyes. I heard the sound of heavy paper being handled. Tilghman moved around the room. "All right," he said. "Open your eyes."

I opened my eyes. He had laid out on the floor two dozen photographs, maybe more—all of Francie.

"These are the ones she wanted back," I said.

Tilghman nodded.

They were astonishing pictures. They were beautiful. We are born in our society to clothes. We're taught clothes. So a photograph of a woman without clothes seems staged and unnatural. But these pictures weren't posed. They weren't alluring in the manner of magazine photographs. They didn't hint or tease. They celebrated dance, though most of them were stills. Francie looked as if she had grown up without clothes, had lived that way for weeks. She was artless and relaxed, wore no makeup. Her forehead and cheeks were lightly freckled. Her body held light and shadow the way water and land hold one another. I was startled by the radiance her body knew.

171

There were enough photographs that you couldn't be impressed by one. No single episode stood out. It was an encompassing story, a day which represented a year or a life.

"We took them at Ellis's last winter," Tilghman said, "when Ellis was in California."

I hadn't looked at the background, but when Tilghman mentioned it, I noticed the terrace, the chandelier, the windows. "It's the sea light," Tilghman said.

But it was not the sea light. It was not the light or the shadow, but the person who held that light and shadow, the person who had an inordinate confidence in the photographer. That was my first inkling about Tilghman.

"I can see why she wants them back," I said.

Tilghman left the photographs on the floor for several days after that, and the box in the kitchen. Every time I walked through the house, I was reminded of Demer and Francie. After a while I collected the photographs and put them in my room.

That same day I collected the pictures, Tilghman decided we should bury the finger bone of Inez Montera.

"You still have it?" I asked.

"Of course I have it." He set the tiny bone on the kitchen table. "I was thinking we'd climb Mount Wrightson."

"What about the backyard?" I asked. "We could make a cross and keep a candle lit."

"Don't joke."

"Or Mount Lemmon. We can drive to the top of Mount Lemmon."

"The bone's not heavy," Tilghman said. "We need to make an effort. We can camp out and conduct a proper ritual."

"What is a proper ritual?"

"We'll invite Francie and Harriet."

"Not Harriet," I said.

"Frank, then," Tilghman said. "You can call her."

I called Francie and told her Tilghman's plan. We'd start out late in the afternoon when the land had cooled a little, and then camp at the saddle in the pines below the summit. At sunrise we'd climb to the top. Tilghman wanted to burn her name into a cross on the top of the mountain.

"What about Friday?" I asked. "Two o'clock. You said once you wanted to go."

"I do," she said.

Francie was on time. Tilghman and I had gathered our gear, and we added what Francie brought. We'd each carry our own sleeping bag, pad, jacket, and idiosyncratic necessities. I brought a deck of cards, a tape recorder for owls, and a pint of Jim Beam. Francie took skin cream, a notebook, and eight packages of M & M's. Tilghman brought a glass box for the tiny bone and was going to carry it in his hands.

Water was a prerequisite, though Tilghman claimed there was a spring halfway up the mountain. I didn't believe him and carried a half gallon with me. He had told us enough lies, though in this case it was true he'd suffer, too, if we didn't have enough water. We divided the remainder—roast beef sandwiches already made, sardines, crackers, a jar of olives, cans of custard, oranges, apples, cheese. Francie wanted to bring a first-aid kit, a flashlight, and sun lotion for the trip down.

I strapped on the camp shovel and two one-by-four boards, one of which we had sawed to a point to drive into the ground. Tilghman packed the hammer and nails and the wood-burning tool he wanted to use to cut Inez Montera's name into the wood.

We loaded the Land Rover, and Francie took Zapata to the neighbor's across the street. Then we were ready. Tilghman and I sat on the curb, while Francie made a last stop in the bathroom. The weather was perfect—a few clouds scudded along the western horizon. We had everything covered.

Then two strange things happened: they always do when you're walking out the door. The first was that Harriet showed up. I recognized the silver Buick when it turned the corner. "Don't look now," I said to Tilghman.

Harriet pulled up and rolled down her window. "Are you going to Mexico?" she asked. "Hello, Scott."

"Climbing Mount Wrightson," Tilghman said. "Want to go?"

"I'm not much of a mountaineer," Harriet said. "No. I thought if you were going to Mexico, you could take something to Ellis." She held out a small paper bag.

"I can take it next week," Tilghman said. "Will it spoil?"

"It won't spoil." Harriet handed the bag to Tilghman.

"Can I look?"

"They're glasses," Harriet said. "Reading glasses."

"Ellis doesn't wear glasses."

"He needs them," Harriet said. "He ought to wear them.

How can you not know that?"

"He drives," Tilghman said. "He goes to town on his motorcycle. He *writes*, for Christ's sake."

"He *types*," Harriet said. "He can't even read what he types. Didn't you watch him fix food? Scott, you were there. You're the birder. Did you notice how he poured a drink?"

"I watched him pour a lot of drinks," I said. I thought about the coffee he'd poured for me the last morning. He'd poured it pretty well, with a little shaking, though he'd asked me to tell him when to stop. He'd fixed the squid. But I remembered how he'd felt for the cuttlebone. He'd had me cut the squid into little pieces.

"That night you were there, Scott, he wanted to read to me. I'd liked *Carte Blanche* and asked what he was working on. Doesn't anyone ever ask him? He offered to show it to me, and I asked him if he'd read."

"In the middle of the night?" I asked.

"It wasn't that late. Maybe a little after ten. You'd gone to bed so early in the living room. Ellis didn't want to bother you, so he came down to my room. But he couldn't see well enough to read. He even brought a flashlight for extra light. Those guest rooms just have kerosene lights. Even with the flashlight he couldn't see the words."

In the background the telephone rang once, twice. Francie must have answered it. In a moment she came to the screen door and called to Tilghman. "For you," she said.

Tilghman got up from the curb and took the paper bag with him inside. I was left alone with Harriet, feeling the fool. "I'm sorry," I said.

"Don't be sorry. For what?"

Francie came out and gave Harriet a hug. I'd forgotten they'd been in Mexico for three days after I left, and they hadn't seen each other since.

Then Tilghman called to me. The telephone is capable of mayhem from long distance. He said it was Lorry on the phone. Something had happened in Casa Grande. Lorry didn't know what was going on, and he couldn't get anyone to take the gas station. His wife was sick. "He wants me to drive up there," Tilghman said. "I have to go now."

"You want me to go with you?"

"You can lend me your car," Tilghman said. "I can make better time on the highway. I want you to bury Inez."

"Inez can wait."

But Tilghman was adamant, and there was no talking him out of it. "Go as high as you can. Be sure to carve her name on the wood. It's rocky on top, but you can find a place."

"Tilghman . . ."

"It's important to me," Tilghman said. "Please."

"We could go tomorrow."

"I'll be gone a couple of days at least. I'll go to Phoenix, too," Tilghman said. "A couple of days, maybe three. It depends on what I find out."

I followed Tilghman outside. It struck me he was making something of nothing. What could be so important about burying Inez then? I knew we were all packed, and Francie was there, but I didn't see the necessity in going immediately. But Tilghman made me feel I would be betraying him if I didn't.

Tilghman pulled his pack from the Land Rover and gave us what we'd need: a few items of food, the hammer and nails, the tool for burning Inez's name into the wood. He set these beside the glass box, which he'd wrapped in a towel. Then he shoved his pack into my Toyota. I gave him the key.

"Don't worry, Scott," he said. He kissed Francie on the cheek and whispered something to her. Then he was gone.

"Are you sure you don't want to go?" I asked Harriet.

Chapter three

The trail began at the end of the Madera Canyon Road. The first several hundred yards led through sycamores along the bank of the creek. It was easy walking. Families were already in some of the picnic places by the stream. Radios blared salsa music and the children, released for the weekend, raced into the water and out again. One picnic spot had twenty people in it—children, parents, grandparents—with a dozen baskets and coolers.

Beyond the picnic area the trail doubled back and started up the hill through the drier scrub oak. Francie went first. As she climbed she held her two hands under the bottom struts of her pack frame, as if she was lifting the weight off her back. She had on blue shorts, and a pale brown shirt with shirtsleeves that rode up under the pack straps to the curve of her shoulder. Her legs were long, slender, finely muscled. Dancer's legs. She kept a good, steady pace. My pack was heavy, too. I was glad I'd been running every day.

I wondered what Francie thought of this trek up the mountain. She hadn't said much on the drive down to Madera. She'd told me about her dancing, her increased exercise regimen, the possibility she had of going to Los Angeles. That's what her plan still was. She liked Harriet. One afternoon in Puerto Peñasco they had played a game with some children on the street, throwing a tennis ball uphill and catching it as it bounced down. Harriet had loved the children.

"She ought to have children of her own," Francie said. "I know she thinks of that."

"And you don't?"

"I don't think of it much right now."

I imagined Harriet playing in the street: the stones, the colors of the children's clothes, the laundry drying across the sky, the word *venceremos* on the wall of one of the buildings. But I heard more in what Francie wasn't saying. She didn't speak about Tilghman. She didn't talk about burying Inez Montera.

In an hour we had climbed up a thousand feet through the scrub oak and into the drier pine forest. We skirted the flank of a ridge and looked down into a ravine where we could hear water flowing. Francie kept a fair distance between us. She was above me on the zigzags, and each time I saw her, I was aware of her avoidance. I expected a glance from her, a word maybe, about how she was faring with her pack or the steepness of the slope, or how it was absurd to be climbing up a mountain to bury the little finger of a woman neither of us knew.

We were still across the gorge from Mount Wrightson, but we could see it plainly now above us—a huge block of granite that already in the late afternoon was absorbing the faint red-orange the sun gave it. Francie rested on the trail at the curve ahead of me, drank from her plastic water jug, and continued on before I reached where she was. I didn't hurry. I was carrying an extra half gallon of water and the fragile glass box.

At Josephine Saddle, 3.2 miles, the trail split. To the right the Agua Caliente Trail led to Rattlesnake Canyon and Agua Caliente, and to the left the Old Baldy Trail went east to the Wrightson massif. We took the left fork, passed a wreath of plastic flowers memorializing two Boy Scouts who had died on the mountain, and continued upward and eastward. Below us now and far away were the billowy deciduous trees of Madera Canyon, the bajadas sloping down to the Santa Cruz River, which cut a line north and south. The Sierritas were tiny hills on the far side of the valley, bordering the vast desert to the west.

Francie's pace slowed in the cooler pines. The steep climb and the thinner air committed us to ourselves, but I felt her mood ease. A breeze sang in the trees, and the air was soft on the skin. A Red-faced Warbler darted among the boughs above us, and once the bright red apparition of an Hepatic Tanager lifted for a moment into the sun and flew across the canyon to shadow.

Mount Wrightson blocked out the whole eastern sky. The serrated rifts, the vertical precipices, the distant summit made me wonder whether we could find a place to bury anything, even a small bone.

Once Francie stopped and gazed at the mountain.

"It's a long way up there," I said, "just to humor Tilghman."

Francie didn't answer.

At the seep Tilghman had told us about, we stopped for water. We filled a spare plastic jug from the half barrel of clear water that ran from the spring. All around us were broad-leafed mountain laurel. Francie drank right from the barrel, dunked her hands and washed her face. She soaked a bandanna and washed her arms. I took off my pack and broke out the Jim Beam for a quick burn. "Want some?" I asked.

She shook her head.

"So what is it?" I asked. I sat down and leaned against my pack.

"Tilghman said you have the photographs."

"I have them," I said. I took another swallow of Beam. "I wasn't hiding them."

"You knew I wanted them back. Why didn't you call me?"

"I thought you'd come by."

"Well, goddamn it, Scott."

"Tilghman left them on the floor for days. Anyone could have come by and seen them. What was I supposed to do? They were his. Or yours. I finally picked them up."

"Did you look at them?"

"Of course I looked at them."

The line of the shadow of the opposite ridge moved up through the trees toward us and toward the summit of Mount Wrightson. From our perspective the pinnacles were disconnected from one another, rock spires that looked like cathedrals. Francie shouldered her pack. A warbler—an Olive Warbler—flitted from a tree to the edge of the barrel and drank.

"I'm sorry you saw the pictures," Francie said. She turned away and started up the trail.

I waited at the spring to see what other birds would come to drink. A Red-faced Warbler didn't trust me, but a Black-headed Grosbeak came in, along with several other warblers, and a Blue-throated Hummingbird hovered in the cool glade and fed on blossoms.

Finally I got up, put on my pack, and climbed higher. The trail led between Old Baldy to the northwest and Wrightson to the south. Several times I stopped to look at some bird—a hummingbird I thought might have been a rare White-eared, or a warbler—

and I thought of calling to Francie, but she was too far ahead. I knew the birds, knew their songs if they'd sung them, the feather colors even when the birds were in shadow. Francie was far ahead, but that was not why I didn't call to her. That was a lie. We were no longer the same as we'd been starting out on our hike. We had been friends before, with Tilghman between us. I had seen the photographs, but that hadn't changed me, hadn't changed anything. What mattered—what was different—was that Francie now knew I had seen them.

The saddle was a curving arc of grass and scree timbered with scattered ponderosa pines. It was level enough for a tent, but we hadn't brought one, so we scouted pine needles and bunched them on a flat spot near where campers before us had built a firepit. We collected tinder and dry twigs, and I broke windfall by cracking the limbs with my foot.

Francie explored the trail a little higher, where in the morning we'd go to the summit. I sat with the Jim Beam and watched the last sun breathe a transparent rose onto the mountain.

Explanations for what we do may come later, in the longer time, or they may never come. I was thinking this as the light worked its way higher onto the spurs. I acted mainly in the present without thought to consequences, and then I would be surprised to learn harm had come to someone else. I let events carry me. That's what I was doing then, as the light ebbed. But Francie was there. Night was falling. I felt the Beam carve into brain and bone.

Francie came down the trail and into the clearing. "Did we bring any matches?" she asked.

The question stopped me. "Tilghman packed them," I said.

We both checked through the compartments in our packs, but couldn't find any, and I emptied my jeans' pockets. "We'll need them to burn in the name," Francie said. "We'll need a fire."

"I'll go down and get some from the picnickers. It's not dark yet."

"And leave me here alone?"

"You can take care of yourself," I said. "I thought you wanted to go to L.A." I paused. "I trust you. You trust me."

The idea of going down and hiking back pleased me. It was only five miles down, ten round trip, and the trail was well maintained. Without a pack I could make it down in about an hour, and back in two and a half. It would kill the evening with Francie.

I found the flashlight in the side pocket of Francie's pack and took a long drink of water to quell the Beam. I left with the sun still on the top of the mountain.

I skipped down the trail, jogged the steeper grades. The Jim Beam evaporated. I thought of what Francie would do in my absence—gather wood, lay out the sleeping bags, eat her sandwich and a couple bags of M & M's, watch colors mix in the west. Maybe she'd climb Old Baldy, where she could see me on the trail opposite. She'd see the night take form and stars emerge, though, of course, they're always there.

And I thought of Tilghman driving my car to Casa Grande. I knew the interior of the car, the sound of the engine, the configuration of the dashboard, *knew what he'd see.* I wondered what he'd think about Francie and me in the saddle below Mount Wrightson, waiting for the night.

It was nearly dark when I reached the streambed. The oaks and sycamores were black above me, closing off the paling sky. A Whiskered Screech Owl sounded its code farther down the stream. There were fires at the picnic spots near the trailhead. Families gathered around the lights. Voices rose and fell, songs. I borrowed matches from the first people I saw. *Fosforo.* I remembered the word from that night at Quitobaquito. A man gave me a small box of them.

I turned right around and began running. I ran three steps, walked three. Ran, walked. In a few minutes I was above the canyon floor again, looking down over the fires of the families and the lights of the summer homes farther down the canyon.

Once, higher up, I heard Francie's voice from across the gorge. She was singing. The wind took the words.

I reached the first saddle well south of where she was, passed the wreath for the Boy Scouts, doubled back to the seep where Francie had asked about the photographs. Tilghman had told the truth about the water. I drank a little. Then I climbed the last pitch more slowly.

When I was closer, Francie called out. "Is that you, Scott?"

"Yes." Saying that one word made me out of breath.

Francie was huddled in her sleeping bag, not by the firepit where we were camped, but on a rock above the trail. It had turned much colder, and the stars had spread over the ridge. The moon hadn't risen yet, but it spawned a halo across the eastern sky.

Chapter four

I set a match in the dry pine needles, and the flame prickled up through the needles to the dry twigs. A hemisphere of light rose around us, expanded up into the huge ponderosas, echoed back. The air was still. We sat forward toward the flame to warm our hands. The small fire sought new wood.

She had never been angry at me, and she hadn't been embarrassed that I'd seen the photographs. What I had seen was part of her, but a part she'd kept hidden. She told me more—of Illinois where she'd grown up, of how she'd been drawn to the sheer motion of ballet. "I wanted to be perfect at it," she said. "Not ballet, but movement. It was painful to be so awkward starting out."

We watched the flames take the larger limbs, leap into the air between us, flash our shadows on the branches of the trees.

"I don't think of that now," Francie said. "The flaws make the dance real—the effort to do what you can't quite do."

I thought of her that day on the bridge over Florida Wash, the careless and careful way she had moved across the pavement. I watched while she told me of love and the absence of love, watched her eyes, the smooth lips moving, the gold skin sketched by flame. And I felt the longing in her that I had seen in the photographs, the longing for whatever she wanted—to dance, to laugh, to forget the past. There are moments when we are lonely, when we are in the great shadow of the earth, and do not know how to lift the darkness. I knew what Francie felt, drifting from Tilghman; what she felt in ways she didn't realize yet. Tilghman in my car, Tilghman who wanted to bury Inez Montera, Tilghman who had left Francie and me together. Neither of us mentioned his name.

I do not remember now how we first embraced, whether slowly or eagerly. I know I extended my hand first. I chose. And once touched, her hand responded. It was as if, in the darkness and the fire, we had each been moving toward the other. We had known this would happen, and all we had had to do was wait. Kiss smooth lips, her throat, her soft breasts. I felt her let go, our bodies in the air. Gentleness, not on purpose, but purposeless, so smooth was the skin of her cheek, her arm, her hand, so smooth her eyes and the curve of her hip, so smooth my cheek on her belly; all the sadness gone.

And already I saw us going through the hours and the days, knowing the longing would never last long enough. I could do nothing to make her love me unless she let herself.

Then we were not waiting anymore, not moving toward one another, but joined. She lay over me, and I held her in a way I was afraid of, afraid I would hurt her, afraid I wouldn't hurt her enough, and I heard my own voice calling from far away, saying words.

Chapter five

We spent a night of shifting illusions: waking, touching, dreaming. We had spread one sleeping bag over two pads and pulled the other bag over us, but the cold seeped in. A bare shoulder exposed, a foot, a hand. The cold slithered between us. Each time either of us woke, the other woke, and we started again the caresses that led after an interlude to exhausted sleep.

I woke finally before dawn in the eerie night light that comes to the top of a mountain. The birds were still silent. To the east the sky had begun to wash the stars, but no sun or color had spun out yet on the horizon. No wind stirred the pines or the sparse high grass near us. The air was cold and still as new love. I slid out naked from the cover and dressed quickly.

I loved the coming morning. I loved the silent birds and the still air and the sleeping woman. I loved the sky and the night, and the day that was appearing, even before it came to us. It was as though until that morning, I had been seeing the events of my life through a darkness, and now, though I understood nothing better than before, I could see the tableau clearly. I saw how foolish I had been, though Tilghman had explained it to me. I saw how pointless it was to have imagined there was an answer. Demer had done nothing more than set me loose to destroy myself if I would, or to save myself if I could find a way. None of my circumstances was different that morning. But I saw the configurations of people, not as I might have glimpsed a bird through binoculars, but as all the parts together—bird, terrain, and air.

Francie woke, and I fanned the embers in the firepit into some dry needles, and we warmed our hands in the cold morning.

There was only a pale early light when we started up the summit trail. I had loaded my pack with pine boughs and dead needles for a fire. I carried the boards, the hammer and nails, the engraving torch. Francie carried in her bare hands the glass box with Inez Montera's finger in it.

We wound through the pines and up the steep switchbacks that ascended the granite rock. The spires beside us, above us, were living things—a soldier unarmed, a lion, a Dutchman with a cocked hat. One crag was a jet rising into tawny air, another Tilghman's gangly form: arms akimbo, blunt nosed, leaping hurdles.

Sun glowed on the rock, and a pink light spread out around us like ether. We were the first ones for a hundred miles in any direction to draw its warmth. We climbed to the top without stopping. At the summit was a small concrete shell of a hut, with a plaque embedded in stone. Beneath us and all around were hazy hills, canyons, the wide desert. There was no place to dig a grave.

We walked back down a few hundred yards and off the trail, where we found a crevice to set the box in. Francie covered it with brush and grass and collected gravel from the edge of the trail to shore up the fragile glass box. I built a fire nearby and heated the torch and burned the name into the wood:

INEZ MONTERA, GUATEMALA

We nailed the cross together and propped it up with stones.

We took our time coming down. We rested, watched birds, rested again, measured how the arc of the sun changed the land beneath us. We got down to the lower canyon around noon and searched the streambed for the trogon. The trogon was a mythic bird—a red breast, long coppery tail, iridescent green back and head, white breast band, yellow bill. We chased what I thought was its call up along the flank of one hill, but never saw the bird.

It was midafternoon by the time we got back on the road to Tucson. A blur settled in. Francie was nodding in the passenger seat before we reached the interstate at Continental. I kept the Rover on line. Ahead of us—sleep, the city, redefinitions. We had not spoken of any of that. I imagined as I drove a conversation with Francie in which she asked, "Scott, would you do whatever I asked?"

"I would," I said.

"Anything?"

"What do you want me to do?"

She smiled at me. "Nothing."

"I'll do anything. Just ask."

I envisioned this going on and on: I agreeing to do whatever she asked, but she not asking. I was ready to give and give, but she wouldn't take, and each day I poured myself into her not-asking.

I didn't know where Francie lived, only that when she'd left Tilghman's house, she'd rented a small studio in the back of a house. It didn't matter. Tilghman wouldn't be home from Casa Grande and Phoenix for another day or two. Besides, she had to get her car and the photographs. I imagined sleep: us curled in Tilghman's double bed, Francie's breath on my shoulder, my arms around her, our legs tangled and untangled. I took the Speedway exit, turned into the neighborhood, passed the park with the palm trees.

I turned again at Tilghman's corner and saw the Toyota parked at the curb. Tilghman was sitting on top of the wall, putting in iron spikes. I pulled the Rover in behind my car, and Francie woke when I turned off the engine.

"We here?" she asked, blinking into the light. "Where are we?"

"Tilghman's."

She sat up. I got out and slammed the door.

The sun glanced from the windshields of cars parked along the curb, reflected from the new wall. The steel gate was in place in the archway. From the outside there was no way to see in.

"Did you bury Inez Montera?" Tilghman asked.

"We did."

"You burned in the name?"

"We burned in the name," I said. "Why didn't you go to Casa Grande?"

"I went to pick up the gate," Tilghman said. "It had been shipped from Mexico City to Nogales. That's what the call was about. I had to go to Nogales to talk to customs."

"You said Casa Grande."

Tilghman grinned. "How was the climb up Wrightson?"

I could have lied to him. I could have given an account exact in its particulars about the canyon and the trail up Mount Wrightson, about the way the trees had changed as we went through the different climatic zones, and which birds had appeared at which elevations. That was what a good bird guide could do. I could have explained about the matches, how I had wanted to leave Francie alone to escape us being together on the mountain with the dark coming. But with Francie there, the lie had no meaning. I couldn't lie. She got out the passenger side of the Rover, and whatever lie I might have told was contradicted in her eyes.

She didn't make a scene. She held Tilghman's gaze for a moment, as if she was accusing him of something. Then she went around and got out her pack and put it into her car. She kissed me good-bye. "Call me," she said. She didn't take the photographs.

Chapter six

That night Tilghman did go to Casa Grande. I had answered the telephone when Martha called. When Tilghman was gone, I read Demer's journals.

I call them journals, though what were in the cardboard box weren't bound ledgers or spiral notebooks, but loose pages of all sizes and colors—white, yellow, pink, blue—some lined, some plain, some pamphlet-sized, some European-sized, some just scraps torn from newspapers or books. Many of the pages were crumpled, as if they'd been carried in a pack or thrust into a suitcase or a pocket at the last minute. Some had been folded and unfolded; some were written in different colors of ink. Tilghman had organized them into ten-by-fourteen manila folders.

Interwoven with the journals were letters to Tilghman: transition pieces, explanations of time and movement which the journal entries did not always reflect or clarify. Sometimes a letter served merely as an epigraph for the journal: *Tilghman, this is what happened at the marketplace last Wednesday. Take care, Demer.*

Most often she collected her impressions over several days or weeks and then wrote Tilghman a letter with the journals. She mailed things sporadically because she was often in the countryside.

I pieced this chronology together a long time after that first night.

The letters began before she had gone to Costa Rica, even before she had left Newbury. I started at the beginning, but decided after a few paragraphs, I would be better served easing into the task, so I skipped randomly to somewhere in the middle, when she'd already been in Costa Rica for several weeks. Some of the details I knew, if only in vague terms—the cloud forests, the rain, the roads, some of the people she was with. Of course the letters were meant for Tilghman, not for me. He was a presence in them in that way. She phrased sentences to him in ways she wouldn't have to me. I tried to detect in Demer's attitude, from these differences in tone, whether, as she had put it, there was "romance." But the letters were noncommittal. The tone was close and friendly, even confiding, but not full of love.

> *There is a purpose for what we do here which obliterates our normal lives as people. Every day we see the need, feel overwhelmed by how great the task is, put our own priorities aside. It's as if for the first time, I am part of other people and not alone.*

That was the kind of paragraph I read in Demer's forward-leaning script. Sometimes she described the mood of a place, like the time she and a friend had watched vultures consume a road-kill dog.

> *The birds had already found the carcass and were descending from all directions. They had widened the anus and pulled out the intestines and internal organs, which they ate first, along with the eyes, squabbling and battering their wings, tugging and fighting over the pieces. As many waited for a chance to feed as could feed, and as soon as one bird hopped away with a prize (a slab of the liver, for which he had to fight again and again), another took his place at the body. In half an hour nothing was left but the head.*

But usually Demer synthesized ideas about what she and the other volunteers were accomplishing. They had gradually assembled and tested the network of contacts along the coast from Costa Rica to Mexico. They were making new connections inside Guatemala, too, on every Amnesty International monitoring assignment. One man had a source in El Salvador. Most often they worked through the church, though sometimes they had liaisons through other relief organizations.

> *It is not necessarily worse to promise what can't be delivered. These people aren't the intellectuals who were ferreted through Europe during World War II. They're not political people. They're uneducated, fearful (not unlike the rest of us,*

*but not so able to choose or get out of the way). They were born
here. Their whole history is here. They want things to be the
same as they were. Here. Not somewhere else. But things won't
be the same if they're dead. So it's worse to say nothing, isn't it,
than to promise what may not happen? Even if there was no
chance, and we said there was? It's not that they don't want to
go to the United States. But there is no other hope for them.*

*So we send them. How many reach the States we have no
way of knowing. I imagine that's the same grief as getting old . . .*

There were many entries like these. Some talked about the
families Demer had met and helped; some mentioned horrific de-
struction of villages, tortures, deaths by mutilation. She wrote
about visiting a model village the government claimed was the
solution to the problems in the countryside, in Quiché Province
especially. The model village had government-constructed
houses, electricity, potable water, a school, a church, postal and
telegraph service, and a health clinic. Whether the one Demer saw
had these amenities or not, she couldn't tell. It did have a military
garrison stationed a quarter mile away, and two soldiers at the
village gate to keep the Amnesty team from entering or talking to
the *campesinos*.

I would be mentioned sometimes, too, often as an after-
thought toward the end of a long letter, as if, when she was tired,
she would remember me:

*Lately I've been thinking about Scott. Maybe it's the same
impulse I've mentioned to you before—wanting to know what
happens to the people you love. What's he doing? Do you know?
Is he still drinking? I wonder whether he's learned anything
that would make a difference to me. I honestly don't know what
that would be. I don't think he understood much when I left.
But that was the trouble. I couldn't explain it in a way that
made sense to him. Nothing gets done by talking.*

And another time she wrote:

*I left Scott, you know, because I loved him. Isn't that odd?
Or is it a rationalization? He was never like you, Tilghman.
You have an instinct to move, to migrate—to use a word Scott
would like—and so do I. It's ironic that Scott, who chased birds
so many years, lacks that desire. But that's not the instinct I
mean really. He has in him the idea of being ordinary. I think
that's what I'm getting at. He sees things out there better than
anyone else I know . . . What I mean is, well, the simplest*

189

example is this: he could touch me in ways I didn't know were possible. I mean that. There have been men here (Tomas, I told you about) who've thrilled me, but only physically. With Scott it was something beyond that. I can't remember what it was now. I can only tell you it's true. Isn't that what love is? Anyone can learn what pleases someone else, but Scott has the instinct. Even that wasn't enough without what I'm doing now, though.

Demer's confessions were hard on me, but even as I began to move backward in time toward the days we were still together in Newbury, the tone toward Tilghman stayed the same. She spoke and wrote to him as a friend, not as a lover.

It was Tilghman who remained the enigma. Reading Demer's letters, I almost got the sense that he had got her to write them not for her reasons, but for his. The detail of place, the men she met, the ideas Demer considered—all these seemed to point to Tilghman.

Did Tilghman understand his power? He had been there, for instance, with Francie and me on the mountain. I remembered how Francie and I had met, when she had come over to get the photographs which Tilghman hadn't told me about. Even then the focus had been on him. He'd deserted us in Mexico, too, at Ellis's house. And he had arranged for us to be together when we buried the finger of Inez Montera.

The next evening, when Tilghman came home from Casa Grande, he was troubled. A Honduran they'd brought across three weeks before had been stopped by the police in Phoenix and questioned about a burglary. It was an incident of mistaken identity, and the lawyer, who had an ear in the police department, had got him released. No harm was done, but it had made Tilghman nervous. "What if they had got him to talk?" Tilghman said. "What if they had checked on him? It would take only one slip."

"But he didn't."

"Not this time."

"Any word on Rodolfo and his mother?"

"They're in Gila Bend," Tilghman said. "The mother is doing well. Martha—that's the woman in Casa Grande you met—went down to see them a couple of days ago. They'll end up in California—Fresno, maybe, or Gilroy. One of the farming towns. The farms are the easiest places to hide, and once people get acclimated, they can move on. They figure things out after a while. We give them a driver's license, papers, all of that, but it takes time. And the language—we can't give them the language."

"You look tired," I said.

"And I have to drive to Guaymas," Tilghman said. "Can I take your car again?"

"To Guaymas? Shit no."

Tilghman barely heard me. "Raul's on his way on the *Estrella*, and he can't raise the network contact. It's the first time the man's missed. Raul thinks no one will meet the boat coming from the south."

"My car has 160,000 miles on it. You're going to trust it to get you to Guaymas?"

"It'll make it," Tilghman said. "The Land Rover's too slow. And that noise that worries you worries me now."

"How long will you be gone?"

"It's serious if the man has gone over," Tilghman said. "It'll take a day to get there, then a couple of days to figure things out. I may have to meet the boat myself. I'll have the car back in a week."

"It's not the car," I said.

"I know," Tilghman said. "Will you feed Zapata?"

Chapter seven

The next day I woke with a headache. Maybe I'd had a bad dream. My head felt as I imagined a hangover would make it feel, though I hadn't drunk anything the night before. Tilghman wasn't there. The Toyota was gone. I assumed Tilghman had driven it to Guaymas, but I understood anything was possible.

I took some aspirin, dialed Francie's number, got no answer. I tried at DuPlooy's too, but his secretary said DuPlooy was out of town and wouldn't be back till midweek. I made coffee, pried open the front door, and sat down on the front step. Zapata ran the border of the yard.

The sun burned along the street, through the palm trees. The dead fronds rattled. I spoke to Zapata about the meaning of life, and what I said meant about as much to him as it did to me. After a while he lay down in the shade.

I finished my coffee, tried Francie again, and then, having postponed the struggle long enough, went to the kitchen to read more of Demer's journals. I started toward the end this time, when Demer had been in transit to Belize. She was still in Guatemala then on her month's visa.

> We're protected at least modestly by our credentials. The government doesn't want to risk international censure by letting something happen to us. How much military aid would the government get if Congress found out Guatemalan troops were murdering Americans? We are probably in more danger from the guerrillas, with whom we have sympathy, than from the government soldiers. The guerrillas could make propaganda by

claiming the government was responsible for our deaths. But they know who controls the media. That's why it's so hard to make others see the truth. In the States you believe what you read in the newspaper, if you read anything at all.

Yesterday we met two men from Maryland at an army checkpoint. They were waiting the normal, unexplained three hours to get through. They were birding—looking for the quetzal in the cloud forests of Huehuetenango. I told them there were no forests anymore. They'd been firebombed. Where had they been the last five years? They pointed to their guidebook, copyright 1980.

We are making routine visits. In each place we call on the nuns and the priests. They're our only hope to reach the ones who might need us. But the clergy feels the extraordinary pressure of who they are and where. "What good are words?" they ask. But to refrain from speaking is tantamount to deserting the faith. One Sunday a priests celebrates mass and urges the truth, the next he does not show up to speak.

(Tilghman, do I sound too bitter? What hope is there? I don't know, truly. There is such a disparity between rich and poor. What can happen in the years to come?)

There were scraps of notes written on the edge of an airline magazine about the Ixil women who walked along the roads balancing their turquoise water jugs on their heads while they carried their children and their possessions in a variety of clothes and shawls. They wore *huipils* of marvelous colors, Demer said, though these were being abandoned in many places because the tribes were identified by the patterns of their colors, and the government troops, therefore, knew whom to kill.

Then I came across this:

I used to be afraid of dying. My own life was so precious. Even when I was a nurse helping people die, I was afraid. Why was this? Why do I not feel afraid now when the danger is so much greater?

And this long account, written on hotel stationery in Belize City. Demer had apparently carried the stationery with her to the pension at San Ignacio, where she had been when she'd written the letter that my uncle had forwarded.

193

San Ignacio
Cayo District
April 21

Dear Tilghman,

After four days of rain, we finally got a break in the weather. (At least I caught up on some notes to friends. I even wrote Scott.) Anyway, during the lull in the rain, Will and I made an excursion to this waterfall somewhere near the border. The pension owner gave us directions.

The border here is ill defined, except at the checkpoint on the road from San Ignacio to Melchor de Mencos and Flores. The jungle doesn't lend itself to borders. But there was a trail, not well used. In some places we could barely see where we were going. Will led with a machete. There were throngs of birds screeching and singing, monkeys, too. But the waterfall was splendid—a thin misty ribbon that fell fifty feet or so into a wide pool. In the U.S. it would have been enshrined with billboards and souvenir stands, maybe even a Holiday Inn. You'd have had to pay to get in. But no one else was there.

I've told you a little about Will. He's the one who writes to all his aunts and uncles in Chattanooga. He's got a girlfriend who's nineteen and wants him to come home. She says all the time she's praying for him, and I'll bet she is.

The day was sweltery. Will brought a Coca-Cola and I'd brought a beer. We sat on the rocks, dazed by the humidity and the sun. The water from the falls misted over us. After so much rain it was good to feel the sun. And then there's the pressure, too—waiting and traveling all the time and the crazy hours. I was enjoying the sun with my eyes closed, when I heard a splash.

You never quite know who or what is around in the jungle. It was Will though. He'd done the unthinkable—he'd stripped off his clothes and jumped into the water. "It was too hot," he said. "Come in. The water's cool."

I didn't need to be asked twice. The water was cooler than the air, and clear. We swam under the falls and back to the rock. I lazed in the shallow stream while Will swam. Some many-colored bird landed in a tree above my head, then a bright yellow one. (Scott would have loved this place. I'm sure he would have known the names of these birds, or would have found out.)

After a while clouds came up, and it looked as though it was *going to rain again. I got out and sat on the rock to dry myself before the sun went under. But Will didn't get out. He swam under the falls again. Finally it dawned on me he was embarrassed. I was naked on the rock, right where his clothes were.*

Until then it had been innocent. I hadn't thought of myself as naked—or Will, either. But he had. It was clear he wanted me to get dressed and turn around. Instead, though, to give him some grief (he can be so goddamn holy), *I picked up his clothes and moved them behind me farther up the rock. The sun went under. Not so far away thunder rolled through the trees. Will swam over and knelt in the stream.*

"Well?" I said. "I think we ought to make tracks."

He didn't answer or need to. He stared at me without moving. It struck me how naive he was: raised in the faith, engaged to a girl who believed the Bible literally. It must have troubled him genuinely to be confronted like that with the evidence of his own desire. I could see his erection in the water.

I hadn't intended to make him suffer. I'd only wanted to tease him a little. He was a friend, right? And we'd spent weeks together. So I turned around to get his clothes. When I turned back, he stood up.

It's difficult for me to look at a naked man and not see his cock. With Will it was impossible. He had such an erection I couldn't take my eyes off it. I was aware how calm the air had become, how heavy, as if movement by either of us would have caused the rain to fall. He stood there six feet away, making no attempt to cover himself or to reach for his clothes. And I didn't give them to him. His cock was glazed marble, his body thin and strong. I knew Will wouldn't do anything. I was the one who couldn't resist. I ached. I trembled. I couldn't breathe. I felt myself flow.

I rocked forward and knelt and leaned toward him. His eyes were closed, as if he was praying. (I knew for what!) This must be God: I remember thinking that. Not Will or Will's cock, but the longing animals have for one another. Will touched my hair lightly. I lifted my hand, slid it over him, down the length of his cock, pressed my cheek against it. He came right then, years of waiting, all warm. His sperm flowed down my shoulder, down my back. I pushed my breast against his cock, which was still hard.

The rain swept over us, stung our skin. It wasn't a storm as it turned out, but more days of rain just beginning.

Love, Demer

After I read this letter, I turned back to the beginning and read straight through all the journals and the correspondence. There was nothing more to wonder about. If I could read that account without feeling jealous, I could read anything. Nothing in any of the letters hinted at an affair with Tilghman. The only thing I found was this passage, written from Newbury about a month after Demer had come back from Steamboat Springs:

I have to leave, though I don't think of it as leaving Scott. I feel the threat of passing my life on this planet by rote. Scott is perfectly willing to do this, says as much every day. Love: isn't that a funny word for the excuse? It's as if love were a shroud. Scott wants me to be a certain way, wants me to behave in ways acceptable to our friends. He likes it when I'm predictable. Why am I not beyond this? Somewhere else, I mean. What makes people accept what they can so easily change?

Seeing you and Clarice struggling with each other has given me courage. I know how Scott will try to talk me out of leaving. He will try to love me out of it, but I know how to use love, too. I can stop him. It's the only way I can think of that will prevent him from begging me to stay. You'll have to forgive me, too, Tilghman, though Scott won't. He won't forgive you, either.

Chapter eight

Running. Mindless steps. The shoes on asphalt over and over again. The sound. The beat of the heart in the ears. I ran my course through the neighborhood, out Speedway toward the mountains, which were opaque blue ahead of me. I loped uphill easily then in the cool evening. The body accustomed itself to repetition.

We respond to reality, to what we perceive as true, even when there's no proof. We can't do anything about this trap of the senses (the bird guide revels in it). When we worry enough about what reality is, we seek out the guidance of someone else—a psychiatrist in the extreme case, or short of that, a friend who might verify or criticize our perceptions.

In college and afterward, that person for me was Tilghman. Then for a while it was Demer. Each of us brought to those moments of perception whatever our peculiar personalities were composed of, together with those fashionings we had made of our pasts. In this way we invested every incident with our separate intelligences. To understand what Tilghman saw, or what Demer felt, was a comfort to me. I thought then there was a constant in this equation. $E=MC^2$. The speed of light was always 186,000 miles per second. $C=2\pi D$; π was always 3.14162 . . . I learned, though, that in human relationships, there were no constants. What I believed immutable was not.

After reading the letters, it was clear that Demer had only asked me what I would do if she and Tilghman had made love so I would imagine it. In a way she had lied to me and implicated Tilghman in the lie, had given him the lie to carry on. And he had done this, guarded the lie, manipulated it, and often, finally, had kept silent. Silence was the biggest lie. That was what else I learned. His silence had forced me to make up the truth, to guess at what wasn't told, to recreate the events. I had imagined Demer with other men, and for a long time, I had imagined her with Tilghman. To read what she had done with Will Terborg was better than not knowing. Silence had to be filled with something else, true or not true, real or unreal. And when I look back now, I understand this was Tilghman's gift. He called on Francie and me to decipher what he did. Always we were too close to see clearly. We could make out the whorls and dabs of color and shadow, but we could not see the whole landscape.

Francie had grasped this first, though she hadn't been able to put it into words. She'd lived with Tilghman, tried to adjust to him, to get him to talk, to see his point of view. She was loyal. She had endured the pain, and then she had chosen not to endure it anymore. She'd rather have lived alone than to accept what Tilghman offered her. Now I had to make that choice, too.

I leaned into the curve on Gates Pass Road, still running on the uphill. The ridges of the Tucsons to my left had darkened, though the sun was still in the clouds. My legs were strong. I turned onto Indigo, ran a mile, touched the silver box, and turned back.

Francie stayed with me at Tilghman's while Tilghman was in Guaymas. We barely left the house. We learned to cook what the other liked to eat. We talked. We listened to music on the radio, and she danced for me. She taught me about utilizing the entire body, from fingertips to toes to tilt of the head. She showed me breathing, the leap and the breath meshing with one another and with the music. There was always something new in the dance and what the music made the dancer do. The body was supposed to mirror the heart. There were power and lightness, balance and loss. It took discipline and will to hold your center, but a willingness to be vulnerable, too.

We laughed. We held one another. We explored the nuances of rooms and light. Once on my way to the kitchen, we crossed paths in the doorway of the hall. She was going to get a book from the bedroom. We kissed. The kiss lasted to a caress. The caress kept on, burst to sighs. I unbuttoned her shirt. She unzipped me. It took us an hour to get through the doorway.

These were extraordinary days when definitions were pointless. Words, languages, what we said or didn't say, had no meaning, and I—repressed, possessed, obsessed—felt the tight wires loosen in my body. I forgot what we meant to do. I danced. I forgot the signs. The exquisite torture or the harsh caress left us both aching for more. These were brilliant days, and the only thing which cast a shadow over them was that we knew Tilghman would come home.

He called from Guaymas on a Thursday. The contact who'd been so reliable had got drunk and had gone to Manzanillo, and had taken with him the money he'd been paid as a retainer. Tilghman wanted me to wire three hundred dollars. Finding another contact would be more difficult than it sounded. He had to make inquiries. And being a gringo didn't help.

"So now when will you be back?"

"I don't know," Tilghman said. "I'll call. Does it matter?"

I paused a moment too long. "I'd like my car back."

Migration had pretty much petered out, and I wound up my fieldwork with my classes. Most of the passerines had moved north, ceding the territory to the indigenous species. There was no sense running the mist nets any longer and catching the same birds. Besides, the desert and the high canyons supported a good variety of native birds. There were six or seven species of owls which responded to tapes, and a dozen hummingbirds that came to feeders at Mile-Hi Ranch in Ramsey Canyon and at the cabins in Madera. I wanted to work the alpine zones, too, on Mount Lemmon. There was still plenty to see.

In transition I met my class a few times in the department, and once, after a lecture, Harriet came to see me. "Can we talk, Scott?"

"Of course."

We walked outside and sat on the grass under a palm tree. Harriet had cut her hair short and she looked younger, not so worn. She had a skirt on, too, unusual for her, and she spread it around her when she sat down. "The Appointments Committee is meeting next week," she said. "Do you want to be considered for the job if it's open in the fall?"

"What about Fred? How is he?"

"Nobody knows whether he'll come back. I don't see why the committee wouldn't renew you."

"I'm interested," I said.

"You don't have to decide right away. I'll suggest your name. Of course Fred has seniority."

Harriet was quiet for a moment, and I looked away. "I have something to tell you," I said.

"I already know, Scott."

"You know?"

"Francie was in love with you in Puerto Peñasco. She didn't tell me that in so many words, but I knew. That's why I didn't want to come back with you that morning."

"I thought you were with Ellis."

"I like Ellis. He's a good man, but I don't think it will work out in the long run."

"You make it sound morbid."

Harriet smiled. "At my age I have to be a little morbid. My chances for the things I've wanted are diminishing. I was fond of you, Scott. I won't deny that. You know many things and see so much. I liked that in you because I like it in me. But I felt your uncertainty from the first night we went to Madera Canyon. You didn't want me the way I wanted you."

"There was Demer," I said.

"But when Francie was there, Demer didn't matter. Isn't that true? It's all right. I don't regret my feelings for you. It did me good." She smiled again, sadly. "I know I can feel something. That night I came to your office, I was afraid you'd say no, and I was afraid you wouldn't. We don't always do what's best for ourselves."

"I didn't mean . . ."

"Ellis likes me," Harriet said. "He's invited me to come down there whenever I want to."

"Will you go?"

"I don't think so. Who would stay with my mother?"

Tilghman called again from Guaymas the following Wednesday afternoon. Whether he intended to reach me or to leave a message on the machine was unclear because at the hour he called, I was scheduled to be at the university. I'd cancelled my class and was in bed catching up on the sleep I'd lost over the days with Francie. "Oh, it's you," Tilghman said. "I didn't think you'd be there."

"How are things?"

"More confusion," he said. The wire crackled, and Tilghman waited for quiet. "I'm going to leave your car here," he said. "I'm coming back on the *Estrella*. Can you meet me in Puerto Peñasco?"

"What kind of confusion?"

"I can barely hear you," Tilghman said. "I'll explain later. We should get there by the weekend—Friday or Saturday. Can you find your way to Ellis's?"

"I think I can."

"Have Ellis get in touch with Leonidas. Leonidas will make arrangements in town. And Ellis should call Lorry."

"All right."

There was a crackle and a pause. "Scott?"

"Right here."

"Francie knows the way. Bring her if you want to."

The line went quiet except for a faint hum. I was shaking. I called Ellis right away.

Later that afternoon I drove over to DuPlooy's to watch Francie at work. I liked to see her in the fancy clothes and the makeup she never wore around me. DuPlooy had asked her to work that weekend in a fashion show downtown. It would be a good fee. Francie had already agreed to do it. I wanted DuPlooy to let her off.

When I got there, Francie and DuPlooy were having a disagreement about a dress he wanted her to wear. "What does sex have to do with a leather belt?" That was Francie's position.

"Everything," DuPlooy said.

"No way will I wear that dress."

"Frank, you've done lingerie ads. What's the difference?"

"Those weren't sexy."

"They were extremely sexy, and you got two catalog deals because of those ads. We aren't talking here about anything new.

"I won't show skin for a leather belt."

"Jesus Maria, a moralist. Just wear the dress. Put it on so Scott can give his opinion. Will you agree to arbitration?"

"No." But she put the dress on behind a Japanese screen. She muttered and swore. The zipper zipped. Then she came out into the bright lights.

I took a deep breath. The dress was dark blue, cut low across the front, slit up the sides. Francie wrapped the leather belt tightly around her waist.

"Stunning," I said. "Very nice."

"See?" Francie said to DuPlooy. "He thinks I'm a piece of ass."

"Would you buy the belt?" DuPlooy asked me.

"I'd buy the belt and tie her up with it," I said. "I'd buy three."

DuPlooy groaned. "We're not after perversion," he said. "This is advertising in the twenty-first century. People buy Pepsi and Diet Cokes and Chryslers because beautiful women offer some fantasy. Big deal. Think of it as art."

"It's not art," Francie said. "You can't think of what it isn't. Advertising and art are contradictions in terms."

"Now she's a philosopher," DuPlooy said. "I like the dress. This is my livelihood. If you aren't going to wear the dress, someone else will. You're not the only woman in Tucson with good legs."

"Be my guest," Francie said. She unbuckled the belt and slung it across the room at DuPlooy. Then she tore the dress right down the front.

"Talk to her, Scott," DuPlooy said. "She's throwing away a good career."

"I'll buy silk scarves," I said. "Chains, soft rubber . . ."

Francie had the weekend free.

Chapter nine

It was early Thursday evening when we got off for Puerto Peñasco. We hadn't brought much except a contribution to the food supply—fresh vegetables, pork, potatoes. You could take anything into Mexico, but you could only bring certain items out. That was how the border worked.

The mountains west of Tucson were bathed in a lilac that obliterated rocks, trees, cacti, gullies. The sun outlined the highest ridges in yellow. Lower down, where the light broke through the valleys, the land seemed to glow with its own dusky orange, which highlighted with shadow and color every spike of ocotillo, every leaf of mesquite. The bulky, misshapen saguaros cast long, monstrous shadows over the ground.

We kept the windows of the Rover down to let the breeze flow through. Francie unbuttoned her blouse while we were still in traffic and took off her bra. She let the blouse flap loose around her shoulders.

"Want a beer?" she asked, leaning back toward the cooler.

I touched her bare breast.

"That's not a beer."

"No, thanks," I said. "I don't know what Tilghman has in mind. I want to be ready."

"Then have two beers."

I hadn't been drinking so much the last few days. I don't know why— whether I'd reached a point of alcohol intolerance or was just tired of it. There was no particular resolve. I'd just lost the urge.

"When do you hear about the job in the fall?" she asked. "Is Harriet going to call you?"

"She says it's up to Fred Bentley. I guess I'd like to stay in Tucson."

"What about L.A.?" Francie asked. "Would you like that?"

"Not much."

"Or New York?"

"I'd like New York less than L.A., and L.A. less than Tucson."

"My time has come, Scott. I'm not going back to work for DuPlooy."

"And you're definitely going to L.A.?"

"I'm going to dance. I'll go wherever I have to."

The light ebbed. We accelerated into the diesel smoke of a Mercedes, and I slowed to let the Mercedes pull away. The idea of Los Angeles had no appeal for me except if Francie was there. I thought I could talk her out of going.

Somewhere near Sells a black-and-white bird, big as a hawk, soared low, left to right, toward the road. At the last minute it swerved at us. We were doing about fifty. Francie ducked, but I didn't have that luxury. I had to hold the wheel. The bird wheeled straight at the windshied, then braced its wing and veered upward, skimming over the top of the car.

"Crested Caracara," I said. "National bird of Mexico, the Mexican eagle. It's more a vulture than an eagle. They're more common in south Texas, but you see them now and then here along the border."

Francie looked around to see where the bird had gone. It was flying north over mesquite and cactus.

We passed the shrine a little way ahead, but we didn't stop. The Budweiser bottle was still there. We couldn't tell whether the candle was burning.

We did stop as usual at the Standard station. Lorry was fixing the tire on the blue van. "Somebody wants to buy it," he said. "Can you believe that?" We discussed briefly the latest conditions in Mexico. Things were as bad as ever, he said. Interest rates were high. Inflation was a disgrace. Mexico City had terrible smog and pollution. "Your best buy down there is vanilla," he said. "It's the real thing." He filled the tank to overflowing. Ellis had already called him.

We were the last people to cross the border that day. The Mexican side was closing early. There weren't even any children to wash the windows of the car.

Beyond Sonoita the light faded quickly. I attributed this to the time of day, but Francie insisted it was the way things were in Mexico. It was darker, she said. The land was more dimly lit. Maybe it was the drone of the Land Rover or the unnaturalness of driving across a darkening desert toward the sea, but the dusk made the air tighter around us. I felt something would happen. The long ridge of mountains was blue, edging to black.

That feeling made me talk. I told Francie how Tilghman and I had become friends, how Demer and I had met, and a few details of our time together, mostly the good things. I told her I had no history, and Tilghman thought that was lucky. I had no parents, and with no likeness of myself, who was I? In that small space I made all the confessions I could think to make. It seemed right to warn her.

Chapter ten

A pale silver-blue rimmed the sea. From the bluff at Las Conchas, the sky and the few stars that glimmered through the curtain of the evening merged with the darker sea. The earth was the only vantage point. Ellis brought out tequila and orange juice for me. He hadn't heard from Tilghman. "So he's coming on the boat?" Ellis asked. "Usually Raul takes that leg."

"Tonight or tomorrow."

"I wouldn't count on days. Certainly not on hours."

"I have class Monday," I said. "That's my only deadline, and I could cancel it. Francie's free for the moment."

"The drink isn't very strong," Ellis said. "Where's Frank gone?"

"To the beach."

"Anyway you can take the motorcycle if you have to get back."

The sea was dark blue cloth spread out in wind—smooth, rippling, shadowy. The house under construction next door was an empty cave, but from the next one over, an arc of honey light sprayed out into the dunes.

"Why here?" I asked. "If you have money, why live here?"

"I wanted to get away from that fame Tilghman was talking about. You think I should live in Acapulco? I wanted quiet, not leisure. I wanted to write another book."

"And you've been alone?"

"Not always by choice. I have friends in other places. What do you think of Harriet? My chances, I mean?"

"You'll have to ask Harriet," I said. I lifted my glass. "Here's to Harriet."

"And Francie," Ellis said. We were quiet a moment. "Harriet thinks the problem is that I can't see well enough. That's not true."

"Maybe it's true a little."

"Writing is a slow process. It's a matter of being ready when the words come to you." Ellis smiled sadly. "I've been ready, but . . ." He took a sip of the margarita he'd been drinking.

We watched two shrimp boats round the point and head toward the islands, which floated calmly now in the dark sea like icebergs.

"Let's not forget Tilghman," Ellis said. He lifted his glass again. "He's the best man I know."

Francie came through the dunes like an apparition. She was barefooted, holding an empty Bohemia bottle. I was not a brave man or a foolish one, but that moment at least, I was glad for who I was.

We had a good dinner—the pork we'd brought seasoned and grilled on the barbecue on the terrace. Francie made a salad. Ellis opened a bottle of red wine, but didn't drink much of it. He was working after dinner, he said. He wanted to leave us alone.

After dinner Francie and I did the dishes and then played a game of gin rummy and listened to Ellis's typewriter clicking through the wall.

After the game—Francie won—we went out onto the terrace. It was dark then without a moon, and the sea was easy. The islands were hidden by black haze. Now and then we heard the skirmishes of cats in the darkness. I wondered whether Demer was still with Will Terborg, but that was all. I hoped she was. I felt no jealousy or longing. She was there in Belize on the other side of Mexico, and I was here.

It was Tilghman who still made me uneasy. Some people, and Tilghman was one of them, liked to see themselves as mysteries. They obscured details, kept secrets, explained nothing. They made other people come to them, made others wait to see what would happen next.

"The last time we were here," Francie said, "you were with Harriet."

"Now I'm not. You were with Tilghman. Do you think of that?"

"No."

"Do you wonder what Ellis thinks?"

"I know what Ellis thinks. I called him the day after we buried Inez Montera on the mountain. I didn't want him to hear stories from Tilghman."

"You think Tilghman knows?"

"Tilghman knows."

"He said I should bring you along. Maybe that means he wants to see you."

Francie smiled. "After what he's done?"

"Would it make a difference if he did?"

"Not to me," Francie said, and her voice threw the question back at me.

We went inside and pulled two pads from the window seats and laid them on the floor in front of the screen door. Francie went to the bathroom. I undressed to my underwear and lay down under the blanket. I closed my eyes, and in minutes I was asleep. I dreamed of the trogon. Every year the trogon found its way from the jungles of Central America to the isolated canyons of southeastern Arizona where water ran—Cave Creek, Madera, Ramsey canyons. I couldn't tell which canyon I was in. Perhaps it was a tropical country, because Demer was there. I had walked across the expanse of desert and found a stream.

Demer was standing knee-deep in the moving water, her naked back to me, her dark hair over one shoulder. She looked down into the water, then lifted her head and saw me behind a boulder, hiding. The trogon gave its hoarse call in the distance, but Demer didn't turn to look.

The trogon flew past her over the stream, its green scapulars, black head, coppery tail unmistakable. Red breast. It perched on a snag, the red vivid against the lush trees and the blue sky. Still Demer did not look.

As I watched, the bird's plumage changed from red and green to colors I had never imagined, no hue or shade I'd ever seen, and the bird sang another song, a low, slurred note which rose in pitch and amplified so loudly I almost didn't hear the rifle shots which came from out of nowhere. At first I thought the shots were aimed at this startling new bird, but the bird, scared from its perch, flew straight up into the heavy blue sky, higher and higher. Demer turned toward me. Her mouth was bloody. Blood flowed from her stomach and her breast and down her legs into the swirling water.

I woke and sat up. Ellis was typing. Francie had come out of the bathroom, and the light from the doorway slid across the slate floor and up into the chandelier. She turned off the light and walked toward me, her bare feet silent on the stone.

The dream dissipated. The rush of my breathing eased. What had made me dream such a thing? I lay back down on the pad, felt the ocean breeze come through the screen. In the dark I listened to Francie slide off her shorts. I heard the brush of her blouse against her skin, the sound it made thrown onto the window seat. She knelt on the pad beside me.

"Scott?" She pulled the blanket away. She touched my shoulder, traced her hand across the rounded muscle, across my bare chest. She slid her hand across my underwear, past the touch I wanted, to the inside of my leg. She trailed her fingernails downward and then back up.

I sighed. She didn't stop where I wanted her to. She touched my cheek, my eyes, ran the back of her wrist over my day's beard, scudded her hand hard over my nipple, paused, pressed two fingers on that small point. I couldn't move.

I don't know how long this went on. Long. I was aware Ellis was typing, but I didn't hear it anymore. The longer Francie touched me, the more I ached, the more I wanted her to touch me. But I understood this language. She didn't want me to touch her. She wanted me to want her. With this gentleness she dissolved reason. She didn't hurry. She kissed my nipples, my neck, my lips gently, touched her tongue on my eyes to keep them closed. She trailed her kiss across my lips, nipples, moved her mouth across my stomach. I arced toward her, but reached nowhere.

"Please," I said.

She kissed my hip, lifted me, slid my underwear down, the white cloth moving with her hand. She touched me softly. "Not yet," she said.

She soothed me. I said the words I could think of—all the empty words which I'd learned, but they were lost in the air. I babbled, I whispered, I canted. I sighed yesyesyes. Still she waited. Then all the words left me, and I glimpsed what I must have known but had never listened to: a new vocabulary of no words or names I could think of or speak.

"Now," Francie said. She covered me with her mouth, and I cried out, careless of who heard.

Later in the night the telephone rang. We woke and knew who it was. Ellis stopped typing and came from his room to answer. "Yes," Ellis said. "Yes, all right. When?" There was a pause.

"We'll be there."

He hung up and stood for a moment in the hall light. "That was Leonidas," he said. "Tilghman wants us now."

"Where? What time is it?"

"It's after midnight," Ellis said. "There's been some kind of trouble."

Francie pulled the blanket over her shoulder like a toga and sat up. "I want to go."

"There's only so much room," Ellis said.

"I can go to the boat."

"It's a free country," Ellis said. "This is Mexico."

We dressed quickly, stuffed down a sandwich, filled our pockets and a cardboard box with whatever Ellis had in the refrigerator and cabinets—crackers, oranges, tortilla chips. We were out of the house in ten minutes.

Ellis took the motorcycle so he and Francie could get back in case I had to drive the Land Rover. We followed him. I remember the mist in the dunes, the layer of smooth cloud which caught the headlights and turned the light back on itself. The motorcycle's single headlamp ahead of us weaved haunting shapes in and out of the smoky mist.

I felt strangely calm. I was confident whatever Tilghman asked, I could do and would do, this for the last time.

Ellis lipped the next hill, skated through the fog on the straightaway. Away from the sea, the fog dissipated. We crested another ridge, and the town was in front of us, a wide swath of lights that ebbed into the desert to the north.

The town was still alive. People were walking on the Boulevard Benito Juárez, leaning against cars, smoking, laughing, drinking. Cars cruised the street. A few cars stopped in front of us, and the occupants leaned from the windows to make conversation with pedestrians. We followed the wide body of a Chevrolet, circa 1970. The Rover's speedometer jiggled at fifteen.

Ellis had passed this car, but I couldn't, and I hoped he'd wait for us ahead. Finally the Chevy cleared through a knot of teenagers and gained a little speed. Ellis made a left by Mister Block.

I followed through the shacks north of the harbor. In a few minutes we were at the rickety pier. Tilghman wasn't there. At least we didn't see him right away. The half-ton truck wasn't there, either. But the *Estrella* was. It was one of a half-dozen boats tied up near the end of the boardwalk. I rolled down the window and smelled fish and dust in the air. The ice maker at the fish factory pounded, and the pounding echoed.

"I'll check around," Ellis said. "Tilghmam may be on the boat."

"But where's the truck?"

"We'll find out." Ellis got out and hustled down the rotting boards toward the boat. I thought how easy it would be for the police to discover us. What were we doing there after midnight? The light at the end of the pier illuminated everything. Ellis made no effort to be quiet or stay in the shadows. But no one paid heed.

"This is the place you came before?" Francie asked.

I nodded. "There was a truck here the last time. We were in and out of here in a few minutes."

"With how many?"

"Maybe twenty people—most in the other truck, some in the Land Rover."

Something was wrong with the *Estrella*. It listed slightly and was deeper in the water than the boats beside it. It barely gave at all when Ellis stepped down onto the stern deck. He ducked under the nets and went across the deck toward a slit of yellow light on the next boat over. We waited five minutes that seemed like twenty.

Once the door opened, and shadows spread around the light. Someone moved to the *Estrella* and back again. Francie and I got out of the Land Rover. Then headlights came down the road through the warehouses. The lights caromed from a corrugated tin roof, then like tracer bullets from a stack of plastic pipe. The truck appeared, and in a second or two, Raul pulled up beside us.

He stepped down quickly from the cab. His eyes were hollow spaces in a face smudged with black. He pulled a few packages from the cab and handed them to me.

"¿Qué paso?" Francie asked.

"Fuego," Raul said. "Hubo un incendio en el bote." He handed another package to Francie.

"They had a fire on the boat," Francie said.

We followed Raul down the pier. Raul jumped onto the *Estrella*, pier to rail, and ducked under the cables.

The deck was full of debris—metal parts, charred wood, tools. Raul crossed to the next boat while we waited. A tarp covered one corner of the stern of the *Estrella*, maybe where the fire had been.

The other boat was the *Pez Gordo*. Ellis took the packages

211

from Raul, and Raul came back and got the ones Francie carried. Francie got aboard the *Estrella* and took the packages from me.

"Over here," Ellis said. A high-powered lantern shone from the cabin below decks on the *Pez Gordo*.

The smell of burn was strongest near the cabin of the *Estrella*. I looked into the dark hole of the engine room, but even leaning down, I couldn't see much except the outline of the big diesel engine and the space that housed it. But that was where the fire had been.

Francie went aboard the *Pez Gordo*. For a moment I paused, stared back at the Land Rover near the cinder-block shed. Cables and riggings of a dozen boats crisscrossed the air. Then I noticed the arc light shiver on the tarp. The tarp moved. I heard hushed voices and went over and lifted the edge.

To see the faces was all it took. Years later, when all these events come to mind, I see those faces first. The faces. Perhaps the police become inured to seeing suffering in the human eye, or maybe in war, soldiers become accustomed to faces in pain. But not I. These were children's faces—ten of them or so: filthy, hungry, bruised, scared, oil stained, burned. But alive. Their eyes turned up to me who had let in the light.

"Scott," Francie called. "Come on." I lowered the tarp slowly.

Two children had been killed in the fire, three others injured. Tilghman had been burned badly, too. His face was seared, and his right shoulder and arm. His hair was singed off one side of his head. The children had been down in the engine room because the *Estrella* had been approached by the Mexican Coast Guard. It was dangerous in the engine room, but where else was there? They carried shrimp in the hold as a cover.

The Coast Guard had circled a few times and asked questions across the water, then had finally left without boarding. The fire had broken out immediately afterward. One of the children had pulled on some wires and hoses, including the fuel line. A spark had ignited the gas. Tilghman and Raul had doused the fire quickly—Tilghman had gone in first. They were afraid the Coast Guard would see smoke, but it was twilight, and the smoke was camouflaged. Or they were lucky. The children had got out, all but the two boys who'd been on the other side of the flames.

The smoke had killed them. Their bodies were on the *Estrella* under a blanket on the bow. The three others who had been burned—two girls about fourteen and a boy of six, the little brother of one of the dead—had been closest to the flash fire. The girls had been burned on their arms and backs, the boy on his face.

Tilghman had tended the children's wounds and his own as best he could on the boat. He'd washed them with cold water, bandaged them with strips of a clean shirt. Raul had fixed the engine. That had taken three hours of jury-rigging wires, splicing hoses, and manufacturing a new fuel line. They'd limped the last sixty miles into port.

Closer in, they'd radioed Leonidas to meet them with a doctor. They hadn't been able to give details for fear of a Coast Guard monitor. That was one of the ways the Mexican government tried to stem the flow of drugs. The doctor had met them, but until she got there, hadn't known the extent of the wounds. She'd sent Raul to get new bandages and antiseptics from the pharmacy. That had taken a good hour. It was late. Leonidas had called Ellis.

The doctor, who spoke good English, thought Tilghman should go to the hospital.

"I'll go in the States," Tilghman said.

"I mean now," the doctor said.

Tilghman shook his head. "We can't wait."

"We can put the children at my place," Ellis said. "We'll watch closely and then move them a few at a time."

"It's foolish to risk infection of these wounds," the doctor said. "The children's wounds, too."

Tilghman shook his head. "There are twenty-three children," he said. "We have to take them all together." He turned and looked at each of us, as if he was including us in the matter at hand. "There are people waiting in Casa Grande and Phoenix. Everything is arranged."

I stepped forward. "The children need rest," I said. "What if . . ." But I stopped there. Tilghman's expression made me.

"The children are already dead," he said. "Think of them that way. All these children are dead, and there are others behind them, too. Remember that. We have a chance to rescue a few of them. We have to go now."

I saw what Tilghman meant. I saw the faces under the tarp and the bandaged, scared face of the little boy and the scared faces of the two girls. I always remember the faces. And if Tilghman, tired as he was, and burned, could go now, then we could all go.

Tilghman insisted on taking the dead children with us. They had no scars on them, no blood, no burns. Their bodies were already stiff. We laid them in the back of the Land Rover and covered them with a blanket.

The doctor had given the injured ones a sedative, and we put them alongside the bodies of the other two. Besides these five I took another four of the children, and Francie, who spoke Spanish, came along to comfort them. She held two girls on her lap in the front seat. The rest of the children rode in the truck. Tilghman drove. Raul rode in back.

The highway was the same one to Sonoita. I followed the truck as before. Ellis came along on his motorcycle in case there was an emergency and someone had to go for help.

The Rover smelled of burns and ointment and sweat. Francie spoke to the children who were awake—did they have brothers and sisters? What did they like to do? She sang songs to them, while the Land Rover clanked and whined in the darkness.

As I drove, I thought about the journey the children had taken. I imagined them then as I would always imagine them from what little I knew. They had come from the decimated villages Demer had written about—from families whose mothers and fathers had been killed by death squads, from hovels in the slums of the capital cities. These children had been spared, but, as Tilghman said, there were others left behind still waiting.

Chapter eleven

We split up in Sonoita. Raul and Tilghman went the back way. Ellis and I stayed on the main road through town. Ellis pulled over by some shops while I went ahead. We met up again on the highway going west. Most of the children in the Land Rover were asleep, some leaning against the side windows, some braced against each other. The two girls in Francie's lap were awake, though, staring out at the blank road. I wondered what the world seemed like to them after midnight, heading toward a country they had only heard of.

We turned off at the same place as before, into the brushy country north of the highway. We scraped over rocks, angled into the deep moon that was rising over the Ajos. The children woke from the jostling and bouncing, and Francie whispered to them in Spanish.

We came to the border at the same strand of wire. Tilghman drove through the fence and went on ahead. Ellis and I, with the headlights off, went back and spliced the fence. When we were through, I shone the flashlight on the ground. There weren't any new footprints I could see, and no snakes. A few drops of rain had fallen weeks ago and had left inch-wide circles in the dust.

"Do you think Tilghman is all right?" I asked Ellis. "Maybe Raul should drive."

"Tilghman is Tilghman," Ellis said. "You can ask and see what he says."

"I will when we stop at the spring," I said.

But Tilghman didn't stop at the spring. He rolled past, and we only saw his headlights along the road in the distance.

I pulled over, and so did Ellis, who edged beside us out of our

215

dust. "Maybe he thinks the truck's so slow he ought to make some headway," Ellis said. "Or he wants to get there. I don't blame him for that."

"We'll catch up," I said. "I think we should see how the children are."

Two of the children needed to pee. We passed around the little food we'd brought. One boy asked Francie if we'd arrived.

There weren't so many sounds that night. Maybe the frogs had found mates. A few insects stirred. Once an Elf Owl called from a dark clump of organ-pipe cactus nearby, and when I shone the flashlight in its eyes, it didn't call again. The moon washed the spring with beautiful shadows.

After Quitobaquito the road was rougher than I remembered it. Stones cracked underneath the car. We jerked over rocks, slid on loose gravel, pitched sideways toward the ditches. Maybe I drove too fast, but I held the wheel. Once we ran over a snake, leaving its body with the nerves still firing, squirming in the road.

Ellis made better time on two wheels, and he went ahead to catch Tilghman. After a mile or two, we could see neither the motorcycle nor the truck—the road rose and fell and skirted the hills. The land changed, but it stayed the same, too. Around each bend was a new panorama of sandy washes and rock outcroppings, tangles of paloverde and cactus along the pale road. We had a clean perspective of the Ajos and the Puerto Blancos and the Quitobaquito Hills, and higher, the moon surrounded by a pelting of stars. It was what I had seen before, but at the same time, it wasn't.

I couldn't help thinking of the longer future, the years when things would be right again. Tilghman and I would talk in the way his father and he never had, and the way my father and I never had. The pain of Demer's leaving would be gone. I would have forgiven her. Something would happen between Francie and me, or it wouldn't. We would love each other as I dreamed it, or we wouldn't. The two dead boys in the back of the Rover would be buried, and crosses would be set over their graves and candles lit for them. The others would recover and lead lives far away. They'd have houses, jobs, wives and husbands, children of their own who would speak English and sit at desks in classrooms. Or not.

I was thinking these things as the desert softened in the moonlight. The rugged granite ridges were smoother hills. The thorny cacti were clumps of gray-green with creamy leaves. We had just emerged from a moonlit white wash and had climbed at an angle to the hill—who could say how far in such a light? The road straightened out, white in front of us.

Francie leaned with the two girls on her lap toward the dash. "Someone's coming," she said. We were maybe a quarter of a mile into the straightaway, and a single headlight wobbled toward us from the right.

"Ellis," I said. I pulled the Land Rover to the side of the road and snapped off the headlights. They had caught Tilghman: that was my first thought.

Francie turned around and spoke to the children.

The light jumped and settled as it cut a line in front of the far hill. Then it curved. It swung to the right, cast its beam into the air, curled farther around until it began moving away from us again, around the flank of the hill.

Appearances deceived. I started up slowly and drove the straight road another mile. We banked down into another wide wash, ascended the next rise, curved back on the U where we had seen Ellis coming at us. Stopping had cost us time. We were a good way behind the others by then, and when we crested the next ridge, doing maybe fifteen on the grade, Ellis's headlight was far away below us, coming up on the lights of the rangers' houses.

"Housing compound," I said. Then I pointed south toward four bright arc lights. "Over there are the monument headquarters and the visitor center. There's a frontage road we have to use from the houses to the main road."

"How far to Lukeville?" Francie asked.

"Five, maybe six, miles."

We could see the sporadic lights at the distant horizon. But we couldn't see the truck. Tilghman must have been farther on near the houses. The last time, I remembered Tilghman had said to turn off the headlights making the pass through the trees.

I shifted to second, braked for the downhill. Then the truck's headlights came on. They fanned out into the margins of brush on the frontage road near where there was a stop sign. Tilghman ran through the stop and kept on toward the visitor center. I let the Rover pick up speed.

Below us Ellis slid under the cover of the trees around the houses, the lone headlight flashing intermittently through leaves, splashing out onto lawns and hedges. Tilghman had reached the visitor center and turned east toward the intersection of the monument entrance and the main highway toward Why.

We bounced on a big rock. A child woke and cried, raising her head up over the backseat. "Esta bien," Francie said, and she smoothed the girl's hair.

I turned for a second to look at the girl's face. Her eyes were sleepy wide, glassy in the pale moonlight. Francie lifted the girl's hair from her face.

When I turned back to the road, everything had changed. That is how I remember it—one second the girl's face, and the next—everything altered. Tilghman was gaining momentum on the highway. Ellis had just veered left at the visitor center, not far behind Tilghman. We were as before, coming down the hill through rocks and cactus. But there was a new array of lights. Lights were on at the rangers' compound. Headlights of trucks moved among the trees. The red flashing lights of Park Service trucks whirled through the air.

"Stop," I said, though I was the one I spoke to. I stopped and turned off the headlights.

Chapter twelve

At the time it was hard to tell what was happening. I prepared to turn around and make a run for it—a useless gesture, I knew, if we'd been spotted. Where would we go? Away. Where we'd come from. We'd go back to the spring, maybe to Mexico. But we couldn't vanish.

The rangers' trucks emptied from the compound and headed south toward the visitor center. We couldn't tell how many men there were or whether they were armed, but there were five trucks. Presumably there was a linkup with the border patrol at Lukeville and with the state police in Ajo. Ellis had a lead of maybe a half mile, and he must have seen the red flashers from the frontage road. But Tilghman was farther ahead. He couldn't know what was going on. He'd already disappeared over a low rise on the main highway. We couldn't see him.

Ellis gave it gas and the motorcycle jumped ahead. We heard the engine all the way up on the hill where we were. He ran north and cleared the low rise. The trucks giving pursuit turned onto the main highway opposite the visitor center. That was all we saw. We figured we hadn't been noticed, so we turned around. It took me five arcs in the narrow road, and each time I shifted from forward to reverse, the gears shuddered. We headed back up the hill slowly, still without our headlights on.

At the top of the hill, I stopped again. There were more flashing lights, probably the border patrol, coming from the south. We drove to Quitobaquito and spent the night there, parked in the brush behind the single cottonwood tree. We rolled down the windows for the air that ebbed and flowed from the hills. The children slept. Francie dozed a little in the driver's seat, but I sat outside on the hood of the Rover, listening to the faint barking of coyotes on distant ridges. Toward morning two deer picked their way through cactus and moon shadows to drink at the spring. Their pale bodies moved like boulders in the light.

I wished I had an answer to fear. Fear was its own punishment, and I longed to be rid of it. But I didn't know how. I sat that night on the hood of the Rover shivering with cold, while the stars shifted and the moon leaned into the black silhouettes of the mountains.

In the morning before first light, Francie changed the bandages of the three injured children, and I doled out what food we had left. Then we moved on. We took the southern loop toward Lukeville. It was longer and came out in town, but it was better than going past the rangers' houses and through the monument, and better than retreating to Mexico. I thought for certain the rangers would check that road first thing that morning.

The terrain was the same as on the other road, but instead of the serene landscape under moonlight, we moved through a stark, alien territory, barren as another planet. At Lukeville no one paid us any attention.

We headed north, paralleling the telephone lines. Cars passed us going south toward Mexico—three travel vans, five or six sedans, two border-patrol trucks. A couple of cars with Sonoran plates overtook us going north. The first sun nudged the day toward hot.

Nothing looked different at the entrance to the monument. There were a few cars already parked outside the visitor center. Off to the west some light clouds expanded into the blue sky. The sun flashed from the tin roof of a maintenance shed. We could see the houses among the trees. We kept on straight. Ajo, 32; Gila Bend, 74. At that time of the morning, the mountains were just beginning to absorb the coming heat.

Six miles past the monument, we came to flares set up on the downslope of a hill. A state police cruiser was parked on the left with flashers on. Francie told the children to stay down. We slowed. Another state patrolman, directing the one-lane traffic, motioned us forward. We fell into line behind a battered Pontiac. A police cruiser with flashers on was parked off the highway on the right, not far from a green Park Service truck overturned in the rocky scree and cactus a little way beyond. A tow truck from Ajo was winching it with a cable. Across the road were two more border-patrol trucks and a brown van. A second patrolman waved us on past the line of oncoming cars stopped in the left lane.

"There's Ellis's motorcycle," Francie said. "My God, look."

I couldn't see it well because I had to drive. The motorcycle was behind the brown van, banged up pretty badly. We didn't see Ellis or the half-ton truck. With the children in the car, we couldn't stop.

Lorry wasn't at the Standard station. I waited at the pump for a minute, and when he didn't come out, I went into the office. A boy, maybe seventeen, was leaning back in the office chair with his feet on the desk, watching cartoons on a small TV. It was 9:45 in the morning.

"Where's Lorry?" I asked.

The boy looked at me as if I was asking his IQ. "We got this accident down the road," the boy said. "And the old man takes off."

"We passed the accident," I said.

"Some fools. I don't know. Probably somebody drinking. Somebody was hurt."

"You know where I can reach Lorry?"

"He's up on the reservation. Went up there with the big truck. Says he wants to salvage some heap." The boy looked back at the TV. "I don't see what he does it for. He wasn't even here when they called to tow. They got somebody out of Ajo. No money, but what do I care?"

"When'll he be back?"

"Afternoon," the boy said.

The cartoon figures on the screen were characters I'd never seen before—flying dinosaurs, a boy with a laser gun. Outside a car pulled up to the gas pump, and the bell in the office rang twice. The boy didn't move. The man at the pump got out of his car and stared toward the window.

"People always want American gas," I said.

"Shit," the boy said. "Same gas in Mexico."

I went around the desk and yanked the TV plug from the wall socket. I picked up the TV and threw it on the floor. The shell splintered and the picture tube broke.

"Hey," the boy said.

"You have a customer," I said. "I'm a friend of Lorry's. No wonder he has such a hard time out here."

The only place I could think of to go with the children was Casa Grande. I had the directions in my head, and we rode the dirt roads of the reservation in nervous silence. Something had happened to Ellis. We'd have called the hospital, but I thought we'd wait to see what they knew in Casa Grande. And at least one of the rangers' trucks had rolled.

It took us a long time to get through those few miles.

Martha had been watching for us out the window, and as soon as we drove up, she came out into the yard. Her eyes were slitted against the sun, and her hair was pulled back from her face. She'd had a long night, too. "I was hoping you'd make it," she said. "You'd better drive into the garage." She opened the bay, and I pulled the Rover in.

"Did the truck get here?" I asked.

"They made it," she said. "We've sent most of the children on to Phoenix already, and Lorry has a couple of them out on the reservation. We still have three here. Two of them are waiting for their sister who's with you."

"We have three kids hurt," I said.

The woman nodded. "Raul told us. We got hold of the doctor, but we didn't know when you'd get here. He can come over right away."

"What about Ellis?"

The woman looked at me. "What about him?"

"We saw his motorcycle wrecked and a ranger's truck sideways on its top."

"Raul came by himself," Martha said. "They got chased, he said, and Tilghman and Ellis went back. Raul didn't know what had happened."

"And Tilghman?"

"We haven't heard."

Francie and Martha helped the three injured children, and I got the others out of the Rover and into the kitchen. Martha had made peanut-butter sandwiches and lemonade. The children sat on the floor and ate. I went back out and carried the two bodies to a corner of the garage in front of the Rover, where I laid each of them on the cool cement. They weren't heavy. I didn't look at their faces.

Later on the doctor came. He dressed the children's wounds and said he'd make inquiries about Ellis. Then I slept. The back room was small, just big enough for one double bed. I remember the sounds of flies, a towhee's singing. I heard Francie's voice and the voices of the children in the living room, and Martha's voice—all the voices blended into the gray air.

I slept the kind of half sleep of the very tired. I saw images floating in the air. I couldn't identify them—were they birds? They alit in a grassy field. I was looking for something without knowing what it was. The dry yellow grass made a harsh noise in the wind, brittle, then eased to a song of sighs.

I heard the telephone ring and more voices and the door opening.

"Scott?" Francie sat down on the bed. I wanted to hold her. "Wake up, Scott," she said. "Tilghman's dead."

Chapter thirteen

Ellis was in the hospital in Ajo for five days before he was moved to Tucson. The doctor at Casa Grande hadn't found out much over the phone except the extent of Ellis's injuries—a broken leg and collarbone, lacerations, a concussion. He didn't know how serious the concussion was. Ellis was under sedation and wasn't having visitors.

We knew even less about Tilghman. The Tucson paper carried this:

UNIDENTIFIED MAN KILLED ON MONUMENT

An unidentified Caucasian man was killed early Saturday morning when he was struck by a ranger's truck on Highway 85 in the Organ Pipe Cactus National Monument. The ranger was traveling north in pursuit of suspected drug traffickers when the accident occurred. Also injured was Ellis Carmichael, no address given, and monument ranger Keith Miller. Carmichael was taken by ambulance to the Ajo Medical Center, where he was listed in fair condition. Miller was treated at the scene and released. State police and drug-enforcement officers are still investigating the incident.

Tilghman was dead. Where there had been someone—acts, words, thoughts—now there was space. Still, even in that absence, I was linked to him, not just because of Francie, though certainly that was true, but because of the past. I had counted on Tilghman to listen to me. I had wanted to listen to him.

I called the state-police barracks in Ajo and asked about the accident. A friend of mine was missing, I told them. He should have been back from Puerto Peñasco where he'd gone for the weekend. Did they have any reports? I gave them a description of Tilghman.

The body had been sent to the morgue in Tucson, and I went down to identify it. It was Tilghman, a version of Tilghman. He had a bruised, purple face, a battered chest, and his eyes were closed. A man wasn't the same dead. I nodded. "That's him."

The investigators interviewed me. Who was Tilghman? What was he doing on that highway at night? Who was Ellis Carmichael?

I lied as much as I told the truth. I said I knew Ellis only slightly. I'd read his book. Tilghman had gone to Puerto Peñasco for the weekend to drink Mexican beer and eat flounder and sit in the sun. His car had been making noises, so he'd left it with me in Tucson—a Land Rover. He'd put a note on the kitchen table that he'd be back Sunday night.

Who was he going to visit?

I didn't know.

"What was a man doing in the desert with no identification, no keys, no money?"

"Maybe he was robbed."

"There was not a trace of alcohol," the investigator said. "Are you sure he went to Mexico to drink beer?"

"Maybe he never got to Mexico. How did the ranger hit him? What happened?"

I knew when I left the investigator's office, they weren't done with me. They knew a truck had disappeared. From phone records they'd figure Tilghman and Ellis were friends. Maybe they'd trace other numbers. Francie's name might surface, though because of me she had an easy alibi. We didn't know who else they might turn up—Raul, Lorry, Martha. Demer's name came to mind.

We were cautious about seeing Ellis. We knew the police had questioned him, and he'd referred all questions to his lawyer. Lawyers were best at delay and obfuscation. The only person who could safely visit Ellis was Harriet, and Harriet enjoyed the intrigue. She knew enough to be on our side, though not enough to give the police much. Maybe reading Ellis's book had given her the same fighting spirit about this that she had about whales.

The danger, of course, was that the police would believe what Ellis had been doing was worse than it was. They were likely to be more tenacious finding out about drug trafficking than about bringing a few Guatemalan and Salvadoran children across the border. In that sense telling the truth made some sense. It would have eased the situation. But there was more to it. By confessing we would be endangering more people than ourselves.

"Ellis says there haven't been any charges filed," Harriet said. "The worst they have so far is entering the country illegally. His story is that the border was closed, so he rode his bike a few miles west. He knew Quitobaquito was close to the road."

"And the truck?"

"What truck?" Harriet asked. "No one's mentioned a truck."

It was almost two weeks before Ellis was released from the hospital in Tucson. Then, finally, we got this story: He'd seen the rangers' trucks coming out of the housing compound that night and had made the obvious deductions. Someone had seen him or the truck, or heard them. He'd been scared first and thought of running. He'd wound the bike up to eighty. You can run, he'd said, but you cannot hide. The road was straight all the way to Ajo. But he hadn't known what to think about the truck. The truck could only do about forty-five, tops.

At best, when he caught Tilghman, only two or three of them could ride on the bike. He'd thought about that racing down the highway. Whom to take? He'd thought of pulling over, too, giving himself up. They didn't have anything on him. But what if they'd gone after the truck?

He'd caught Tilghman in a couple of minutes and motioned for him to pull over. There wasn't time to discuss anything. He'd only been able to give Tilghman the gist of the pursuit.

"It was as if Tilghman already knew what to do," Ellis said. "He just *knew*. He grabbed the lantern from the front seat, that bright one we'd had down in the boat. 'Maneja,' he told Raul. '¡Vamanos!' He jumped out of the truck, threw his wallet and keys on the floor, and took off running. Raul jumped over into the driver's seat and revved the engine.

"I didn't know what to make of it. I remember the truck headlights shining in the red reflectors on the bridge—they'd stopped by a bridge over a wash. The lights skimmed across the metal posts. When Raul shifted to second, the lights dimmed and surged. I didn't know what else to do but turn around and go get Tilghman.

"He'd covered a quarter mile by the time I reached him. He was sprinting, holding the unlit lantern in one hand. He had on dark clothes, so even in the moonlight I barely saw him. I shouted for him to get on. He told me to turn off my fucking headlight. What was I trying to do?

"I turned off the light. We were coming up a long incline. I could feel the engine pull, and I shifted down. We went through a pocket of cooler air. The yellow highway line, the dotted white passing stripes—I remember all that. The red flashers and head-lights appeared over the rise—just halos.

"Tilghman moved to the left of the center line. 'Wait till I give the signal,' he shouted. I didn't understand. I moved the bike toward him, up close, but he motioned me away. 'Other side,' he shouted.

"Then I got what he was doing. At least I thought so. I moved to the right of the center line a little ways. We were going to decoy the lead truck—make the driver think there were two headlights coming straight down the middle of the highway.

"The flashers showed first, then the headlights funneled up through the air. When the high beams crested the hill, Tilghman gave the word. He turned on the lantern and I snapped on the bike's headlight. You could feel the oncoming truck hesitate. The driver lowered his beams. Tilghman weaved left, and I went with him. Then we weaved right. The driver of the truck must have braked. He must have thought something was up, because he slowed way down. We were pretty close, then, maybe fifty yards apart. Tilghman and I swerved left again, right, left. The truck angled off toward the side of the road. I was surprised when it went up on two wheels. It hung that way for a few seconds and then caught a washout and tipped over. It rolled once. The flashing light smashed—you could hear that.

"We didn't have time to do anything. The next truck came right behind. He'd seen what had happened and slowed, or maybe he saw us. Tilghman and I had split up by then. But the second truck was *there*. It came down the wrong side of the highway and was smack in front of me. He braked and I heard the tires screech; then the truck came around sideways. I veered right and felt the bike go off the road. The engine surged in midair. I remember trying to keep the wheels straight and thinking I was dead."

That was as much as Ellis knew. He'd hit the ground hard and bounced through brush until the bike spun down. The pain in his leg was all he remembered.

We learned the rest finally from the police reports and from the statements of the rangers at the inquest. The second truck, the one that had forced Ellis off the road, had stopped on the pavement backward. Two men had been in that truck, and both of them were shaken up, but okay. They'd seen Ellis fly off the road and hit the ground and fall. Then they'd jumped out to wave down the others coming behind. Farther up the hill they'd heard a snap like a tree limb breaking, and brakes squealing. The lights had stopped except for the flashers.

Perry Ellman, a ranger from Chula Vista, California, had hit Tilghman.

Q: *You were the driver, Mr. Ellman?*

A: We came over the hill, and the first thing we saw right off was Jeff spin out on the highway. We never saw the first truck go over.

Q: *By "we" you mean you, the driver?*

A: Yeah, there were three of us in the truck, but I mean me. I never saw the lead truck go off the road. I saw the headlights cut out into the brush, but it had already turned over. Things happened so fast.

Q: *Let's slow them down.*

A: Jeff's headlights did a near three-sixty and angled back toward us to the left—our left, that is. *My* left. I only got a glimpse of the motorcycle. That was off the highway pretty far.

Q: *So you saw the motorcycle?*

A: Out in the cactus, yes, sir.

Q: *How fast were you going?*

A: You mean me?

Q: *What was your speed?*

A: I guess coming up the hill on the other side, we were doing maybe seventy, just keeping up. It's an '80 Chevy truck with some hard miles on it. I had the flasher on. At the top of the hill, we braked right away, seeing Jeff and what all was going on ahead. The man was right in front of the truck when we hit him.

Q: *So how fast?*

A: Maybe about fifty.

Q: *What do you mean he was right there in front of the truck?*

A: I mean right there. It was like a deer had jumped out from the brush at the side of the road. I didn't have time to adjust. I didn't even put on the brake.

Q: If you were looking at the motorcycle . . .

A: He ran in front of the truck. Steve'll tell you. I didn't have a chance to blink. One second he's not there, then he was. Boom.

This statement was corroborated by Steve McKeown and Feanie Lewis, the passengers in Ellman's cab. They hadn't seen Tilghman, either, until just before impact. McKeown said Tilghman had run into the path of the truck deliberately.

A: I was sitting far right and I saw him first. Feanie was next to me and Perry was driving. I happened to be looking more to the right, and I saw this man running—staggering off on the shoulder. He was carrying something that looked like a weapon, and I thought, "oh, oh, where's my pistol?" But later we found out it was a lantern. He threw it at us, but it bounced under the truck. Then he jumped out into the road at us.

Q: And you hit him?

A: Perry did. If you ask me, the man hit us. That's how it was really.

Raul had continued on to the Standard station. By the time the highway patrol from Ajo had gone past, the half-ton was in one of the garage sheds, and the children had been transferred to the salvage rig and the blue van. No one had been looking for those vehicles, which were the ones Lorry and Raul drove to Casa Grande.

Chapter fourteen

Tilghman's mother wanted him buried in St. Cloud in the family plot, but we discovered Tilghman's will and instructions in the event of his death in his safety-deposit box. They'd been written that spring. He wanted to be cremated and buried with Inez Montera on the top of Mount Wrightson.

Mount Wrightson was national forest so burial was prohibited, but we got permission to scatter his ashes. There was no hurry for that. We wanted to wait and see whether Ellis would recuperate enough to go up with us. And I thought Demer would want to come.

I called the pension where she'd been staying at San Ignacio in Belize, and when I got hold of the owner, I put Francie on the phone. Demer wasn't there. The man remembered her, but he had no idea where she'd gone. She hadn't left an address. He knew she'd left with somebody called Guillermo, but not when. He didn't keep a guest register.

The U.S. Embassy in Belize knew nothing about her. Visas weren't necessary for travel in Belize. Guatemala was a different story. I should call the Guatemalan Embassy for information. Yes, it was possible to enter Guatemala illegally, but it wasn't advisable. The border checkpoint was on alert, and there were random checks along the roads.

Francie telephoned the Guatemalan Embassy in Belize and in Washington, but could never find out whether they had a record of Demer.

After that I called all the Terborgs in Chattanooga. It didn't take too long to get Will's number. Will's mother answered. I explained who I was, how Will was the friend of a friend, and that he and Demer had been traveling together in Belize.

"He was alone last we knew," his mother said.

"I'm trying to reach the woman," I said. "Demer Hayes."

"Will hasn't written so much in the last several months," his mother said. "We got a postcard from Belmopan two weeks ago. That's been all. It'll be his sister's birthday on May seventeenth, and he always calls."

"If he calls, tell him to ask Demer to call Scott. I'll give you my number."

"Scott . . ."

"Scott Talmadge. I'm in Tucson. (602) 555-8645."

"Who is Demer?" Will's mother asked.

"Demer Hayes. She's my ex-wife. A friend of ours died and left her a half-a-million dollars."

Tilghman had left Demer the money. He left Francie the house. He left me Zapata and the Land Rover and the photographs of Francie.

Grief naturally tilts perception. Tilghman had offered me a sounding of myself, and that was what I missed most, especially at first. It was like being without the place that echoes. But after that I began to think about it in a different way. Francie and I didn't talk about it much. In some ways that was better. Each of us had to find a balance for what had happened. Whatever motives Tilghman had had, whatever his life had been, couldn't be changed anymore except in the ways we changed it ourselves by looking back. Francie had lived with Tilghman almost two years, had watched him day to day, had suffered his arrogance and his silence in close quarters. Tilghman had elicited from her that initial, powerful love, then anger, and finally hopelessness. But she still loved him in ways that never quite ended. I felt that way about Demer, too.

Perhaps Francie was puzzled, and that was why she didn't say much. I read that in her expressions sometimes, in her pauses at certain moments when Zapata barked, or when she read something in a book or a newspaper, or when she looked at the wall in the backyard.

For myself I saw Tilghman in many attitudes. I remembered the time on the island when he'd asked me to swim with him across the channel. Or the time he had been alone in the yard, thinking about the girl with the sweaters and coats and the beret. Or the moment in the cabin of the *Pez Gordo* when he had insisted on taking the children across the border. I thought sometimes I understood what Tilghman had been up against—too late, then, of course—that fear of suffocation, a past dominated by a father who left him nowhere to go, and his own perceived failure. He had swum the strait and dived from the cliff to show he could do such things. Failure was the veil he was trying to bring down and which always fluttered above the magician's bullet.

But had he been a failure?

Ellis recuperated slowly. He was in the hospital a long time, and then, for outpatient therapy, he stayed with Francie and me at Tilghman's for another month. Harriet came to see him every day. She brought food and books and her final exams to grade. During this time she sent her mother to her brother's in Chicago.

The term ended. Whether my classes had learned anything about birds, whether they took from our hours in the field any useful lessons, I could only hope. They said they liked the class, and I liked them. Teaching suited me. It was work that mattered.

One Sunday in early June, Demer called. She was in Tennessee with Will, and she'd just got the message about Tilghman. I was shocked to hear that familiar voice, and surprised, too, at my recognition of it after so long. Her voice had an odd cadence. And yet though it was the voice I remembered, it was a voice that was different, too. She wanted to know, first of all, about Tilghman.

I told her what had happened, as near as I knew. I told her about the accident on the boat, and our flight across the border at Quitobaquito, and the pursuit by the monument rangers and then the border patrol.

"You were there, Scott?" she asked.

"I was there more than once," I said. "But that night I was a little behind the truck on a hill above the rangers' compound. We saw most of it, except the last."

"Who's we?" Demer asked.

"Francie and the children we had in the Land Rover. When Tilghman got to Puerto Peñasco after the fire at sea . . ." I paused, realizing that what I knew and what I could tell her were different. Too much had happened, and over the telephone, I could not say the right words. "Anyway there were children in the truck Tilghman was in, and he didn't want the truck to be stopped. It was at night. Tilghman sent the truck ahead with someone else, and not long after, one of the rangers ran over Tilghman by accident."

There was a long pause on Demer's end. "You mean he was flagging down the ranger?"

"We don't know. Maybe something like that. All of the children made it through. Another friend of ours was hurt pretty badly." My voice trailed off, then rose again. "Did you hear about the half million?"

"I got the message. If that's true, the money isn't for me. It's for the work. What's happened to the lifeline?"

"Raul's in Guaymas," I said. "That's the last I've heard from people here. They can't cross anymore at Quitobaquito. But I understand Raul has some contacts down near Bisbee."

"The problem is that what we're doing is such a small part. It's like a thread that barely starts a tapestry. Will and I are thinking we need to be in Washington. That's where the real trouble lies. The government doesn't believe the horror is true."

I thought of the children's faces under the tarp. "I believe," I said.

"Good."

"So you're all right?" I asked Demer.

"I'm tired, but all right."

There was a pause.

"Tilghman . . . We're going to carry Tilghman's ashes up a mountain out here. We'll wait for you if you want to come out."

"No, Scott. I can't. No."

"I thought I would ask."

"Tilghman was a friend," Demer said. "I trusted him, and I sent him my journals. I sent them to him because he already knew so much about the work. And who else could I send them to? I couldn't keep them, traveling the way I was. I don't know what I would have done without Tilghman."

"But what?"

"I was afraid of him. I don't know why." Demer coughed and then continued. "Did you know Tilghman flew down to Costa Rica once? It was just after he'd moved to Tucson. Even now I'm not sure what he wanted. He wanted to see me—that's what he said. He wanted to learn about what I was doing. It was Tilghman's idea to run the lifeline."

"Tilghman's?"

"No one else could have done what he did. I knew a few people in Costa Rica and Guatemala. Some other workers knew people in Honduras and El Salvador. We would meet many more people as we went from place to place. He wanted to be able to give them something. Meanwhile Tilghman worked things out in Mexico. I came up once as far as Manzanillo to make sure what I was saying to these people was true. And it was. It was all true."

Demer stopped, and I knew she wanted to get off the phone. I had a hundred questions I might have asked her, and I thought of more later. But I asked only one. "What about Inez Montera?"

"Inez," Demer said, "my friend, Inez. One of the *'disappeared'*. God, when will someone do something?"

I was going to tell her about the finger bone and Tilghman's idea—or was it obsession?—and what I knew from reading her journals and letters to him. But all that seemed gone now, part of the past. Instead I asked, "So you won't come out for Tilghman?"

"I can't, Scott."

Demer and I made small talk for another few minutes. I told her about Francie. She said Will had got sick, and that's why they'd come home. But it was time for a rest anyway. Neither of us knew what would happen, but we were content for the moment. I didn't say much more. I told Demer the lawyer would write her about the money if she had an address. She gave me Will's.

"Do you want me to send your journals?"

"I'd like them back. Yes."

"Stay in touch," I said.

"I will."

When we went up Mount Wrightson finally, there were only three of us. Ellis couldn't go because his leg hadn't healed right, and he had to have corrective surgery. Harriet decided she hadn't known Tilghman well enough not to feel like an interloper. Tilghman's mother didn't come, either. She was nearly seventy, and I think she was disappointed by Tilghman's wish to have his ashes scattered so far from the family. Tilghman had two brothers. One of them had committed suicide in college (Tilghman had always blamed his father), and the other brother Tilghman had alienated in his brief time with the family insurance company in St. Cloud.

So there were just three—Francie and me and Martha, who drove down from Phoenix where she'd been staying since the lifeline had been shut down. She had loved Tilghman. She thought he was a great man.

We didn't make much of a ritual of it. We hiked up early in the morning before the clouds started in over the mountains. It was a pretty morning of blues and grays in the Sierritas and the Rincons. We could see Tucson's haze in the far distance, and the cloud shadows on the desert all around us. The sun was warm, but the breeze up high was cool. Francie said a few words. Martha said a prayer. Each of us tossed some of Tilghman's ashes into the wind.

Chapter fifteen

Raul picked up my car in Guaymas and drove it to Puerto Peñasco, and one day Francie and I drove down to visit Ellis and Harriet to get it. On the way we circled over to Quitobaquito to look for birds. It was hot though, and even at the pond, few birds were active at midday when we arrived. We had a Vermilion Flycatcher on a snag over the water, several towhees in the damp ground under the bushes, and a covey of Gambel's Quail. A small sandpiper flew from the edge of the reeds, but it winged in the other direction so fast I had only a glimpse of it.

We didn't stay long. We held hands and walked a little way around the pond, until the path gave out in the cactus and the dry thorny brush that was the beginning of the Cabeza Prieta Wildlife Refuge, an immense stretch of desert without water or roads.

Francie reminded me I'd promised to tell her about the time I had taken Tilghman birding: "You said you would sometime."

"All right." I smiled thinking of it. "It was in Minnesota," I said. "We were still in college. One night I had a date with a friend of Tilghman's—Maggie Delaney."

"I'm not jealous," Francie said.

"We'd been to a movie and were out parking near this marsh outside of St. Cloud. It was a warm night, and we had the car windows open. Are you sure you want me to tell you this?"

"I'm sure it gets better."

So I told her the story: Maggie Delaney and I were parking at that marsh and in the midst of our grappling, I heard this sound, like someone tapping two rocks together. I sat up.

"You hear that?" I asked.

Maggie hadn't heard anything. We waited. "Come on," she said, and she pulled my arm toward her.

But I heard the sound again. Tick-tick, tick-tuck-tick. Margaret heard it that time, too, and it scared her. "Let's go somewhere else," she said.

So I started the car and drove her home. Tilghman was asleep when I got back to his house. It was three o'clock in the morning and I woke him up.

"What the fuck, Scott?" Tilghman said.

"We're going to find a bird," I said. "The Yellow Rail. We'll be back before daylight. You won't even know you were awake."

Tilghman humored me that once and rolled out of bed. We took two flashlights, put on the plaid Land's End jackets his family kept on hooks in the vestibule, and found rubber waders and two lengths of chain in the garage. Tilghman made a thermos of black coffee. I packed my birding gear into a day pack—binoculars, book, tape recorder. He made me drive the Jeep.

It was cold, especially moving through the clear night air. Black space was frozen over us. The stars were icedrops. I swore the dew was frozen, but the pavement hissed wet under the tires. We drove the empty streets and out into the countryside. We drank coffee.

"I don't get this," Tilghman said.

I explained my idea—how we'd lay the chains out over the marsh grass to hold it flat. Then we'd lure the rail with a taped call. It would cross the matted-down grass, and we'd get a glimpse of it.

"That part I get," Tilghman said. "It's the motive I don't understand."

"The motive?"

"Why do you want to do this?"

"I haven't seen the Yellow Rail."

"You haven't seen the Great Wall of China," Tilghman said.

"We aren't in China."

"You haven't seen the Metrodome. Why do you want to see a bird? That's the question."

I was driving through a low woodland where a sudden patch of fog had webbed the trees on both sides of the road. Water dripped from the leaves. I might have said birds were beautiful in their myriad forms—the delicate hummingbirds with gleaming iridescent throats of red or violet or green; the mottled feathers of owls, which wove such perfect, intricate patterns; the vivid yellows and oranges and blacks of orioles and warblers; the blues of buntings and reds of tanagers; the power of falcons and hawks and eagles.

I might have said I was fascinated by flight, like Icarus or da Vinci or the Wright Brothers. A hawk rising on a thermal or an eagle soaring on motionless wings made me shiver with joy. And migration was a marvel of instinctual calculation: birds moved to survive, and they navigated unerringly across land and sea. The New England passerines headed toward Africa, for example, to catch the tradewinds south, and certain petrels and the Arctic Tern traveled halfway around the world between winter and summer. And who would not be mesmerized by the dizzying mating flights of the snipe or the aerobatics of hummingbirds?

Or I might have said the songs of birds enthralled me—the gentle whistle of the White-throated Sparrow, the sweet trill of the Parula Warbler, the flutelike music of the Veery, and the soft moan of the dove.

But the Yellow Rail was not a bird of beauty or grace or power. It was not even yellow, but rather a tawny brown and drab ocher, with blackish cross-hatching on its back and wings; it had a dull yellowish bill, and a white wing patch visible only when it flew. And it was a poor flyer. If flushed from its habitat in the reeds, which was nearly impossible to do, it paddled the air a few feet and flopped back down into cover. It was hard to imagine it at all as a migrant, but despite the odds, it made its way from puddle to pond, from marsh to ditch, along the midsection of the country from Minnesota to Texas, flying low, skulking like a wanted man, crossing hundreds of roads and telephone wires, slipping past thousands of houses in the dark.

It did not have a pretty song, either, just the sharp ticking I'd heard that night parked with Maggie Delaney. It happened to be breeding season, and that was the only time the rail called.

I couldn't give Tilghman an answer then. We came through the low woodland, and the Jeep leaned on the unbanked hill. I could have said that birds had been my obsession since childhood. Up to then I had checked off in the back of my bird guide 592 species, and there would be more to come. There were over 800 species recorded in North America, including nesters, visitors, and vagrants, and 9,000 in the world. Was I going to see them all? No.

We rose through the green halo of leaves, and then Tilghman said, "My father is leaving."

I looked over. "Leaving for where?"

"Leaving my mother," he said.

I didn't know what to say to him. "When did you find this out?" I asked.

"Last night," he said. "You were there."

I thought back to the previous night. The conversation at dinner had been mostly about fishing at the lake cabin the Myres owned, and whether they needed a new boat. I couldn't think of anything that had been said that could have given Tilghman that idea. After dinner I had got ready for my date with Maggie, and as I was leaving, Mr. Myre had come out of the den and asked who my date was. Tilghman had been standing there.

"Maggie Delaney," I had said.

Mr. Myre had got a funny smile on his face. "I know Maggie," he had said. "I know her parents."

That was all. I didn't see how Tilghman could draw any conclusions from that. Tilghman knew he was right, though. And he was. A year later his father told Tilghman he was getting divorced.

But that morning we continued to the marsh. I parked where Maggie and I had parked the night before. In the early morning darkness, there were fewer sounds than just after dusk and in the first of night. A single frog whimpered in the low, pale fog over the pond. A few cicadas whirred in the distant trees. We got out and pulled on the waders, and I put the bird book and tape recorder into a day pack I'd brought.

Tilghman got out the chains. "Now what?" he asked. He turned on his flashlight and shone it out into the marsh.

"Follow me," I said.

We skirted the marsh through an inch of water. It was spongy under the reeds. The thick stalks scythed our legs as we moved through. The sound was like tearing cloth. I stopped once or twice to shine the light around, thinking I'd heard something, but all there was to see were the reeds and the shadows of the reeds.

I made a wide swath through the back of the wetland, away from the road, where a small creek fed the marsh. We laid out the chains across a section of the reeds, stringing them parallel to one another, bending the grass down flat under their weight. I took the tape recorder out, but didn't play it right away. I first wanted our presence to settle into the quiet.

When I think of it now, it was the only time I'd ever known Tilghman to let himself be absorbed by what was around him. He was quiet. He listened. He understood, I think, that our movement through the marsh had disrupted the life there, and the only chance of seeing the rail was to let the place return to itself. What I felt so keenly was that Tilghman wanted to see the bird more than I did. For me there would be other early mornings in other marshes, other nights, other chances, but for him there was only this one time, and he wanted it to be perfect.

So we waited. I don't know how long it was—ten minutes, perhaps fifteen. We couldn't blend fully with the marsh, of course. By being there, we had already changed it. We had bent the grass down. We smelled of deodorant soap, exhaust fumes, coffee spilled on a sleeve. Our waders carried mud from a stream two hundred miles away. Our breathing wasn't the breath of frogs or birds. Even the noise of our passing, though gone already, lingered in the hearts of unseen creatures.

Still the grass we'd walked through eased back to its former height. A heron splashed on the far end of the marsh. A frog once again signaled its territory. A faint light seeped from the east, though it only made visible the black trees scalloped around us against the sky.

I was in no hurry. I wanted to hear the rail call again before I played the tape. But it didn't call. I was about to start the machine, when Tilghman held up his hand. "Not enough time," he whispered.

I patted the air down. "Shhh."

Our voices drifted away. We waited another few minutes. Nothing. I played the tape. The rail didn't respond. We watched the narrow patch of flattened grass where the chains were laid out. The bird didn't cross.

Finally the light widened around us. Colors rose into the day—greens, yellows, a blue sky. The pale mist melted away. A Yellowthroat called at the perimeter of the reeds and made me aware we were being observed. A Marsh Wren scolded us.

The sun rose through the trees and flooded the marsh with light, and then it was too late. I put the tape recorder away in the day pack. "The rail won't respond now," I said.

"I'll circle around," Tilghman said. "I'll ambush it."

"It's no use," I said. "You can't flush it, either."

But Tilghman wouldn't listen. He beat a path around through the reeds. His idea was that he could outflank the bird, get on the other side of it somehow, and push it toward me. There was no chance of that. The rail was too wary. When someone walked through a marsh, it would slither out to the side through the tall stalks. It almost never flew. Or else it would sit tight and not move.

That morning, though, the Yellow Rail didn't behave as I had thought it would. Tilghman circled wide, and as he came toward me, waist deep in the green reeds, the rail moved ahead of him and across the place where the chains pressed down the grass. I had the binoculars on it before it ducked into cover—black speckled back, white wing patch visible when it flapped twice across the open space. Yellow Rail—my life bird. Tilghman never got to see it.

Francie was quiet for a moment when I had finished this tale. We had reached the Land Rover, and she paused in one of those moments she had, when I imagined she was thinking of Tilghman. "And what about the motive?" she asked. "Why did you want to see the Yellow Rail?"

"I think I know now," I said. "I wanted to see the rail because birds are in me. They are in my blood, like a language. They were what I first knew how to love."

Chapter sixteen

We took the loop road to Lukeville, got across the border at Gringo Pass, and drove the highway to the sea. We hadn't seen very much of Harriet and Ellis that summer, after Ellis had recovered enough to go home. No charges were brought against him, though no one ever said why not.

We arrived in Puerto Peñasco in the midafternoon. It was good to feel the sea air. I knew the way to the house.

Ellis wasn't back to himself even then, and he walked with a bad limp. Harriet took care of him, helped him dress, did his exercises with him. She cooked all the meals. But he was writing well. He had a new project, he said, and it was taking good shape.

One evening when I came up from the beach, he was sitting on a dune in front of his house having a drink of mescal. "Want one?" he asked. "Harriet and Francie are in town."

"No, thanks. You know me."

"Straight shooter these days."

I sat down beside him. The islands off in the distance floated, and in that summer light, I could see gulls and terns circling in the sun. "So you're writing about Tilghman," I said.

"Who told you that?"

"No one."

Ellis smiled. "It's fiction," he said. "In the book his name is Madison Stroud. I'm making him up."

I tried to hear Tilghman in that name, but nothing came to me. Ellis drank. The sea was that calm, endless blue it gets when wind slacks at the end of the day, and the light is right. The smaller island, the one Tilghman had dived from, was oddly like the larger one, and suddenly I saw the islands as goats, hoofs below the water, bodies swimming, heads—goat heads—raised above the sea. The light made them appear that way.

"So how far are you along?" I asked Ellis.

"It's something I've worked on a long time. Years, really, without knowing it. It's only been recently that it's made sense. When it made no sense, I hurried, but now I can take my time."

"What makes sense?"

"Madison Stroud," Ellis said.

I didn't want to ask about the book, so I changed the subject. "How is Harriet?"

"She makes sense, too. She's been wonderful to me. I don't know what she wants, taking care of an old man. Did she tell you she's taking a leave from the university to collect material on whales?"

"No."

"She's already written to the committee."

"And would she work here?"

Ellis sipped his mescal and nodded. "That would make a place for you in the department, even if the regular man comes back. Harriet thought of that."

"I'd like the job," I said.

"You'd have Tilghman's place to live in. It would work out."

"It would have its advantages," I said, "except Francie's going to Los Angeles."

"You mean for good?"

I shrugged. I didn't know whether anything was for good.

"When?"

"Anytime now. The fall maybe. She says your friend, the dance teacher, Elena Valdez, can put her in a show she's going to do."

"And you'd stay in Tucson?"

"There's Tilghman's house. I can stay there until it sells. Francie has a small stake to get to L.A., and selling the house would make it easier. I think she has that in mind. She doesn't want to be reminded of Tilghman."

"Tilghman again."

"It's time for changes," I said.

On the way back to Tucson on that trip, we stopped and got gas for both cars at the Standard station at Why. Lorry was glad to see us.

"How's it going?" he wanted to know.

"All right," I said. "How about you?"

"Oh well, people always buy gasoline."

"That's what I hear."

"Security's been tightened on the border now. They got in two light planes, and they fly a good ways along the fence on both sides of Lukeville. I guess if the government thinks there's something to look for, they'll get the people to do the looking."

"Are they finding anything?"

"Oh no, we're over in Naco now, down by Bisbee. I'm going down there myself in a few weeks."

"And leave the station?"

"My nephew's going to run it. Remember him? He's been paying off on that TV set, and he wants to see if he can make this place work. You did him a favor that day, and me, too."

"Naco," I said. "I've been over a lot of Arizona, but I haven't been there. You have any use for the Land Rover?"

Lorry smiled and shook his head. "You keep it," he said. "We have the blue van, and I'll take the big truck rig for something to do. That Land Rover's going to fall apart pretty soon." He stopped and looked off toward the white scar of the copper mine in the distance. "We figure things will be quiet in Naco for a while. That's what we hope anyway. I know one thing. When people have to get out, they will."

Epilogue

Ellis's book was called *The Blue Revolution.* It was published
the next spring when Francie was in Los Angeles, and I had moved
to Austin, Texas. I ran across it in Garner & Smith before Harriet
sent me a copy, and I bought it. Tilghman, or Madison Stroud, was
a man for the eighties: principled, but misguided, a rebel with a
lost cause. It began in a town by the sea. I read the first several
chapters—enough so I had an idea of the people and the places (I
could feel *Carte Blanche* in the pages), and then I put it down and
didn't read any more. I didn't want to know how it turned out.

    I talked to Harriet a few times after that on the telephone.
The book had got good reviews, but it hadn't sold so well as *Carte
Blanche*, and Ellis was disappointed. He drank too much, she said.
She supposed she'd spoiled him by doing too much for him while
he was recovering from the accident, and then while he was writing
the book, but he'd had a long time to practice spoiling himself
before she'd met him. He spent a good bit of his time on his new
motorcycle. Or else he stayed alone in his room. When he was
with her, he drank, and she didn't know what to do for him. She
was going back to her job in the biology department the next fall.
Her research on whales was still a long way from being complete,
and she needed the resources of the university to finish up. She
hadn't told Ellis yet, but she was going to try to get him to go with
her. She thought maybe he'd be better if he could spend more time
around other people.

    I liked Austin all right. I'd moved there at the end of the fall
term, even before Tilghman's house had sold. Fred had come back
from his illness then, and instead of ornithology courses, they'd

offered me a couple of baby science sections. I liked teaching, but I had decided to take the job Jack Watkins had made for me at Top Flight in Austin. It was just office work because Jack had his guides lined up for the spring, but if something came up, he'd use me. In the meantime I sorted applications and wrote letters to prospective clients.

On the weekends I explored the birding places I knew in Texas. I visited the Rio Grande Valley—Bentsen State Park, San Ygnacio, the Sabal Palm Sanctuary east of Brownsville. Twice I went to Galveston, Bolivar Flats, and High Island. I drove to Big Bend once and to the Davis Mountains. I took a weekend trek into the Big Thicket. The Land Rover kept running.

Francie and I wrote letters back and forth, short notes which, for me anyway, who'd always used the telephone, were acts of love. She found Los Angeles to be rough territory, even with Elena's help. Elena had a few contacts and some influence, but not so much as Francie had hoped. Anyway, once that first show had closed, Francie had wanted to earn her own way. But there were lots of dancers, and good ones, and the competition was cutthroat. She'd thought her desire would be enough, but like other successes and failures, it so often depended on whom you knew. She'd expected a challenge, but not the dirty tricks.

Later that spring, a year after Tilghman died, Francie came to live with me in Austin in the little walk-up I had on Nueces Street near the Capitol. She had the money from selling Tilghman's house, and with the interest on that, together with what I made at Top Flight, we did all right. It was May, then, and warm and humid in Texas. The mornings were sunny, but in the afternoons, the clouds boiled up in the Hill Country to the west, and the rains came. Creeks filled in minutes, but in the next day or two they were trickles again, the current sliding smoothly over rocks.

One day my uncle called. He'd taken ill – nothing too serious, he said, just a hernia that had to be fixed up. But in his absence the company had virtually stopped. He wanted me to come back to Amesbury. He'd thought it over. He'd give me a percentage share in the company with the idea that, when I knew the ropes, he could retire and more down to Bradenton, Florida, where his sister lived.

"When's the operation?" I asked. "Are you okay?"

"I already had the operation," he said. "It's too late to help now. I'm talking about the future."

"Can I think about it?"

"Sure. Think it over. But you know, time's getting on Scott. You have to decide some things."

Jack Watkins had offered to put me on as a guide the following summer. He had enough clients signed up to stretch one more group to Colorado in July. He'd let Francie go too, if the tour didn't fill up.

I was pondering all of this one night when Francie and I took a walk down to the Capitol. The dome was illuminated by big spotlights, like the cathedral I remembered at Montmartre. It shone. The tops of the tall live oaks around it were lighted, too, brush strokes of leaves and shadows against the starless sky. Far away, lighting shivered in the west so far away we couldn't hear the thunder, but the lightning opened the gray clouds.

Then the earth where we were calmed to absolute stillness, as if the promise of the storm sapped the air of its strength to resist the movement of the clouds, or the rain that would fall, or the days ahead. Francie was unusually quiet. We stood on the steps of the Capitol and looked up Congress Street toward the city. She put her arm around me.

"Are you all right?" I asked her.

"I love you, Scott," she said. "I'm glad I'm here."

"I love you, too."

"I'm pregnant, Scott. We're pregnant."

I felt the lightning in the distance run up inside me. I put my arms around her and held on.

Sometime in the night we wakened to the rain battering the roof just over our heads, and we rolled to one another in that easy embrace and listened to the rain. The heat of her body flowed into mine. I loved the way we fit together as if that touching were part of the learning we had to do. I knew the meanings of words then, words which did not exist, though they were in me the way birds were in me. To love, to hope, to feel sane and right and peaceful —that was for me the beginning of another journey.

In the morning the storm had moved on. I woke early and had coffee and went down to buy a newspaper while Francie slept. I bought an *American-Statesman* at a vending machine at Congress and 11th in front of the Capitol, and then I circled through the Capitol grounds. Birds were everywhere on the grass and in the trees—Summer Tanagers, Painted Buntings, yellowthroats, Bay-breasted Warblers, catbirds. Birds were everywhere I looked, hundreds of them, all exhausted by the storm and driven down into the huge oak trees which had been illuminated in the night by the spotlights on the dome. There were sixty Indigo Buntings on the lawn in front of the legislators' parking lot, two dozen Mourning Warblers and fifteen Overbirds in the hedge at the east entrance, Grasshopper Sparrows and Lark Sparrows clinging to the low bushes along the perimeter. Warblers fluttered on every branch overhead. A Great Blue Heron strode majestically across the entrance to the rotunda.

At the beginning of that summer, we agreed in principle with my uncle to buy part of the lighting company, and we moved to Amesbury. With the child coming, I didn't want to be too far away from Francie for days at a time leading tours, and the upheaval of that life—the moving and the searching all the time—had for me, at least then, lost its glamor. Perhaps it was a temporary feeling, but I suppose, finally, it was part of that adjustment I had had to make after Tilghman died. My uncle's proposition was fair enough. We could renege within eighteen months if Francie didn't like the East, or if I found the business more than I could manage. Francie and I got married that fall, and the baby was born in November. We named her Inez.

Ellis died a year later, before Terence was born (Terence after my father). Ellis had lived with Harriet in Tucson, but Harriet said he'd been difficult right up to the end. She had no regrets. "It was the book that killed him," she said. "If he'd never finished it, he'd have gone on working and been all right. With nothing to do he drank himself sick."

Francie was pregnant and couldn't fly, and I was swamped at the company, but I flew out for the funeral. Quite a few people showed up—writers, teachers, friends, including Elena Valdez. It was good to see Harriet. She said she was going to quit teaching and take a job in Seattle, treating whales which were diseased or had been wounded at sea. Her mother was well and tormenting her brother.

We heard from her every so often after that, at Christmas, and maybe once or twice during the year. She was well and happy with her job. The whales, she said, were great friends.

I heard only once more about Demer. Francie and I had been married about three years then, and one afternoon I went to Newburyport to a bank meeting. I called Paige Jones. Paige was divorced and still working in Boston, but for a brokerage company instead of Amnesty International. The edge she'd always had in her voice when she spoke to me was gone, and she was quite pleasant. She'd visited Demer in Washington, D.C., not too long before I called. Demer had started a group called Truth in the Americas, dedicated to educating Congress and the public about what was going on in Central America and how ruinous United States policy was for the people there. "She wasn't fanatic," Paige said. "She was businesslike. The group had brochures, and statistics from the AFS and AI, from the governments themselves and from the United Nations. Demer had put together a book of photographs and testimonials by the people. But she was frustrated by how slowly it was going, how hard it was to reach the people who decided policy. Even the media weren't interested in finding out what was going on in the world."

"But she was going to stick with it?"

"The last thing I heard, she was traveling back to Central America."

"Where?"

"This was a month ago, Scott. That's a long time with Demer. I don't know where she is now."

"Alone?"

"I think three or four people from the group in D.C. were going with her. I don't remember the names."

That was all I knew. I had thought Demer might write after I sent the journals and after she got Tilghman's money, but after a while, I had realized she wouldn't. That's how things are. We lose track of people, even the people we once loved. People move, begin to care about other things which make up the foreground of their lives. We keep our eyes on the task at hand, and our caring sifts into what we have to do.

Sometimes for me, though, the background came into sharp relief, and the days with Tilghman reverberated in me with such force I was stunned to tears. I saw the faces of the children, and the vivid circumstances of those days made me feel weightless and lost, even in my own sphere in Amesbury, where my days were routine. I felt then as if I were still in the clear light, moving across the serrated rocky hills of the Ajos and the Growlers. I saw powder blue ridges, intricate shadows, the moonlight, and I felt the hot islands in the Gulf and the pale pink dawn on the top of Mount Lemmon. I wondered whether the lifeline had come back to Lukeville, and whether it still worked for others as it had for me.

The great and the evil and the artists are the breakers of rules. Tilghman was a breaker of rules. Was he great? I sometimes pondered that question as certain details occurred to me in retrospect. I thought of the way he had dived from the cliff, and how he had run down the highway in the desert on the way to Puerto Peñasco that first time. I thought of the photographs he had taken of Francie (which I still had, but was afraid to look at), and of the wall he had built that cut off the sun from his backyard. These memories came to me at odd moments, flashes now and then, but I could never quite focus the whole picture.

Francie liked New England. I thought after the children were born, she might get depressed by the close-in trees and the long winters, but she said Illinois, where she'd grown up, wasn't so much different. She'd gained a little weight after the two children, but she seemed cheerful, and she loved Inez and Terry. Once I mentioned moving back to the West. The light was better out there. But she wouldn't hear of it. The company couldn't just pick up stakes, and she was content where she was. I had work I liked. The children were prosperous. She didn't care the way I did about light and space.

For those first couple of years, she stayed home, and then she came to work for the company as a designer. She was good at it, too, good with colors and shapes, and she had an instinct, perhaps from dance, for what people found pleasing to the eye. Two of our best-selling lamps were ones she developed. Meanwhile I had pressed for and won a line of designs with broader appeal than my uncle's arctic klieg lights. My argument to him was that if we made a healthy profit on one product, the money could be used to finance more experimental research. My uncle resisted, but finally he gave way, and after a year or so of haggling with me, he retired and moved to Florida. Still I had to implement my ideas with new marketing strategies. I made better contacts with more stores and outlets, and I refinanced some of our existing loans and found new capital for expansion and upgrading of our plant. That was how I spent my days.

With the money from Tilghman's house, we bought a piece of land—ten acres next to a working apple orchard, just across the state line in New Hampshire. We had the notion of building there someday, if things kept on as they had.

Occasionally we went birding with the children on weekends,

usually in the spring or the fall down at Plum Island along the Parker River. Inez and Terry liked to watch the boats on the river and to wade in the surf at the beach. They were too small to learn the distinctions among the gulls and shorebirds, or the various songs or field marks of the warblers. Francie became proficient, but I didn't press the children. Sometimes I made up names of birds for them—the Rain Crow or the Cheery Flyer or the Bird of Light.

The days were good to me. When I got home at night, I was tired, but I found time to help a boys' club Wednesday evenings, and to do some volunteer work for Audubon and the Sierra Club. I gave money to Amnesty International and Demer's group in Washington. At night Francie was there to hold me, and I was there to hold her.

Once I heard from Rodolfo. He was the only one. He wrote me a letter in care of the Department of Birds, The University of Arizona. Fred Bentley got it and sent it to Harriet, who sent it to me. Rodolfo wrote in English. Did I remember him? he asked. He was fourteen and living outside of Fresno with his mother and his sister, who had come up from Guatemala a year after they were settled. His mother worked in a factory making clothes. He was doing pretty well in school. He liked to draw and paint, and he hoped someday to work in the movies. He thanked me for doing something to help them.

I wrote back a long letter and told him about my life. I wasn't in Arizona anymore. I said I was married and had two children and was happy. I was glad his mother and sister were well. I told him about my job building lights. I remembered him, I said. I thought about him often when I drove the Land Rover to work in the mornings and home again in the evenings. Someday I would tell my own children about him, when they were old enough to understand. I would tell them about Rodolfo at college or in the movies or in Guatemala, if things were different and he went back there. I sent the letter to the address he had given me, but I got no answer. It didn't matter. For a long time I kept Rodolfo's letter in the glove compartment of my car.